Race and Entrepreneurial Success

Race and Entrepreneurial Success

Black-, Asian-, and White-Owned Businesses in the United States

Robert W. Fairlie and Alicia M. Robb

The MIT Press
Cambridge, Massachusetts
London, England

For information about special quantity discounts, please e-mail ⟨special_sales@mitpress.mit.edu⟩.

This book was set in Palatino on 3B2 by Asco Typesetters, Hong Kong.
Printed and bound in the United States of America.

Library of Congress Cataloging-in-Publication Data

Fairlie, Robert W.
Race and entrepreneurial success : Black-, Asian-, and white-owned businesses in the United States / Robert W. Fairlie and Alicia M. Robb.
   p.   cm.
Includes bibliographical references and index.
ISBN 978-0-262-06281-7 (hardcover : alk. paper)
1. Minority business enterprises—United States. 2. African American business enterprises. 3. Asian American business enterprises. 4. Entrepreneurship—United States. 5. Small business—United States. 6. Success in business—United States. I. Robb, Alicia M. II. Title.
HD2358.5.U6F35   2008
338.6′420890973—dc22   2008005535

10 9 8 7 6 5 4 3 2 1

Contents

Preface

Interest in entrepreneurship is growing around the world. Although our understanding of what leads to entrepreneurial success has improved, we know less about why some racial groups succeed in business while others struggle. In writing this book, we were interested in figuring out why Asian American-owned businesses perform relatively well on average and the businesses owned by African Americans typically do not perform as well. An important concern is whether these racial patterns in business performance are both a symptom and cause of broader racial inequalities in the United States. Along the way, we also became very interested in exploring the more general question of why some small businesses succeed and others fail and how success is related to the human-capital, financial-capital, and family-business background of the entrepreneur.

The main goal of the book is to provide a comprehensive comparative analysis of the performance of African American-, Asian American-, and white-owned businesses in the United States. We hope that it will serve as a useful informational source for policymakers and business leaders as well as a valuable research and instructional tool for professors and students. In researching the book, we were surprised to learn that there were no studies or reports in the literature that provided thorough information on recent trends in minority-business ownership rates and outcomes. We present a new compilation of data on minority entrepreneurship over the past few decades as well as a detailed analysis of confidential data from the U.S. Census Bureau. We hope that anyone interested in learning more about racial trends in business ownership and outcomes, the determinants of successful entrepreneurship, and the causes of racial disparities in business performance will find what they need in this book.

We started this research project many years ago when we applied to the Center for Economic Studies to use the confidential and restricted-access Characteristics of Business Owners data. Given a project of this length, there are many people to thank for providing comments, suggestions, and criticisms. We thank Timothy Bates, Ken Brevoort, Anthony Caruso, Ken Couch, Mark Doms, Tom Dunn, Lingxin Hao, Brian Headd, James Jarzabkowski, Leora Klapper, Lori Kletzer, Rebecca London, Ying Lowrey, Justin Marion, Kevin Moore, Richard Moore, Chad Moutray, Charles Ou, Robert Strom, Valerie Strang, Kathryn Tobias, John Wolken, and Donald Wittman.

We also thank participants at the numerous conferences, workshops, and seminars at which we presented the research discussed in this book. They include the American Economic Association Meetings; Baruch College; Board of Governors of the Federal Reserve System; California State University Moss Landing Marine Laboratory; Consulate General of Sweden at the University of Southern California; Dartmouth College; Federal Reserve System's Community Affairs Research Conference; Harvard University; National Academy of Sciences Panel on Measuring Business Formation, Dynamics, and Performance; National Bureau of Economic Research Workshop on Entrepreneurship; United States Association for Small Business and Entrepreneurship Meetings; RAND; United States Small Business Administration; SBA and the Kauffmann Foundation Conference on Entrepreneurship in the Twenty-first Century; University of Amsterdam Entrepreneurship and Human Capital Conference; University of California at Santa Barbara; University of California at Santa Cruz; University of Maryland; University of North Carolina Minority Entrepreneurship Boot Camp; University of North Carolina Research Conference on Entrepreneurship among Minorities and Women; University of Washington Business Diversity Conference; Urban Institute; Yale University.

We thank Bill Koch, Garima Vasishtha, Oded Gurantz, and Matt Jennings for providing excellent research assistance. We are also grateful for funding from the Russell Sage Foundation and Kauffman Foundation. The views expressed here are solely ours and do not necessarily reflect the views of either foundation. Finally, we thank Rebecca London, Zoe and Jessica Fairlie, and Mark Doms for their patience and support during the past several years of writing this book.

Race and Entrepreneurial Success

1   Introduction

Racial inequality in education, income, and wealth are well known. Less understood are the large and persistent racial disparities in business ownership and performance in the United States. The lack of attention is surprising, given the magnitude of these racial differences and the importance of business ownership as a way to make a living for many Americans. More than one in ten workers, or 13 million people, in the United States are self-employed business owners. These 13 million business owners hold an amazing 37.4 percent of total U.S. wealth (Bucks, Kennickell, and Moore 2006). Yet only 5.1 percent of African American workers and 7.5 percent of Latino workers own businesses compared with more than 11 percent of white and Asian workers. Low rates of business ownership among African Americans have also persisted over the entire twentieth century, and recent trends indicate that racial disparities in business-ownership rates will not disappear in the near future.

Racial Patterns in Business Outcomes

Although racial disparities in business ownership are troubling, perhaps a more important concern is that businesses owned by disadvantaged minorities tend to be smaller and less successful than nonminority-owned businesses. On average, black- and Latino-owned businesses have lower sales, hire fewer employees, and have smaller payrolls than white-owned businesses (U.S. Census Bureau 2006b). Firms owned by African Americans also have lower profits and higher closure rates than those owned by whites (U.S. Census Bureau 1997). For most outcomes, these disparities are large. For example, white-owned firms have average annual sales of $439,579, compared with only $74,018 for black-owned firms (U.S. Census Bureau 2006b). There certainly are a large number of very successful black-owned businesses in the United States, many with revenues of more than $250,000 per year.[1] But a substantial proportion of black firms are less successful, leading to average outcomes that are worse than for white firms. In contrast to these patterns, Asian American-owned firms have average outcomes more similar to—and in some cases better than—those of white-owned firms. Overall, these racial patterns in business outcomes have remained roughly unchanged over the past two decades.

Improving the performance of minority-owned businesses in the United States is a major concern among policymakers. Although they are sometimes controversial, various federal, state, and local government programs offer contracting set-asides, price discounts, and loans to businesses owned by minorities, women, and other disadvantaged groups (Boston 1999b; Joint Center for Political and Economic Studies 1994). One of the goals of these programs is to foster minority-business development, which may have implications for reducing earnings and wealth inequalities (Bradford 2003). Self-employed business owners earn more on average than wage and salary workers (Borjas 1999), and disadvantaged business owners have more upward income mobility and experience faster earnings growth than disadvantaged wage and salary workers (Holtz-Eakin, Rosen, and Weathers 2000; Fairlie 2004b). It has also been argued that some disadvantaged groups facing discrimination or blocked opportunities in the wage and salary sector—such as Chinese, Japanese, Jewish, Italian, and Greek immigrants—have used business ownership as a source of economic advancement.[2] More recently, the economic mobility of Koreans has been linked to business ownership (Min 1996).[3]

Another concern, which is often overlooked, is the loss in economic efficiency resulting from blocked opportunities for minorities to start and grow businesses. Business formation has been associated with the creation of new industries, innovation, job creation, improvement in sector productivity, and economic growth (Reynolds 2005). If minority entrepreneurs face liquidity constraints, discrimination, or other barriers to creating new businesses or expanding current businesses, there is some loss of efficiency in the economy.[4] Although it is difficult to determine the value of these losses, barriers to entry and expansion that minority-owned businesses face are potentially costly to U.S. productivity, especially as minorities represent an increasing share of the total population. Barriers to business growth may be especially damaging for job creation in poor neighborhoods (Boston 1999b, 2006b).

Minority firms in the United States hire more than 4.7 million employees, a disproportionate share of them minorities (U.S. Census Bureau 1997, 2006b), and many of these jobs are located in disadvantaged communities.

A growing body of literature attempts to address these concerns by exploring the causes of racial disparities in business ownership. Human, financial, and social capital appear to be the main driving forces behind racial differences in rates of business ownership. For example, previous research focusing on blacks indicates that relatively low levels of education, assets, and parental self-employment are partly responsible for their low rates of business ownership (Bates 1997; Fairlie 1999; Hout and Rosen 2000). Less is known about the underlying causes of racial differences in business outcomes such as profits, sales, and employment. The lack of evidence is surprising given that the benefits of improving minority-business performance are unambiguous compared with the benefits of simply increasing rates of business ownership among minority businesses.[5] The limited previous research on the topic indicates that the owner's education level and startup capital have been found to contribute to racial differences in business closures and profits (Bates 1997).

To get an idea of the potential importance of access to financial capital in contributing to racial disparities in business ownership and outcomes, one only has to look at the alarming levels of wealth inequality that exist in the United States (U.S. Census Bureau 2005a). Half of all blacks have less than $6,200 in wealth. Wealth levels among whites and Asians are *11 times higher*. Low levels of wealth among disadvantaged minorities are likely to translate into less successful businesses because the owner's wealth can be invested directly in the business or used as collateral to obtain business loans. Lending discrimination can exacerbate this problem by further restricting access to capital (Blanchflower, Levine, and Zimmerman 2003; Cavalluzzo, Cavalluzzo, and Wolken 2002).

Another contributing factor is racial disparities in education. Fewer than 20 percent of blacks have a college education, compared with nearly 30 percent of whites. Asians have even higher levels of education: nearly 50 percent of Asians, whether born abroad or in the United States, are college educated. The general and specific knowledge and skills acquired through formal education may be useful for running a successful business. If this is the case, racial differences in the education levels of the owners will lead to racial disparities in business outcomes.

The legacy of slavery and historical discrimination underlies another concern about current disparities in the performance of black- and white-owned firms. Blacks made scant progress in rates of business ownership throughout the twentieth century, even in light of their substantial gains in education, earnings, and civil rights. The ratio of white to black self-employment rates remained roughly constant at 3 to 1 over the twentieth century (Fairlie and Meyer 2000) with only slight improvements shown in the past several years. Why was there no convergence in racial self-employment rates over the twentieth century? Early researchers emphasized the role that past inexperience in business played in creating low rates of business ownership among blacks. Du Bois (1899) and later Myrdal (1944), Cayton and Drake (1946), and Frazier (1957) identify the lack of black traditions in business enterprise as a major cause of low levels of black business ownership at the time of their analyses.

The argument for the importance of black traditions in business relies on evidence of a strong intergenerational link in business ownership; that is, the children of business owners are more likely than those of nonbusiness owners to own businesses. We might expect the intergenerational link to be strong because working in a family business is an excellent way to acquire general business or managerial experience that is later useful for starting and running a successful business. Children who choose to work in an industry similar to that of their family's business may also acquire industry- or firm-specific expertise (learning how to run a restaurant by working in their parents' restaurant, for example). The inheritance of a family-owned business and correlations among family members in entrepreneurial preferences may also contribute to intergenerational links in business ownership. Indeed, a few recent studies find that the likelihood of being a self-employed business owner is substantially higher among the children of business owners than among the children of nonbusiness owners (Lentz and Laband 1990; Fairlie 1999; Dunn and Holtz-Eakin 2000; Hout and Rosen 2000). Current racial patterns in self-employment rates are also in part determined by racial patterns of self-employment rates in the previous generation (Fairlie 1999; Hout and Rosen 2000).

Although the previous literature provides evidence that racial disparities in financial-capital, human-capital, and family-business backgrounds contribute to the likelihood that some minority groups will not own businesses, less is known about whether these factors also contribute to racial differences in business performance. The standard theoretical model of entrepreneurship posits that human capital and access to financial capital are two of the most important determinants of the entrepreneurial decision (Evans and Jovanovic 1989), and these types of capital are clearly inputs in the production process potentially affecting performance. But we know little about the business consequences of racial disparities in these factors. Although owner's education and access to financial capital have been identified as contributing to racial differences in closure rates and profits, the relative importance of these factors is unknown. Ideally, one would like an estimate of how much of the racial differences in several business outcomes can be explained by each factor and whether, for example, racial differences in access to startup capital are more detrimental to business success than are racial differences in human capital.

Knowledge about the importance of family-business backgrounds is especially lacking. In particular, the intergenerational transmission of business ownership is found to contribute to racial disparities in *rates* of business ownership, but whether it also contributes to racial disparities in business *outcomes conditioning* on ownership is unknown. For example, can differences in family-business backgrounds explain why black-owned businesses underperform white-owned firms on average? Can they explain why Asian-owned firms have better outcomes than other racial groups? If they do contribute to racial disparities in outcomes, how do they contribute? Do family businesses primarily provide an opportunity for would-be entrepreneurs to acquire general and specific business human capital, or are inheritances and correlated preferences more important? Very little is currently known about the exact mechanisms that drive the intergenerational relationship in business ownership and outcomes.

The previous literature has not explored these questions in depth partly because of the lack of available data. The primary difficulty is finding a nationally representative dataset that includes a large enough sample of minority-owned businesses, information on business outcomes, and the family-business background of the owner. An exception is the Characteristics of Business Owners (CBO), conducted by the U.S. Census Bureau, which contains detailed information on the characteristics of owners and firms. To our knowledge, it is the only dataset that includes large samples of minority-owned firms and information on family-business ownership, prior work experience in family businesses, prior work experience in similar businesses, and business inheritances.

In this study, we use CBO data to explore the role that racial differences in financial-capital, human-capital, and family-business backgrounds play in contributing to racial disparities in small business outcomes, such as closure rates, profits, employment, and sales. Low levels of education and wealth may limit the ability of disadvantaged minorities to start successful businesses. The inability of minorities to acquire general and specific business human capital through exposure to businesses owned by family members may also contribute to their limited success in business ownership. The richness of these data allows us to examine the contributions of many additional owner and business characteristics in racial disparities in business outcomes. Unlike individual-level datasets, such as the Census of Population and the Current Population Survey, the CBO contains detailed information on both business and owner, allowing us to explore the determinants of several different business outcomes.

Although the CBO provides an excellent dataset for exploring the underlying causes of racial differences in business outcomes, it has been used by only a handful of researchers. The lack of use appears to be due primarily to difficulties in obtaining access, using, and reporting results from these confidential and restricted-access data. All research using the CBO must be conducted in a Census Research Data Center or at the Center for Economic Studies (CES) after approval by the CES and the Internal Revenue Service (IRS), and all output must pass strict disclosure regulations.

Another contribution of the study is to provide a new compilation of estimates of racial patterns of business-ownership rates and business outcomes. Surprisingly, there is no comprehensive source of information on recent trends in minority businesses in the literature. Combining estimates from the most widely used and respected sources of government data, we provide an assessment of the state of minority business in the United States. Estimates of business-ownership rates and performance are generated from public-use and restricted-access microdata taken from published sources and obtained from special tabulations prepared for us by the U.S. Census Bureau.

The focus of the analysis is on African American- and Asian American-owned businesses. Estimates presented later in this study indicate that Asian American-owned businesses have the best average outcomes of all major racial groups. In contrast, the average outcomes of businesses owned by African Americans are at the low end of all groups. Although a sizeable body of research has focused on why there are few black-owned businesses, very little research focuses on the causes of their relative underperformance. Furthermore, relatively little research using business-level data focuses on the performance of Asian American-owned firms. We also present statistics on recent trends in business outcomes for Latino-owned businesses but do not explore the causes of differences between firms owned by Latinos and those owned by whites because we do not find notable differences in average outcomes in the CBO data used. Thus, the analysis of CBO microdata focuses on identifying why Asian-owned businesses have the best and black-owned businesses have the worst average outcomes of all major racial and ethnic groups. The answers to these questions have important policy implications, given the importance of successful business ownership for income generation, wealth accumulation, job creation, and economic development.

Outline of This Book

The main goals of this book are to (1) document recent trends in business ownership and outcomes by race using the most up-to-date and respected sources of government data, (2) identify the owner and business characteristics associated with business success, (3) explore potential explanations for the relative underperformance of black-owned businesses, and (4) explore potential explanations for the relative success of Asian-owned businesses. The findings from this analysis of racial differences in business outcomes are useful for characterizing the state of minority-owned businesses in the United States.

Chapter 2 documents recent trends in racial patterns in business ownership and performance using the most up-to-date and widely used government data on minority-owned businesses, the Survey of Minority-Owned Business Enterprises (SMOBE) and the Survey of Business Owners (SBO), and on self-employed business owners, the Current Population Survey (CPS). These datasets are described in detail in the book's data appendix. We first provide new estimates of recent trends in business ownership rates by race and ethnicity from the CPS and a brief review of previous literature examining the causes of racial differences in business ownership. Estimates from CPS micro-data improve on published estimates from the same source by the U.S. Bureau of Labor Statistics that do not include incorporated business owners. Using the SMOBE, SBO, and CBO, we provide estimates of recent trends in business outcomes by race. Racial differences in sales, profits, employment, payroll, and closure rates are documented and discussed. Estimates from published sources, public-use and restricted-access microdata, and special tabulations created for us by the Census Bureau are combined to provide a comprehensive picture of the performance of minority-owned businesses in the United States. The compilation of estimates of business outcomes by race over the past two decades presented here is new and makes definitions as comparable as possible over time.

Although a large body of literature examines the causes of racial differences in rates of business ownership, much less is known about the causes of racial differences in business outcomes, such as survivability, profits, employment, and sales. Examining the factors associated with successful businesses is the first step in identifying the causes of racial differences in business outcomes outlined in chapter 2. Chapter 3 provides a detailed analysis of the determinants of small business success using confidential and restricted-access CBO microdata. We examine the owner and business characteristics associated with higher sales and profits, more employment, and a lower likelihood of closure among small businesses. In addition to examining more traditional determinants, such as owner's education and financial capital, we examine whether family-business backgrounds are important in predicting business success. We estimate the independent effects for small business outcomes of having a self-employed family member, of having prior work experience in that family member's business, and of inheriting a business. The results have implications for the importance to business success of general and specific business human capital and of correlations in entrepreneurial preferences across family members. To identify measurable and causal factors affecting business success, we focus on parsimonious models for business outcomes common in the economics literature.

Building on the findings from chapter 3 on the determinants of business success, chapter 4 employs a special decomposition technique to identify the underlying causes of differences in business outcomes between African American- and white-owned firms. The decomposition technique provides estimates of how much each factor explains of the racial gaps in business outcomes. Black-owned businesses are found to have lower revenues and profits, to hire fewer employees, and to be more likely to close than white-owned businesses. We explore the role that owner's education, financial capital, family-business backgrounds, and other owner and firm characteristics play in creating racial disparities in small business outcomes. Do black business owners have limited opportunities to acquire general and specific business human capital by working in a family-owned business or inheriting a business, in addition to having less education and less access to financial capital?

Estimates from CBO microdata indicate that Asian-owned businesses have better outcomes, on average, than white-owned businesses. Chapter 5 explores why Asian-owned firms have higher sales and profits, are more likely to hire employees, and are less likely to close than white-owned firms. The oversample of Asian-owned firms in the CBO allows us to explore whether the relative success of these firms is because of higher levels of human and financial capital, advantaged family-business backgrounds, or other factors. We use estimates of the determinants of small business outcomes identified in chapter 3 and the decomposition technique described in chapter 4 for this analysis. The results for Asian Americans are important because only a few previous studies in the literature explore business outcomes for this group using nationally representative business-level data.

Chapter 6 concludes by reviewing the findings from our analysis of racial patterns in business outcomes from CBO, SMOBE, SBO, and CPS data. Policy implications of the results are also briefly discussed.

Main Findings of the Research

The main findings from our analysis of racial differences in business outcomes are as follows.

1. African Americans and Latinos are substantially less likely to own a business than are whites and Asian Americans. Estimates from 2006 CPS microdata indicate that 11.1 percent of white workers and 11.8 percent of Asian workers are self-employed business owners, whereas only 5.1 percent of black workers and 7.5 percent of Latino workers are business owners. In the past few years, however, there is some evidence of rising black and Latino business-ownership rates.

2. Black-owned businesses have lower sales and profits, hire fewer employees, have smaller payrolls, and have higher closure rates than white-owned businesses. For most outcomes, the disparities are extremely large. For example, estimates from the 2002 SBO indicate that white-owned firms have average sales of $439,579 compared with only $74,018 for those owned by blacks.

3. Although white firms generally outperform Asian firms when examining data for all businesses, Asian firms clearly have the strongest performance among all major racial and ethnic groups after removing small-scale businesses. Estimates from 1992 CBO microdata indicate that Asian-owned firms have higher sales and profits, are more likely to hire employees, and are less likely to close than white-owned firms.

4. Estimates from the SBO/SMOBE data also indicate substantially worse outcomes among Latino-owned firms than white-owned firms. Latino-owned businesses have lower average sales, are less likely to hire employees, and hire fewer employees than white-owned businesses. Estimates from our CBO sample, however, do not reveal large disparities in business outcomes between Latino-owned firms and white-owned firms.

5. Trends in minority business outcomes do not indicate improvement relative to white business outcomes in the past two decades.

6. Intergenerational links in business ownership are strong. Estimates from the CBO indicate that more than half of all business owners had a self-employed family member prior to starting their business. Where there was a self-employed family member, fewer than half of small business owners worked in that family member's business. On the other hand, only a very small percentage of all small businesses were inherited.

7. Estimates from regression models for small business outcomes *conditioning* on business ownership indicate that having a self-employed family member plays only a minor role. In contrast, prior work experience in that family member's business has a large positive effect on business outcomes. Working in a family member's business may provide opportunities for acquiring valuable specific and general business human capital. Regression estimates also indicate that inherited businesses are more successful on average than noninherited businesses, but their limited representation in the population of small businesses suggests that they are not a major determinant of business outcomes.

8. We also find evidence that other forms of human capital and business human capital—the owner's education level and prior work experience in a business whose goods and services were similar to those provided by the owner's business—are important determinants of business outcomes.

9. Estimates from the CBO indicate a strong positive relationship between startup capital and business outcomes. Firms with higher levels of startup capital are less likely to close and are more likely to have higher profits and sales and to hire employees. The estimated positive relationship is consistent with the inability of some entrepreneurs to obtain the optimal level of startup capital because of liquidity constraints.

10. The median level of wealth for blacks is $6,166, compared with $67,000 for whites. We find that black-owned businesses start with substantially lower levels of financial capital than white-owned firms. Using a nonlinear decomposition technique, we find that the black/white disparity in startup capital is the largest single factor contributing to racial disparities in closure rates, profits, employment, and sales.

11. Estimates from the CBO indicate that black business owners have a relatively disadvantaged family-business background compared with white business owners. Black business owners are much less likely than white business owners to have had a self-employed family member owner prior to starting their business and are less likely to have worked in that family member's business. We do not find sizeable racial differences in the inheritance of businesses.

12. We find that the relatively low probability of having a self-employed family member prior to business startup among blacks does not generally contribute to racial differences in small business outcomes. Instead, the lack of prior work experience in a family business among black business owners, perhaps by limiting their acquisition of general and specific business human capital, negatively affects black business outcomes. We also find that limited opportunities for acquiring specific business human capital through work experience in businesses providing similar goods and services contribute to worse business outcomes among blacks.

13. Only 17.6 percent of blacks have a college education compared with 28.2 percent of whites. Black business owners are also found to have lower levels of education than white business owners, on average. Estimates from our decomposition technique indicate that these racial differences in education contribute significantly to the observed racial disparities in business outcomes.

14. The most important factor in the higher survival rates, profits, employment, and sales of Asian-owned firms is that Asian Americans

invest more startup capital in their firms than whites. This factor alone explains 57 to 100 percent of the difference in outcomes between Asian and white firms.

15. Nearly half of all Asian American business owners are college educated, which follows the pattern of high levels of education in the Asian American population more generally. Higher levels of education among Asian business owners, who are 80 percent foreign born, explain a large fraction of the better outcomes in Asian- compared with white-owned businesses.

16. The relative success of Asian-owned businesses is not due to having advantaged family-business backgrounds. In fact, Asian business owners are less likely than white business owners to have a self-employed family member prior to business startup and are less likely to work in that family business.

Overall, our findings indicate that large racial disparities exist in business ownership and business outcomes in the United States. There is also no evidence suggesting that these patterns will disappear in the near future. Our analysis of the confidential and restricted-access CBO reveals several important determinants of success in small business ownership. The analysis focuses on the business and owner characteristics that are likely to be the most important inputs into the firm's production process as suggested by economic theory. In addition to more traditional explanations, such as the owner's education level and access to financial capital, we find evidence suggesting that family-business backgrounds are important. In particular, prior work experience in a family business has a positive effect on business outcomes, possibly through the acquisition of specific and general business human capital.

Turning to explanations for disparities in business outcomes, we find that racial differences in these factors are important. The relative lack of success among black-owned businesses is attributable in part to owners who have less startup capital, disadvantaged family backgrounds, and less education. Conversely, the relative success of Asian American-owned businesses in the United States appears to be mainly due to their relatively high levels of startup capital and owner's education.

2 Racial Disparities in Business Ownership and Outcomes

In the United States, African Americans and Latinos are less likely to own businesses than whites, and the businesses that they own are less successful on average. In contrast, Asian Americans have similar business-ownership rates as whites, and Asian-owned businesses outperform white-owned businesses for most outcome measures. In this chapter, we lay out the facts about business ownership and performance among minorities.

We create new estimates of racial patterns of business-ownership rates using the most recently available microdata. Estimates of recent trends in minority business ownership are also generated and discussed. To explore recent trends in minority business outcomes, we put together a new compilation of estimates that are as comparable over time as possible. Our goal is to provide a comprehensive picture of the state of minority business in the United States based on estimates from the most widely used and respected sources of government data. Estimates of recent trends in business ownership and outcomes from these sources that are presented here are generated from public-use and restricted-access microdata, taken from published sources, and obtained from special tabulations prepared for us by the U.S. Census Bureau.

To examine current levels and trends in business-ownership patterns by race, we use microdata from the 1979 to 2006 Outgoing Rotation Group Files of the Current Population Survey (CPS). The survey, conducted by the U.S. Census Bureau and the Bureau of Labor Statistics, is representative of the entire U.S. population and interviews approximately 50,000 households and more than 130,000 people per month. The CPS provides the most up-to-date estimates of the rate of business ownership in the United States. The new estimates of minority business-ownership rates from CPS microdata presented here also improve on published estimates from the CPS by the U.S. Bureau of Labor Statistics (BLS) because these latter data do not include incorporated business owners. More details about the CPS microdata are provided in the book's data appendix.

After examining racial differences in business ownership, we provide estimates of racial differences in business outcomes. Trends from the past two decades are presented. A detailed comparison of several measures of performance among white, black, Asian, and Latino businesses sets the stage for the analyses contained in the later chapters. Estimates of business outcomes are taken from the 2002 Survey of Business Owners (SBO) and the Surveys of Minority-Owned Business Enterprises (SMOBE) from 1982, 1987, 1992, and 1997. We also present estimates from our sample of businesses taken from the confidential and restricted-access 1992 Characteristics of Business Owners (CBO) Survey and published estimates from the same source. The SBO/SMOBE is considered the most up-to-date, comprehensive dataset on minority businesses. The CBO, which is a more detailed subsample of the SMOBE, is used in later chapters to analyze the determinants of business success and causes of racial differences in business outcomes. The book's data appendix includes a detailed discussion of all these datasets.

Racial Differences in Business Ownership

Although the focus of this study is on explaining racial disparities in business performance, it is useful to first discuss racial business-ownership patterns and briefly review the literature on potential explanations. Microdata from the 2006 Outgoing Rotation Group File to the CPS are used to examine racial patterns of business ownership. These are the latest available national data on business ownership in the United States. Estimates of nonagricultural self-employed business-ownership rates are reported in table 2.1. The self-employed business-ownership rate is the ratio of the number of self-employed business owners to the total number of workers. Business ownership in the CPS captures all types of businesses including incorporated, unincorporated, employer, and nonemployer businesses.[1] Agricultural industries are excluded, but they represent only 6 percent of all business owners. The owners of side and small-scale businesses are also excluded because self-employment status is defined for the main job activity and

Table 2.1
Self-employment rates by ethnicity or race, Current Population Survey, Outgoing Rotation Group Files (2006)

	Self-Employment	
	Rate (percent)	Sample Size
White non-Latino	11.1%	132,786
African American	5.1	15,988
Latino	7.5	19,357
Asian	11.8	8,206
Total	9.9%	181,071

Notes: (1) The sample consists of individuals age sixteen and over who work fifteen or more hours during the survey week. (2) Self-employment status is based on the worker's main job activity and includes owners of both unincorporated and incorporated businesses. (3) Agricultural industries are defined using the North American Industry Classification System classifications and are excluded. (4) Estimates include only individuals reporting one race. (5) All estimates are calculated using sample weights provided by the Current Population Survey.

only workers with at least fifteen hours worked in the survey week are included in the sample.

A clear ordering of self-employment propensities across ethnic and racial groups emerges.[2] Asians and white non-Latinos have the highest self-employment rates, Latinos have the next highest rates, and blacks have the lowest rates. Among whites, 11.1 percent of the workforce is a business owner. The Asian self-employment rate is slightly higher at 11.8 percent, but it varies from year to year, as noted below. In the past few years, the Asian self-employment rate has been roughly similar to the white rate. The rate of business ownership among Latinos is 7.5 percent, which is only 68 percent of the white rate. The black self-employment rate is even lower at 5.1 percent, which is 46 percent of the white rate.[3] The ordering and general levels of self-employment rates across ethnic or racial groups are similar to those reported in previous studies using alternative data sources and years.[4]

Recent Trends in Business Ownership

We now turn to an analysis of the major trends in minority business ownership that have occurred in the past few decades. Figure 2.1 and table 2.2 provide estimates of self-employed business-ownership rates by race from 1979 to 2006. The white non-Latino self-employment rate

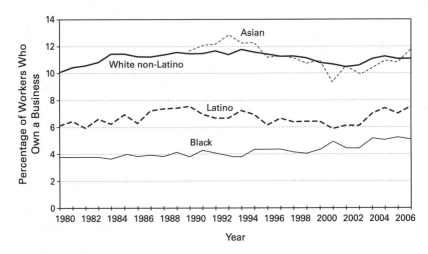

Figure 2.1
Self-employed business ownership rates for all workers, Current Population Survey, Outgoing Rotation Group Files (1979 to 2006)

rose by just over one and a half percentage points from 1979 (10.1 percent) to 1993 (11.7 percent).[5] It then started a downward trend, which did not end until 2001 (10.5 percent).[6] Since then, the self-employment rate has risen by slightly more than a half percentage point and has remained steady around 11.2 percent over the last few years. Over the entire period from 1979 to 2006, the white non-Latino business-ownership rate increased by one percentage point.

The estimates displayed in figure 2.1 indicate that the black self-employment rate remained roughly constant in the 1980s and early 1990s. The self-employment rate was slightly higher in the middle to late 1990s and rose to 4.9 percent in 2000. The black self-employment rate then fell, rose to a high of 5.2 percent in 2003, and has remained at 5.1 to 5.2 percent in recent years. The current rate of business ownership for blacks is substantially higher than it was only two and a half decades ago. The percentage of black workers who are business owners increased by 1.3 percentage points over the past twenty-five years. These trends indicate that business ownership for blacks is rising at a faster rate than for whites, suggesting that the racial gap is closing if measured as a ratio. The black/white ratio in self-employment rates increased from 0.38 in 1979 to 0.46 in 2006. At the same time, however, it is clear from figure 2.1 that blacks had lower self-employment rates than any other group for the entire period and have a long way to go

Table 2.2
Trends in self-employed business ownership rates by race, Current Population Survey, Outgoing Rotation Group Files (1979 to 2006)

Years	White non-Latino Self-Employment Rate (percent)	Number of Self-Employed (000s)	Labor Force (000s)	Black Self-Employment Rate (percent)	Number of Self-Employed (000s)	Labor Force (000s)	Latino Self-Employment Rate (percent)	Number of Self-Employed (000s)	Labor Force (000s)
1979	10.1%	7,066	70,168	3.8%	297	7,907	6.1%	241	3,956
1980	10.4	7,298	69,988	3.8	300	7,960	6.4	270	4,205
1981	10.6	7,589	71,827	3.8	309	8,203	5.9	269	4,533
1982	10.8	7,663	70,896	3.8	300	7,960	6.6	292	4,430
1983	11.4	8,220	71,953	3.6	298	8,213	6.2	281	4,515
1984	11.4	8,608	75,386	4.0	352	8,908	6.9	337	4,868
1985	11.2	8,497	75,697	3.8	357	9,285	6.3	362	5,774
1986	11.2	8,670	77,401	3.9	374	9,627	7.2	450	6,248
1987	11.4	8,949	78,818	3.8	388	10,179	7.4	496	6,743
1988	11.5	9,294	80,533	4.1	429	10,446	7.4	533	7,203
1989	11.4	9,376	81,915	3.8	406	10,711	7.5	562	7,454
1990	11.5	9,374	81,822	4.3	471	11,040	7.0	600	8,627
1991	11.7	9,405	80,675	4.1	451	10,976	6.7	574	8,614
1992	11.4	9,210	80,993	3.9	424	11,007	6.7	581	8,723
1993	11.7	9,653	82,164	3.8	431	11,322	7.2	652	9,032
1994	11.6	9,687	83,826	4.3	507	11,704	6.9	659	9,522
1995	11.4	9,732	85,336	4.3	526	12,134	6.1	592	9,645
1996	11.2	9,550	85,032	4.3	538	12,386	6.6	661	9,953
1997	11.3	9,738	86,490	4.1	530	12,828	6.4	697	10,935
1998	11.1	9,710	87,353	4.1	544	13,407	6.4	734	11,466
1999	10.8	9,545	88,536	4.3	602	13,999	6.4	759	11,819
2000	10.7	9,510	89,108	4.9	697	14,220	5.9	732	12,490
2001	10.5	9,273	88,560	4.4	629	14,251	6.1	785	12,848
2002	10.6	9,290	87,788	4.4	621	14,062	6.1	782	12,842
2003	11.1	9,658	87,305	5.2	710	13,717	7.0	1,032	14,777
2004	11.2	9,880	87,919	5.1	705	13,926	7.4	1,135	15,348
2005	11.1	9,842	89,065	5.2	751	14,308	7.0	1,115	15,900
2006	11.1	9,955	89,833	5.1	745	14,635	7.5	1,275	16,958

Notes: (1) The sample includes individuals age sixteen and over who work fifteen or more hours during the survey week. (2) Self-employment status is based on the worker's main job activity and includes owners of both unincorporated and incorporated businesses. (3) Agricultural industries are defined using the North American Industry Classification System classifications and are excluded. Estimates for 1979 to 1991 also exclude veterinary services. (4) Race and Spanish codes changed in 1989, 1996, and 2003, and the Current Population Survey was redesigned in 1994. Estimates starting in 2003 include only individuals reporting one race. (5) All estimates are calculated using sample weights provided by the CPS.

Table 2.2
(continued)

Years	Asian			Total		
	Self-Employment Rate (percent)	Number of Self-Employed (000s)	Labor Force (000s)	Self-Employment Rate (percent)	Number of Self-Employed (000s)	Labor Force (000s)
1979				9.3%	7,724	83,503
1980				9.6	8,016	83,694
1981				9.7	8,380	86,587
1982				9.9	8,460	85,405
1983				10.4	9,056	86,946
1984				10.4	9,568	91,568
1985				10.2	9,494	93,327
1986				10.2	9,786	95,998
1987				10.3	10,175	98,691
1988				10.5	10,617	101,292
1989	11.7%	319	2,734	10.4	10,711	103,432
1990	12.1	372	3,088	10.3	10,881	105,248
1991	12.1	381	3,147	10.5	10,880	104,114
1992	12.9	418	3,254	10.2	10,690	104,687
1993	12.2	394	3,218	10.5	11,201	106,498
1994	12.2	362	2,953	10.4	11,287	108,801
1995	11.2	298	2,661	10.1	11,217	110,594
1996	11.3	460	4,074	10.0	11,258	112,238
1997	11.1	488	4,375	10.0	11,525	115,537
1998	10.8	494	4,595	9.8	11,557	117,730
1999	10.9	521	4,771	9.6	11,483	120,015
2000	9.4	466	4,977	9.4	11,460	121,743
2001	10.5	534	5,077	9.3	11,287	121,707
2002	9.9	502	5,077	9.3	11,268	120,803
2003	10.4	590	5,647	9.8	12,176	123,830
2004	11.0	641	5,851	10.0	12,558	125,533
2005	10.8	661	6,116	9.8	12,571	128,033
2006	11.8	754	6,419	9.9	12,960	130,459

before catching up with white levels. Furthermore, the gap in percentage points or as a difference between the two rates decreased only slightly (from 6.3 to 6.0 percentage points).

The Latino rate of business ownership increased dramatically over the 1980s. The rate was 6.1 percent in 1979 and rose to 7.5 percent by 1989. The Latino self-employment rate then fell over the next decade. In the early 2000s, roughly 6 percent of Latinos were self-employed business owners. In the past few years, however, the rate of business ownership has increased sharply. The Latino self-employment rate is now 7.5 percent, which is 1.4 percentage points higher than it was twenty-five years earlier. Similar to the trends for blacks, Latino business-ownership rates are rising faster than for whites, indicating that the ratio of Latino to white self-employment is rising over time.

Estimates of business-ownership rates for Asians fluctuated more than for other groups from 1989 to 2006. Unfortunately, the CPS does not allow identification of Asians prior to 1989. The fluctuation in the self-employment rates is party driven by smaller sample sizes for Asians than for other groups. Although the group's self-employment rate has declined somewhat from the early 1990s to the current period, Asians continue to have the highest rate of business ownership among minority groups and have rates that are roughly comparable to white rates. More than one out of every ten Asian workers is a self-employed business owner.

Although there is little evidence in the literature on what has contributed to these trends in recent years, there is some evidence that suggests the causes of racial differences in earlier periods. Using a dynamic decomposition technique, Fairlie (2004b) explores the causes of racial differences in trends in self-employment rates from 1979 to 1998. Several interesting patterns are revealed. For example, increasing levels of education among black men relative to white men contributed to the narrowing of the white/black self-employment rate gap from 1979–1981 to 1996–1998. In contrast, Latino men did not experience gains in education relative to white men over this period, and the white/Latino gap increased. Differential trends in the age distribution of the workforce across racial groups also contributed to relative trends in self-employment rates. For all minority groups, the workforce aged less rapidly than for whites, reducing the self-employment rates of these groups relative to the white self-employment rate.

Examining trends in business ownership among black and white men for a limited set of cities, Chay, Fairlie, and Chatterji (2005) find evidence of increasing rates for blacks in the mid-1980s that are likely due to the creation of affirmative action contracting programs. The staggered introduction of set-aside programs across U.S. cities during the 1980s is used to estimate their impact on minority self-employment rates. Large increases in black self-employment rates relative to white self-employment rates are found soon after program implementation concentrated in those industries, such as construction, that were most heavily affected by contract set-asides from city governments. Boston (1998) also examines the growth rate in the number of black-owned businesses in cities that implemented affirmative action programs in the 1980s relative to cities that did not and finds weaker results. He finds that the average growth rate from 1982 to 1992 was 65 percent in cities with programs and 61 percent in cities without programs but that the difference was not statistically significant.

Racial Trends over the Twentieth Century

African American self-employment rates were lower than white self-employment rates throughout the twentieth century. Figure 2.2 displays black and white male nonagricultural self-employment rates and the ratio of the two rates from 1910 to 1990 generated from Census of Population microdata. During this period, the black self-employment

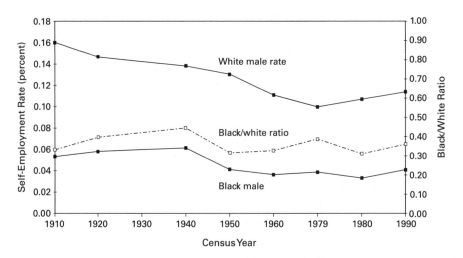

Figure 2.2
Long-term trends in white and black male self-employment rates, Census of Population (1910 to 1990)

rate generally followed the same time pattern as the white self-employment rate. The main difference was that the decline in black self-employment continued until 1980 and reversed only after 1980. The similar trends in the racial self-employment rates resulted in a roughly constant black/white ratio during most of the twentieth century.[7]

Examining these long-term trends in racial self-employment rates, Fairlie and Meyer (2000) find that the large gap between the black and the white self-employment rates is due to the lower self-employment rates of blacks in all industries and not due to the concentration of blacks in low-self-employment-rate industries.[8] Another finding was that major demographic changes that occurred during the twentieth century, such as the great black migration out of the U.S. south (1914 to 1950) and the racial convergence in educational attainment, did not have large effects on the racial self-employment rate gap. Furthermore, relative self-employment rates among more recent cohorts of black men are not found to be higher than among older cohorts, suggesting that business-ownership patterns are not changing rapidly across generations.

Explanations for Racial Differences in Business Ownership

A large body of research investigates the causes of current racial differences in business-ownership rates using individual-level datasets, such as the CPS and Census of Population.[9] Given the large size of this literature, we do not provide a comprehensive review. Instead, we provide a brief review of the main findings focusing on previous studies that provide estimates of the relative importance of explanatory factors before turning to the focus on this study on racial differences in business performance.[10] Previous studies focusing on the causes of low rates of business ownership among blacks and Latinos are discussed here, leaving a more detailed discussion of the Asian self-employment literature to chapter 5.

The standard economic model of the self-employment decision posits that individuals choose the work sector that provides the highest utility—wage and salary work or self-employment (Kihlstrom and Laffont 1979; Evans and Jovanovic 1989). The main component of this comparison is potential earnings in the two sectors. Blacks and Latinos may be less likely to choose self-employment than whites and Asians due to the perceived lower relative earnings in the self-employment sector. A comparison of earnings in self-employment and the wage and salary sector, however, does not provide evidence that blacks and Latinos have lower relative self-employment earnings than whites and Asians (Fairlie 2006).

Although the earnings comparison is a key component of the standard theoretical model of entrepreneurship, the decision between wage and salary work and self-employment is actually based on a comparison of utility in the two sectors, suggesting that the characteristics of the type of work may be important (Rees and Shah 1986; Blanchflower and Oswald 1998). A potential explanation for low rates of business ownership may be that minorities have less of a preference for entrepreneurship. Available data on preferences for self-employment among young blacks, however, indicate a strong interest in self-employment. More than 75 percent of young blacks report being interested in starting their own business (Walstad and Kourilsky 1998). For comparison, 63 percent of young whites are interested in starting a business.[11] These findings suggest that blacks may have a stronger desire for entrepreneurship than whites, at least when they are young.

Evidently, the simple economic model of entrepreneurship does not explain basic differences in business-ownership rates between racial groups. Racial differences in business-ownership rates appear to be driven by factors other than just differences in earnings differentials and preferences. Thus, much of the previous literature has focused on analyzing potential constraints limiting the ability of minorities to start businesses.

The importance of personal wealth has taken center stage in the literature on the determinants of self-employment. Numerous studies using various methodologies and measures of wealth explore the relationship between wealth and self-employment for different countries. Most studies find that asset levels (such as net worth) measured in one year increase the probability of entering self-employment by the following year.[12] The finding has generally been interpreted as providing evidence that entrepreneurs face liquidity constraints, although there is some recent evidence against this interpretation (Hurst and Lusardi 2004). Several previous studies also show that blacks have substantially lower levels of wealth than whites.[13] Although less research focuses on Latinos, disparities in asset levels are also large (see Wolff 2001; Cobb-Clark and Hildebrand 2006). Estimates from the Survey of Income and Program Participation (SIPP), discussed more thoroughly in chapter 4, indicate that median levels of net worth are $6,166 for blacks and $6,766 for Latinos. In contrast, the median net worth for white non-Latinos is $67,000 (U.S. Census Bureau 2005b). Asians are found to have wealth levels that are roughly similar to those of whites (Hao 2007).

These findings from the previous literature suggest that relatively low levels of wealth among blacks and Latinos and relatively high levels of wealth among Asians may be a source of racial differences in rates of business ownership. Indeed, recent research using statistical decomposition techniques provides evidence supporting this hypothesis. Using matched CPS Annual Demographic Files (ADF) data from 1998 to 2003, Fairlie (2006) finds that the largest single factor explaining racial disparities in business-creation rates are differences in asset levels. Lower levels of assets among blacks account for 15.5 percent of the difference between the rates of business creation among whites and blacks. This finding is consistent with the presence of liquidity constraints and low levels of assets limiting opportunities for blacks to start businesses. The finding is very similar to estimates reported in Fairlie (1999) for men using the Panel Study of Income Dynamics (PSID). Estimates from the PSID indicate that 13.9 to 15.2 percent of the black/white gap in business start rates can be explained by differences in assets.[14]

Fairlie and Woodruff (2007) examine the causes of low rates of business formation among Mexican Americans. One of the most important factors in explaining the gaps between Mexican Americans and non-Latino whites in rates of business creation is also assets. Relatively low levels of assets explain roughly one quarter of the business entry rate gap for Mexican Americans. Lofstrom and Wang (2006) using SIPP data also find that low levels of wealth for Mexican Americans and other Latinos work to lower self-employment entry rates. Apparently, low levels of personal wealth limit opportunities for Mexican Americans and other Latinos to start businesses.

Education has also been found in the literature to be a major determinant of business ownership. Low levels of education obtained by blacks and Latinos are partly responsible for their lower business-ownership rates. Using CPS data, Fairlie (2006) finds that 6.0 percent of the black/white gap in self-employment entry rates is explained by racial differences in education levels. Similar estimates from the PSID are reported in Fairlie (1999). Mexican Americans have even lower levels of education than blacks, which translates into a limiting factor for business creation. Estimates from the CPS indicate that education differences account for 32.8 to 37.9 percent of the entry-rate gap for Mexican Americans (Fairlie and Woodruff 2007). Lofstrom and Wang (2006) find that education is important in explaining differences in business-creation rates between Mexican Americans and whites, as well as the types of businesses entrepreneurs are likely to pursue. The high rate of business ownership by Asians is in part due to their relatively high levels of education (Fairlie 2006).

Another measure of human capital relevant for Latinos and Asians is language ability. Limited English-language ability may make it difficult to communicate with potential customers and suppliers and learn about regulations. On the other hand, lack of fluency in English may limit opportunities in the wage and salary sector, resulting in an increased likelihood of becoming self-employed. Previous studies provide some evidence that a better command of the English language is associated with more self-employment (Fairlie and Meyer 1996; Fairlie and Woodruff 2007). But there is also a literature that points to blocked opportunities in the wage and salary sector because of language barriers increasing self-employment among Asian immigrants (Kassoudji 1988; Min 1989, 1993; Bates 1997).

Research also indicates that the probability of self-employment is substantially higher among the children of the self-employed (Lentz and Laband 1990; Fairlie 1999; Dunn and Holtz-Eakin 2000; Hout and Rosen 2000).[15] These studies generally find that an individual who had a self-employed parent is roughly two to three times as likely to be self-employed as someone who did not have a self-employed parent. There is evidence that this strong intergenerational link in business ownership is detrimental to disadvantaged minorities. Hout and Rosen (2000) note a "triple disadvantage" faced by black men in terms of business ownership. They are less likely than white men to have self-employed fathers, to become self-employed if their fathers were not self-employed, and to follow their father in self-employment. Fairlie (1999) provides evidence from the PSID that current racial patterns of self-employment are in part determined by racial patterns of self-employment in the previous generation.

Previous research also indicates that the size and composition of social networks are associated with self-employment (Allen 2000). If minority firms have limited access to business, social, or family networks or have smaller networks, then they may be less likely to enter business and create successful businesses. These networks may be especially important in providing financing, customers, technical assistance, role models, and contracts. These same networks, however, are also likely to be useful for finding employment in the wage and salary sector, creating a dampening effect on self-employment.

Ethnic enclaves represent one method for creating and facilitating entry into networks. Of particular importance is that locating in an ethnic enclave may provide a market for special products and services and access to coethnic labor.[16] Using a measure of enclave at the Standard Metropolitan Statistical Area (SMSA) level, Borjas (1986) finds that self-employment among Mexicans, Cubans, and "other Hispanics" is increasing in the percentage of Hispanics in an SMSA. The effect is larger among the immigrant population than among the population born in the United States. Using 2000 U.S. Census data, Fairlie and Woodruff (2007) find that Mexican-immigrant self-employment rates are higher in ethnic enclaves. The evidence is more mixed on whether black self-employment is higher in areas with larger concentrations of blacks (Boyd 1990; Dawkins 2007). Ethnic enclaves may explain why some ethnic groups have high rates of business ownership, but enclaves can also dampen opportunities for entrepreneurs by creating intense competition among coethnics (Aldrich and Waldinger 1990; Razin and Langlois 1996).

Additional factors that might explain differing rates of business ownership across ethnic and racial groups are labor-market, lending, and consumer discrimination. Labor-market discrimination may increase business entry for some minority groups. Wage and employment discrimination represent disadvantages in the labor market, causing some groups to favor self-employment (Light 1972, 1979; Sowell 1981; Moore 1983). On the other hand, Coate and Tennyson (1992) present a theoretical model positing that labor-market discrimination can reduce the incentive for minorities to enter self-employment. This happens because lenders provide less favorable terms in the credit market, such as higher interest rates, to the discriminated group because of the difficulty in observing entrepreneurial ability. Empirical evidence for sixty detailed ethnic or racial groups presented in Fairlie and Meyer (1996) indicates that more advantaged ethnic or racial groups (measured by wage and salary earnings, self-employment earnings, and unearned income), not the more disadvantaged groups, have the highest self-employment rates. Finally, discrimination may occur directly in self-employment through limited opportunities to penetrate networks, such as those in construction (Bates 1993a; Feagin and Imani 1994; Bates and Howell 1997).

Using microdata from the 1980 U.S. Census, Borjas and Bronars (1989) explore whether the large observed variances in self-employment rates across racial groups are partly due to consumer discrimination. They find that minorities negatively select into self-employment, with the most able minorities remaining in the wage and salary sector, whereas whites positively select into self-employment and negatively select into wage and salary work. These findings are consistent with the most able minority businesses avoiding self-employment because of white consumers' distaste for purchasing goods and services from minority businesses. Using recent panel data from the CPS, Kawaguchi (2004) finds that among African Americans low earners are the most likely to enter into business ownership, whereas both low- and high-earning whites are the most likely to enter self-employment. He notes that this finding is consistent with the theoretical predictions of consumer and credit-market discrimination against blacks. In contrast to these results, Meyer (1990) does not find evidence supporting the consumer-discrimination hypothesis. Using data from the 1987 Characteristics of Business Owners (CBO), he finds that black businesses are relatively more common in industries in which white customers more frequently patronize black businesses.

Several previous studies use data from the Federal Reserve's Survey of Small Business Finances (SSBF) to study lending discrimination and find that minority-owned businesses experience higher loan-denial probabilities and pay higher interest rates than white-owned businesses, even after controlling for differences in creditworthiness and other factors (Blanchard, Yinger, and Zhao 2004; Blanchflower, Levine, and Zimmerman 2003; Cavalluzzo, Cavalluzzo, and Wolken 2002; Cavalluzzo and Wolken 2005; Coleman 2002, 2003; Robb and Fairlie 2006). We discuss these results more fully in chapter 4. Although this empirical evidence is focused on more established businesses, lending discrimination is likely to deter business creation among minorities because of the effect on startup loans.

Related to the issue of discrimination, government jobs have been very attractive to black workers because of stricter antidiscrimination policies, universal hiring standards, and affirmative action. Previous research indicates that black self-employment is lower in areas in which higher percentages of blacks are employed in the public sector (Boyd 1990). Although would-be black entrepreneurs may have gone into the public sector instead of starting businesses, the total impact has to be relatively low because only 6.4 percent of the black workforce is employed in the public sector compared with 4.3 percent of the white workforce. Even if the entire difference in public-sector employment rates was added to the black self-employment rate, a substantial gap in self-employment rates would remain between blacks and whites.

To summarize, the previous literature identifies several explanations for racial disparities in business-ownership rates. These include racial differences in wealth, education, and parental self-employment. Consumer and lending discrimination against some minority businesses may also limit business-ownership rates. Ethnic enclaves, language ability, and networks may also contribute to ethnic and racial disparities in business-ownership rates. Although the determinants of business ownership might differ from those for business performance, these factors are a good place to start looking for explanations.

Trends in the Number of Minority-Owned Businesses

We now turn to examining business-level data on minority-owned businesses in the United States. We present results from the most commonly used sources of data on minority-owned businesses—the SBO, SMOBE, and CBO. All of these surveys are conducted by the U.S. Census Bureau. Estimates reported here are taken from government publications, special tabulations prepared for us by U.S. Census Bureau staff, and generated from restricted-access microdata (see the book's data appendix).[17] The data provide information on the number of minority businesses and on business outcomes (such as closures, profits, employment, and sales) that are not typically found in household survey data, such as the CPS.

Estimates of the number of minority businesses from the SMOBE and SBO are discussed first. The SMOBE and SBO are considered the most up-to-date and comprehensive data on minority-owned businesses. These data have experienced several changes in sample criteria and definitions, however, making them not directly comparable over time (see more details in the book's data appendix). Estimates were also revised in many cases by the Census Bureau, and we attempted to find the most recently available data.[18] With these concerns in mind, the analysis focuses on relative trends.

Estimates from the SMOBE and SBO indicate that the number of minority businesses grew rapidly over the past two decades (see table 2.3). In 1982, there were 308,260 black-owned businesses. By 2002, the

Table 2.3
Number of businesses by race, Survey of Minority-Owned Business Enterprises (1982 to 1997) and Survey of Business Owners (2002)

	Includes C Cor- porations	All Firms	White- Owned Firms	Black- Owned Firms	Latino- Owned Firms	Asian- and Pacific Islander- Owned Firms
1982	No	12,059,950	11,318,310	308,260	233,975	187,691
1987	No	13,695,480	12,481,730	424,165	422,373	355,331
1992	No	17,253,143	15,287,578	620,912	862,605	603,426
1997	No	18,278,933	15,492,835	780,770	1,121,433	785,480
1997	Yes	20,440,415	17,316,796	823,499	1,199,896	912,960
2002	Yes	22,480,256	18,326,375	1,197,567	1,573,464	1,132,535

Sources: U.S. Census Bureau, Economic Census, Survey of Minority-Owned Business Enterprises (1982, 1987, 1992, 1997), U.S. Census Bureau, Survey of Business Owners (2002), and special tabulations prepared by the U.S. Census Bureau.
Notes: (1) All firms excludes publicly held, foreign-owned, not-for-profit, and other firms, which are not included in the estimates by race. (2) See the book's data appendix for changes in sample criteria and definitions. Estimates are not directly comparable over time. (3) The white category is equal to all firms minus all minority firms for 1982, 1987, and 1992 and all white firms minus Latino-owned firms in 2002. (4) The most recently revised estimates are reported when applicable.

number quadrupled to nearly 1.2 million. The growth rates and increases in the number of Latino- and Asian American-owned businesses are even larger. Latino-owned businesses grew from 233,975 in 1982 to 1.6 million in 2002, and Asian-owned businesses grew from 187,691 to more than 1.1 million in 2002. The total number of businesses and the number of white-owned businesses also grew substantially over the period but at a much slower rate (from 11.3 million in 1982 to 18.3 million in 2002).[19] For example, the total number of businesses in the United States grew by 86 percent from 1982 to 2002, compared with a growth rate of 288 percent for black-owned businesses.[20] Growth rates for Latino and Asian businesses were even higher—572 and 503 percent, respectively.

One major reason for these rapid growth rates in the number of minority businesses is population growth, especially for Latinos and Asians. The estimates of much slower or nonexistent rates of growth in business-ownership rates from the CPS reported above provide support for this point. The roughly constant business-ownership rates over the past two decades found in the CPS imply that the rate of growth in the population kept pace with the rate of growth in the number of business owners over this period. Trends in the number of businesses to population ratios from 1997 to 2002 also indicate low growth rates for Asians and Latinos but not for blacks (U.S. Small Business Administration 2007a).

Growth rates in the reported number of minority-owned businesses are also partly due to changes in the sample universe of included businesses in the SMOBE and SBO data (see table A.1 in the book's data appendix). The biggest change over this period is that the SMOBE began including C corporations in 1997. Thus, part of the growth in the number of firms from 1982 to 2002 is due to the addition of these corporations. This change, however, does not have a substantial effect on trends in the number of black- and Latino-owned firms. Table 2.3 reports two separate estimates of the number of businesses by race in 1997, which exclude or include C corporations. The exclusion of C corporations is consistent with the sample criteria used in earlier years, and the inclusion of C corporations is consistent with 2002.[21] The difference in reported estimates implies that only 5.2 percent of black firms and 6.5 percent of Latino firms were C corporations in 1997, indicating that the addition of C corporations contributed only slightly to the estimated growth rates over the past two decades. A larger share of Asian firms are C corporations (14.0 percent), but they also represent only a small fraction of the growth in the reported number of Asian-owned businesses from 1982 to 2002.

Focusing on the most recent period, 1997 to 2002, estimates of the total number of businesses including C corporations indicate rapid growth rates in the number of minority-owned businesses. The number of black-owned businesses grew by 45.4 percent from 1997 to 2002. The number of Latino and Asian businesses also grew at rapid rates of 31.1 percent and 24.1 percent, respectively. In contrast, the number of white businesses grew by 5.8 percent from 1997 to 2002.

But are these estimates of phenomenal rates of growth for the number of minority-owned businesses reasonable? The CPS estimates of the rates of business ownership showed more modest rates of growth over the past several years. In fact, the recent growth in minority business-ownership rates shown in the CPS data occurred primarily after 2002.

Comparison of SBO/SMOBE and CPS Estimates

We next compare estimates of the number of minority businesses to the number of minority self-employed business owners. Estimates of the number of businesses from SBO/SMOBE data and the number of self-employed business owners from the CPS reveal different levels and trends in minority business activity in the United States. Differences between the current number of businesses and number of business owners are expected, but large differences in trends for the two measures are unexpected. The CPS estimates indicate much slower recent growth rates in the number of minority business owners than the SBO/SMOBE estimates.

Table 2.4 reports estimates of the number of businesses from the SBO and SMOBE and the number of business owners from the CPS by race for comparable years. The CPS estimates indicate that there were 11.3 million self-employed business owners in the United States in 2002. In contrast, estimates from the SBO indicate that that there were 22.5 million businesses in the United States in 2002. The large discrepancy between the number of businesses and business owners from the two sources holds for each racial group in almost every year. Discrepancies between the two measures of business activity are due to the inclusion or exclusion of small businesses, side businesses owned by wage and salary workers, multiple owners of businesses, individuals who own multiple businesses, and workers in occupations such as sales and real estate agents (see the book's data appendix for more details).[22] The measurement of business ownership at the survey date in the CPS and at any time during the year in the SBO/SMOBE also creates a discrepancy in estimates.

To address the issue of whether the difference in treatment of smaller businesses account for the difference in estimates, we remove the hours-worked restriction imposed in the CPS estimates of the number of business owners. In the bottom panel of table 2.4, we report estimates of the number of business owners who report self-employment as their main job activity and have any number of hours worked in the survey week. This includes many but not all smaller-scale business activities. Individuals who report working at a wage or salary job for more hours than they worked in their business (that is, a side business), however, will not be classified as self-employed business owners. Thus, the estimates are still not fully comparable to the SBO and SMOBE estimates.[23] The modified CPS estimate of the total number of business owners in the United States is 12.9 million in 2002, which remains substantially lower than the estimate of 22.5 million businesses from the 2002 SBO. Estimates of the number of minority businesses are more similar, but large differences remain in the past few years.

Table 2.4
Comparison of number of businesses and business owners by race, Survey of Business Owners (2002), Survey of Minority-Owned Business Enterprises (1982 to 1997), and Current Population Survey (1982 to 2002)

	Includes C Corporations	All	White	Black	Latino	Asian
Total number of businesses, SBO and SMOBE:						
1982	No	12,059,950	11,318,310	308,260	233,975	187,691
1987	No	13,695,480	12,481,730	424,165	422,373	355,331
1992	No	17,253,143	15,287,578	620,912	862,605	603,426
1997	No	18,278,933	15,492,835	780,770	1,121,433	785,480
1997	Yes	20,440,415	17,316,796	823,499	1,199,896	912,960
2002	Yes	22,480,256	18,326,375	1,197,567	1,573,464	1,132,535
Total number of business owners, CPS (15+ hours worked in survey week):						
1982	Yes	8,459,840	7,662,950	300,470	291,610	
1987	Yes	10,175,150	8,949,320	387,800	496,120	
1992	Yes	10,689,690	9,209,860	423,790	581,030	418,200
1997	Yes	11,525,030	9,737,880	530,120	697,200	487,620
2002	Yes	11,268,230	9,290,020	620,840	782,160	501,700
Total number of business owners, CPS (no hours restriction):						
1982	Yes	10,060,270	9,104,320	379,280	344,660	
1987	Yes	11,696,510	10,303,410	470,180	552,900	
1992	Yes	12,379,770	10,676,570	517,320	654,880	463,320
1997	Yes	13,462,580	11,453,560	615,220	779,500	526,610
2002	Yes	12,932,580	10,693,920	719,160	880,590	546,980

Sources: U.S. Census Bureau, Economic Census, Survey of Minority-Owned Business Enterprises (1982, 1987, 1992, 1997), U.S. Census Bureau, Survey of Business Owners (2002), special tabulations prepared by the U.S. Census Bureau, and authors calculations using the Current Population Survey.
Notes: (1) All firms excludes publicly held, foreign-owned, not-for-profit, and other firms, which are not included in the estimates by race. (2) See the book's data appendix for changes in sample criteria and definitions. Estimates are not directly comparable over time. (3) The white category is equal to all firms minus all minority firms for 1982, 1987, and 1992 and all white firms minus Latino-owned firms in 2002. (4) The most recently revised estimates are reported when applicable. (5) The CPS samples consist of individuals age 16 and over. Only self-employed business owners working fifteen or more hours in the survey week are included in the second panel. The third panel does not impose the hours worked restriction. (6) Self-employment status is based on the worker's main job activity and includes owners of both unincorporated and incorporated businesses. (7) All estimates are calculated using sample weights provided by the CPS.

Estimates from the CPS indicate rapid growth rates for the number of minority business owners over the past two decades but not nearly as rapid as the estimated growth rates in the number of minority-owned businesses from SBO/SMOBE data.[24] The CPS estimates indicate that the number of black business owners roughly doubled from 1982 to 2002, compared with a threefold increase in the number of black-owned businesses estimated from the SBO/SMOBE data. The number of Latino business owners increased by 155 percent from 1982 to 2002, and the number of Asian business owners increased by 18 percent from 1992 to 2002. Estimates from SBO/SMOBE indicate much faster growth rates for the number of Latino and Asian firms over comparable time periods.

The recent release of the 2002 SBO data received a lot of attention in the press and among policymakers. The press release by the U.S. Census Bureau noted the 45 percent increase in the number of black-owned businesses since 1997, the 31 percent increase in the number of Latino-owned businesses, and the 24 percent increase in the number of Asian-owned businesses (U.S. Census Bureau 2006b). These estimates were viewed as positive news for the state of minority business, especially in light of the much slower growth rate in the number of all businesses of 10 percent. Estimates of the number of minority business owners from the CPS, however, provide evidence of more modest growth in minority business activity over this five-year period. CPS estimates indicate that the number of black business owners grew by 17 percent, the number of Latino business owners grew by 12 percent, and the number of Asian business owners grew by 3 percent from 1997 to 2002.

Although focusing on businesses that represent the owners' main work activity reduces the absolute growth rates in the number of minority-owned businesses, the CPS estimates also indicate rapid growth rates relative to all business owners or white business owners. From 1982 to 2002, the total number of business owners increased by only 33 percent and actually decreased by 2 percent from 1997 to 2002. The rates of growth in the number of minority business owners are substantially higher over similar time periods. Thus, both estimates of business owners in the CPS and businesses in the SBO/SMOBE indicate that the number of minority businesses increased much faster than the number of white businesses over the past two decades.

Racial Patterns and Trends in Business Outcomes

Table 2.5 reports estimates of sales and receipts by race from the 2002 SBO and prior SMOBE surveys (1982 to 1997) for minority-owned, white-owned, and all firms. These data provide the most up-to-date and commonly used sources of information on minority business performance. The tables reported here represent a new compilation of estimates of recent trends in business outcomes by race. We report separate estimates for 1997 that both include and exclude C corporations, but there were other changes over that time period that make estimates not directly comparable as noted above and in the book's data appendix.

The 2002 SBO data provide the most recent estimates of annual firm sales for minority-owned firms. Black-owned firms have much lower average sales than white-owned firms. Average annual sales and receipts are $74,018 for black-owned firms compared with $439,579 for white-owned firms.

Latino firms also have lower average sales than white-owned firms. Average annual sales are $141,044 for Latino-owned firms in 2002, 32 percent of average annual sales of white-owned firms. Asian-owned firms have lower average sales than white-owned firms, but the difference is much smaller. Average annual sales and receipts are $292,214 for Asian-owned businesses.

Racial disparities in annual sales are not new. Throughout the past two decades, black- and Latino-owned firms have had substantially lower average sales than white- and Asian-owned firms. In every year reported in table 2.5, black and Latino firms had lower sales than white-owned firms. Asian firms also had lower average sales than white firms, but the differences were notably smaller.

Trends in annual sales for black- and Latino-owned firms also do not indicate recent improvements when compared with trends in average sales for white-owned firms. Average sales of black firms were 25 percent of white average sales in 1992 and dropped to less than 20 percent in 1997 and 2002. The decline also does not appear to be due to the inclusion of C corporations in which black firms are underrepresented. Average sales for black-owned firms drop from $86,478 to $54,652 in 1997 after excluding C corporations, but average sales for white firms drop by a similar percentage. The result is that black average sales are roughly 20 percent of white average sales with or without C corporations in 1997.

Table 2.5
Sales and receipts by race, Survey of Minority-Owned Business Enterprises (1982 to 1997) and Survey of Business Owners (2002)

	Includes C Corporations	All Firms	White-Owned Firms
Total number of firms:			
1982	No	12,059,950	11,318,310
1987	No	13,695,480	12,481,730
1992	No	17,253,143	15,287,578
1997	No	18,278,933	15,492,835
1997	Yes	20,440,415	17,316,796
2002	Yes	22,480,256	18,326,375
Total sales and receipts:			
1982	No	$967,450,721	$932,996,721
1987	No	$1,994,808,000	$1,916,968,057
1992	No	$3,324,200,000	$3,122,188,579
1997	No	$4,239,708,305	$3,904,392,106
1997	Yes	$8,392,001,261	$7,763,010,611
2002	Yes	$8,783,541,146	$8,055,884,659
Mean sales and receipts:			
1982	No	$80,220	$82,433
1987	No	$145,654	$153,582
1992	No	$192,672	$204,230
1997	No	$231,945	$252,013
1997	Yes	$410,559	$448,294
2002	Yes	$390,722	$439,579

Sources: U.S. Census Bureau, Economic Census, Survey of Minority-Owned Business Enterprises (1982, 1987, 1992, 1997), U.S. Census Bureau, Survey of Business Owners (2002), and special tabulations prepared by the U.S. Census Bureau.

Notes: (1) All firms excludes publicly held, foreign-owned, not-for-profit, and other firms, which are not included in the estimates by race. (2) See the book's data appendix for changes in sample criteria and definitions. Estimates are not directly comparable over time. (3) The white category is equal to all firms minus all minority firms for 1982, 1987, and 1992 and all white firms minus Latino-owned firms in 2002. (4) The most recently revised estimates are reported when applicable.

	Black-Owned Firms	Latino-Owned Firms	Asian- and Pacific Islander-Owned Firms
Total number of firms:			
1982	308,260	233,975	187,691
1987	424,165	422,373	355,331
1992	620,912	862,605	603,426
1997	780,770	1,121,433	785,480
1997	823,499	1,199,896	912,960
2002	1,197,567	1,573,464	1,132,535
Total sales and receipts:			
1982	$9,619,055	$11,759,133	$12,653,315
1987	$19,762,876	$24,731,600	$33,124,326
1992	$32,197,361	$76,842,000	$95,713,613
1997	$42,670,785	$114,430,852	$161,141,634
1997	$71,214,662	$186,274,581	$306,932,982
2002	$88,641,608	$221,927,425	$330,943,036
Mean sales and receipts:			
1982	$31,204	$50,258	$67,416
1987	$46,592	$58,554	$93,221
1992	$51,855	$89,081	$158,617
1997	$54,652	$102,040	$205,151
1997	$86,478	$155,242	$336,195
2002	$74,018	$141,044	$292,214

The same finding holds for Latino-owned businesses, except that the disadvantage and relative decline are smaller. In 1992, average sales for Latino-owned firms were 44 percent of the average sales for white firms. In 1997, average sales for Latinos dropped to 35 percent of white average sales if C corporations are included or 40 percent if C corporations are excluded.

For both black and Latino firms, these trends represent disappointing news. Although there has been substantial growth in the number of businesses relative to white businesses, the average sales of these firms relative to all firms have not improved over time and, in fact, have actually lost ground. From 1992 to 2002, average sales among Asian firms also fell relative to average sales among white firms, although this is partly due to the inclusion of larger C corporations. On

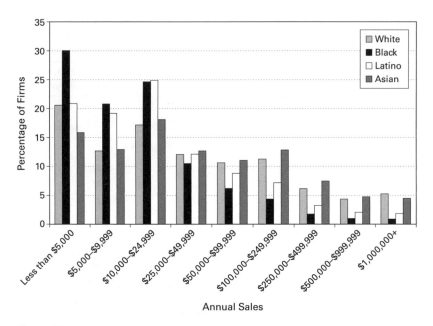

Figure 2.3
Sales distribution by race, Survey of Business Owners (2002)

average, Asian firms have lower sales than white firms, but the comparison changes when we investigate this further below.

A comparison of average levels of sales can mask important racial differences. In particular, the higher average sales among white and Asian businesses may be driven by a few businesses with very high revenues even though most of these businesses might have roughly similar sales levels as black and Latino businesses. To investigate this question, figure 2.3 displays the distribution of sales by race using the 2002 SBO. The estimates clearly indicate that white- and Asian-owned firms are much more likely to have high sales levels than are black- and Latino-owned firms. For example, 27.0 percent of white-owned firms and 29.5 percent of Asian-owned firms have sales of $100,000 or more. In contrast, only 8.0 percent of black-owned firms and 14.3 percent of Latino-owned firms have revenues at this level. Racial disparities in the percentage of firms with higher levels of sales are even larger.

Black and Latino firms are overrepresented at the bottom of the sales distribution. Thirty percent of black-owned firms grossed less than $5,000, compared with approximately 20 percent of white and Latino firms and just over 15 percent of Asian-owned firms. More than 85 percent of black-owned firms grossed less than $50,000. Black firms make up the largest group in each of the smallest revenue-size classes. Latino firms are also overrepresented in the lower sales classes except for the similar percentage of Latino and white firms with less than $5,000 in sales and receipts.

Overall, white and Asian firms have substantially higher sales and receipts than do black and Latino firms. Large racial disparities are revealed when comparing either average levels or the entire distribution of sales. Asian firms do not have higher average sales than white-owned firms, but this appears to be driven by a small percentage of white firms that have extremely high sales. In comparing the distribution of sales, a larger percentage of Asian firms can be found in each of the largest revenue classes except the $1 million and more level.

Estimates from the SBO and SMOBE also indicate that black- and Latino-owned firms are less likely to hire employees and hire fewer employees on average than white- or Asian-owned firms (see table 2.6). Most businesses in the United States do not hire any employees— slightly less than one quarter of firms had employees in 2002. Whether or not a firm has employees, however, varies substantially by race.[25] Only 7.9 percent of black-owned firms have paid employees, compared with 12.7 percent of Latino-owned firms and 28.5 percent of Asian-owned firms. Just under one quarter of white-owned firms have employees with a mean employment level of 2.8. In 2002, black-owned firms averaged under one employee, and Latino-owned firms averaged only one employee. Asian businesses hired an average of two employees.

Racial disparities in employment levels are evident throughout the period covered by the SBO and SMOBE data. Black and Latino firms are less likely to hire any employees and hire fewer employees on average than white or Asian firms in every year with available data. The differences exist even after the inclusion of C corporations in 1997.

Conditioning on employment, racial patterns differ somewhat, and there is evidence that black- and Latino-employer firms have gained some ground on white-employer firms. Table 2.7 reports estimates of mean annual payroll and payroll per employee by race for the subsample of employer firms. It is important to keep in mind, however, that these are larger, more successful firms to begin with and represent only a small fraction of all businesses in the United States. Black-, Latino-, and Asian-employer firms have made some gains relative

Table 2.6
Employment statistics by race, Survey of Minority-Owned Business Enterprises (1982 to 1997) and Survey of Business Owners (2002)

	Includes C Corporations	All Firms	White-Owned Firms	Black-Owned Firms	Latino-Owned Firms	Asian- and Pacific Islander-Owned Firms
Total number of firms:						
1982	No	12,059,950	11,318,310	308,260	233,975	187,691
1987	No	13,695,480	12,481,730	424,165	422,373	355,331
1992	No	17,253,143	15,287,578	620,912	862,605	603,426
1997	No	18,278,933	15,492,835	780,770	1,121,433	785,480
1997	Yes	20,440,415	17,316,796	823,499	1,199,896	912,960
2002	Yes	22,480,256	18,326,375	1,197,567	1,573,464	1,132,535
Percentage of firms with paid employees:						
1982	No	N/A	N/A	12.3%	16.8%	N/A
1987	No	25.5%	26.0%	16.7%	19.6%	26.1%
1992	No	18.2%	18.5%	10.4%	13.4%	N/A
1997	No	17.9%	18.5%	8.1%	13.5%	23.6%
1997	Yes	24.6%	25.3%	11.3%	17.7%	31.8%
2002	Yes	23.0%	24.6%	7.9%	12.7%	28.5%
Mean number of paid employees:						
1982	No	N/A	N/A	0.4	0.7	N/A
1987	No	1.4	1.5	0.5	0.6	1.0
1992	No	1.6	1.7	0.6	0.8	N/A
1997	No	1.6	1.8	0.5	0.7	1.6
1997	Yes	2.9	3.1	0.9	1.2	2.4
2002	Yes	2.5	2.8	0.6	1.0	2.0

Sources: U.S. Census Bureau, Economic Census, Survey of Minority-Owned Business Enterprises (1982, 1987, 1992, 1997), U.S. Census Bureau, Survey of Business Owners (2002), and special tabulations prepared by the U.S. Census Bureau.
Notes: (1) All firms excludes publicly held, foreign-owned, not-for-profit, and other firms, which are not included in the estimates by race. (2) See the book's data appendix for changes in sample criteria and definitions. Estimates are not directly comparable over time. (3) The white category is equal to all firms minus all minority firms for 1982, 1987, and 1992, and all white firms minus Latino-owned firms in 2002. (4) The most recently revised estimates are reported when applicable.

Table 2.7
Employment statistics by race for employer firms only, Survey of Minority-Owned Business Enterprises (1992 to 1997) and Survey of Business Owners (2002)

	Includes C Corporations	All Firms	White-Owned Firms	Black-Owned Firms	Latino-Owned Firms	Asian- and Pacific Islander-Owned Firms
Total number of employer firms:						
1982	No	N/A	N/A	37,841	39,272	N/A
1987	No	3,487,454	3,239,305	70,815	82,908	92,718
1992	No	3,134,959	2,823,264	64,478	115,364	N/A
1997	No	3,277,510	2,860,580	63,010	151,571	185,357
1997	Yes	5,027,208	4,372,817	93,235	211,884	289,999
2002	Yes	5,172,064	4,512,577	94,518	199,542	323,161
Mean annual payroll for employer firms:						
1982	No	N/A	N/A	$25,055	$31,573	N/A
1987	No	$85,786	$89,423	$38,990	$39,120	$37,770
1992	No	$167,011	$175,342	$74,547	$93,340	N/A
1997	No	$206,087	$219,711	$103,673	$101,540	$116,642
1997	Yes	$298,237	$319,051	$153,615	$140,785	$159,240
2002	Yes	$314,533	$333,494	$185,680	$183,980	$175,984
Payroll per employee for employer firms:						
1982	No	N/A	N/A	$7,812	$8,010	N/A
1987	No	$15,069	$15,232	$12,524	$12,246	$9,967
1992	No	$19,106	$19,390	$13,924	$15,582	N/A
1997	No	$22,739	$23,173	$17,266	$18,350	$17,653
1997	Yes	$25,454	$25,796	$19,938	$21,480	$20,961
2002	Yes	$29,381	$29,842	$23,277	$23,888	$25,352

Sources: U.S. Census Bureau, Economic Census, Survey of Minority-Owned Business Enterprises (1982, 1987, 1992, 1997), U.S. Census Bureau, Survey of Business Owners (2002), and special tabulations prepared by the U.S. Census Bureau.
Notes: (1) All firms excludes publicly held, foreign-owned, not-for-profit, and other firms, which are not included in the estimates by race. (2) See the book's data appendix for changes in sample criteria and definitions. Estimates are not directly comparable over time. (3) The white category is equal to all firms minus all minority firms for 1982, 1987, and 1992, and all white firms minus Latino-owned firms in 2002. (4) The most recently revised estimates are reported when applicable.

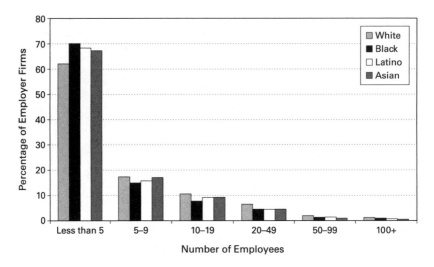

Figure 2.4
Employment size distribution of employer firms by race, Survey of Business Owners (2002)

to white-employer firms in recent years, although all three groups had lower average payrolls and payrolls per employee than white-employer firms. In 2002, all three minority groups had average payrolls that were less than $200,000 compared with an average payroll of $333,494 among white firms. Much of the difference is due to the number of employees hired. Payroll per employee was $29,842 for white-employer firms compared with $23,277 for black-employer firms, $23,888 for Latino-employer firms, and $25,352 for Asian-employer firms.

Because the comparison of average employment may be driven by a few very large employers, it is also useful to examine racial distributions of employment levels. Figure 2.4 displays employment distributions by race for employer firms in 2002. Most employer firms have fewer than five employees. This is true across all racial groups. Very few firms had twenty or more employees, and only a very small fraction had fifty or more employees. White-employer firms are the least likely to hire fewer than five employees and are the most likely to hire large numbers of employees. The employment distributions for black-, Latino-, and Asian-employer firms are not substantially different, although black firms are most likely to be located in the smallest employment-size class.

Table 2.8

Small business outcomes by race, Characteristics of Business Owners (1992)

	All Firms	White-Owned Firms	Black-Owned Firms	Latino-Owned Firms	Asian-Owned Firms
Percentage of firms in 1992 no longer operating in 1996 (closure)	22.5%	22.6%	26.9%	22.2%	17.9%
Percentage of firms with a net profit of at least $10,000	30.1%	30.4%	13.9%	28.2%	38.0%
Percentage of firms with a positive net profit	74.5%	75.1%	60.7%	73.6%	72.5%
Percentage of firms with 1 or more paid employees	21.3%	21.4%	11.3%	20.7%	29.9%
Mean number of employees	1.77	1.80	0.63	1.72	2.20
Mean sales	$212,791	$219,190	$59,415	$167,698	$245,481
Mean log sales	10.10	10.10	9.43	10.14	10.71
Sample size	38,020	15,872	7,565	7,390	6,321

Notes: (1) The sample includes businesses that are classified by the IRS as individual proprietorships or self-employed persons, partnerships, and subchapter S corporations, have sales of $500 or more, and have at least one owner who worked at least twelve weeks and ten hours per week in the business. (2) All estimates are calculated using sample weights provided by the Characteristics of Business Owners.

Racial Differences in Business Outcomes: Evidence from the CBO

Estimates from the 1992 CBO also indicate large racial disparities in business outcomes. Table 2.8 reports estimates of 1992 profits, employment, and sales as well as closure rates between 1992 and 1996 from confidential and restricted-access CBO microdata. We use a sample of businesses with a substantial hours-worked commitment by the owners for these estimates (see the book's data appendix for more details). This restriction rules out the large number of very small businesses in the United States that are included in the SBO and SMOBE estimates. By restricting our sample to include only firms in which at least one owner worked at least twelve weeks during the year and at least ten hours per week, we reduce the number of firms in our sample by 22.1 percent.[26] As expected, the resulting sample has higher sales and employment on average than the SMOBE estimates for 1992, which is the underlying sample frame for the CBO.

We first discuss the results for black-owned businesses and make comparisons to white-owned businesses. The magnitude of the disparities in business outcomes found in our CBO sample is striking. For example, only 13.9 percent of black-owned firms have annual profits of $10,000 or more, compared with 30.4 percent of white-owned firms. In fact, the entire distribution of business net profits before taxes for black-owned firms is to the left of the distribution for white-owned firms (with the exception of the largest loss categories).[27] Surprisingly, nearly 40 percent of all black-owned firms have *negative* profits. Black-owned firms also have lower survival rates than white-owned firms. The average probability of business closure between 1992 and 1996 is 26.9 percent for black-owned firms, compared with 22.6 percent for white-owned firms.[28]

Estimates from CBO microdata confirm the findings from SMOBE data on black/white differences in sales and employment. Black-owned firms are substantially smaller on average than are white-owned firms. Mean sales among black-owned firms were $59,415 in 1992. Average sales among white-owned firms were nearly four times larger. The difference is due not simply to a few very large white firms influencing the mean. Median sales for black firms were one half that of white firms, and the percentage of black firms with sales of $100,000 or more was less than half the percentage of white firms. Estimates from the CBO also indicate that black-owned firms hire fewer employees than white-owned firms. In 1992, they averaged only 0.63 employees, whereas white-owned firms hired 1.80 employees. Only 11.3 percent of black-owned firms hired *any* employees. In comparison, 21.4 percent of white-owned firms hired at least one employee. As was shown earlier, these trends have continued through the more recent surveys.

Unexpectedly, estimates from our CBO sample do not reveal large disparities in business outcomes for Latino-owned firms. We find very similar rates of closure, profits, employment, and mean log sales as white firms. The only business outcome showing a nonnegligible difference is average sales. We do not have an explanation for these patterns, as the outcomes for Latino-owned businesses presented above from the SBO and SMOBE data clearly indicate worse outcomes than for white-owned businesses. One potential explanation for the discrepancy in results is that the two sets of estimates differ in their treatment of businesses with low hours-worked commitments by the owners. This appears to be part but not all of the reason for the discrepancy. Published estimates from the 1992 CBO, which do not exclude smaller-scale businesses, indicate that Latino firms have lower sales, are less likely to hire employees than are white-owned firms, but have only slightly lower profit levels and slightly higher closure rates than white-owned firms (U.S. Census Bureau 1997).

To follow up on this question, we estimate business outcomes from the 2003 Survey of Small Business Finances (SSBF) and 2000 U.S. Census. Estimates from the 2003 SSBF indicate that Latino firms have lower sales, profits, and employment levels than white firms. Latino business owners are also found to have lower earnings than white business owners using data from the 2000 census. These results are different than those from our CBO microdata but are consistent with the SMOBE/SBO estimates.

Robb (2000) also found evidence that the CBO may have problems capturing Latino firms. While her research showed statistically significant differences between survival rates of Hispanic- and white-owned firms using the SMOBE data, those differences did not appear in the CBO data, which is problematic because the CBO is a representative subsample of the SMOBE. Although there is uncertainty over whether the lack of differences in business outcomes that we report from our CBO sample is real, we cannot explain gaps that do not exist in our data. Thus, we do not focus on explaining the causes of differences in business outcomes between Latino and white firms in our analysis of CBO microdata in the following chapters. Instead, we focus on identifying the causes of differences in outcomes between black-, Asian-, and white-owned businesses.

Although estimates from the SBO and SMOBE provide mixed results on the performance of Asian firms relative to white firms, the evidence from our CBO sample of more active businesses is clear. Asian firms outperform white firms on every business outcome measure reported in table 2.8. Asian-owned firms are 16.9 percent less likely to close, 20.6 percent more likely to have profits of at least $10,000, and 27.2 percent more likely to hire employees than white-owned firms. Asian firms have mean annual sales that are also higher than the mean annual sales of white firms. The difference in log annual sales, which lessens the influence of large outliers, implies that Asian firms have annual sales that are roughly 60 percent higher than the mean sales of white firms. The exclusion of smaller businesses in which the owner is providing only a minimal hours- and weeks-worked commitment leaves little doubt about whether Asian businesses perform better on average than white firms.

Using the published CBO results, we can also examine the distribution of profits by race. Unlike estimates that we generate from CBO

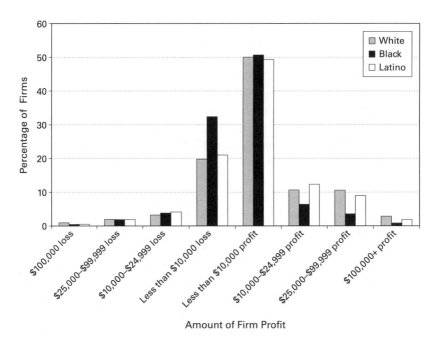

Figure 2.5
Firm profit distribution by race, published estimates from the Characteristics of Business Owners (1992)

microdata, published CBO estimates include all businesses and do not rule out ones with low hours or weeks worked by the owner. Figure 2.5 displays racial distributions of firm profits. We do not report separate estimates for Asians because in the published CBO data they are grouped with Native Americans.[29] The distribution of profits indicates that the majority of firms (about half in each race category) received positive profits up to $10,000. The next-largest category, again across all race groups, was a loss of up to $10,000. Black firms are clearly overrepresented in the less-than-$10,000-loss category and underrepresented in the large-profit categories relative to white firms. On the other hand, the profit distribution for Latino businesses does not differ substantially from the white profit distribution.

Estimates from previous waves of the CBO generally indicate similar racial patterns in business outcomes. For example, using the 1987 CBO, Bates (1997) found that closure rates were higher among black-owned firms compared with other minority-owned businesses and white-owned businesses. Bates also found that Asian-owned firms have somewhat lower average sales than white-owned firms but slightly higher survival rates and profits than white-owned firms.

Estimates from Other Business-Level Data Sources

Focusing on employer firms, two recent studies use special administrative longitudinal data on minority-owned businesses to examine survival and other dynamic outcomes. Robb (2002) links Business Information Tracking Series (BITS) data from 1992 to 1996 to SMOBE microdata from 1992 and examines new firm-survival rates by race. Estimates from the linked data indicate that 48.7 percent of new white-employer firms and 51.7 percent of new Asian-employer firms survive from 1992 to 1996. In contrast, only 34.8 percent of new black-employer firms and 43.7 percent of new Latino-employer firms survive over this period. Boden and Headd (2002) also used this matched dataset and find similar results.

Lowrey (2005) uses a special U.S. Census dataset that tracks 1997 SMOBE respondents over time to examine racial differences in survival, contraction, and expansion among employer establishments from 1997 to 2001. She finds lower survival rates among black- and Latino-owned establishments than among nonminority and Asian-owned establishments. In contrast to these results, however, she finds that Latino establishments had a higher expansion rate and that black and Latino establishments had lower contraction rates than white establishments. Asian establishments had a higher expansion rate but a slightly higher contraction rate than white firms.

Estimates from the 2003 Survey of Small Business Finances (SSBF), which is conducted by the Federal Reserve and is known to include a larger share of more established firms than the SBO, indicate similar racial patterns for business outcomes. Asian firms have much higher sales, profits, and employment levels than white firms. Black and Latino firms have substantially lower business outcomes. Similar patterns for black and Latino firms are found using the 1998 SSBF (Robb 2005). These results confirm the rankings of business performance by race generally found in the CBO and SBO/SMOBE data.

Differences across Asian and Latino Groups

We briefly discuss the differences within the Asian and Latino groups. Table 2.9 reports estimates of the number of firms, average sales, and

Table 2.9
Business outcomes among detailed Asian groups, Survey of Business Owners (2002)

	All Asians and, Native Hawaiian, and Other Pacific Islander	Asian Indian	Chinese	Filipino
Total number of firms	1,132,535	223,212	286,041	125,146
Mean sales and receipts	$292,214	$394,818	$367,261	$113,110
Mean number of paid employees	2.0	2.7	2.3	1.1

	Japanese	Korean	Viet-namese	Other Asian	Native Hawaiian and Other Pacific Islander
Total number of firms	86,910	157,688	147,036	89,118	28,948
Mean sales and receipts	$352,354	$297,808	$105,501	$272,400	$147,837
Mean number of paid employees	2.4	2.0	0.9	1.8	1.0

Source: U.S. Census Bureau, Survey of Business Owners (2002).

average employment for several Asian subgroups from the 2002 SBO. Each of the three largest Asian subgroups of business owners—Asian Indians, Chinese, and Koreans—has average sales and employment that are not substantially lower than for all firms. Average sales range from $297,808 to $394,818 and average employment ranges from 2.0 to 2.7 employees. Japanese and other Asian firms also fall in this range. Filipino, Vietnamese, and Native Hawaiian and other Pacific Islander firms are less successful on average. Average sales for these groups range from $105,501 to $147,837, and average employment from 0.9 to 1.1. Although businesses owned by these three Asian subgroups are less successful than the larger Asian subgroups, they represent only 26 percent of all Asian-owned businesses.

Overall, there exists some variation in business outcomes across Asian subgroups. These estimates, however, indicate that businesses owned by most Asian subgroups are successful relative to other minority groups. We do not focus on Asian subgroups in the main analysis of this study because of sample sizes, time constraints, and confidentiality restrictions. Combining Asian subgroups for the analysis, how-

Table 2.10
Business outcomes among detailed Latino groups, Survey of Business Owners (2002)

	All Latinos	Mexican American	Puerto Rican	Cuban	Other Latino
Total number of firms	1,573,464	701,078	109,475	151,688	596,125
Mean sales and receipts	$141,044	$137,980	$112,723	$233,660	$124,503
Mean number of paid employees	1.0	1.0	0.7	1.4	0.8

Source: U.S. Census Bureau, Survey of Business Owners (2002).

ever, is not likely to create serious problems based on this comparison of outcomes.

Examining business outcomes for more detailed Latino groups, we find a few differences (table 2.10). Puerto Ricans have the lowest average sales ($112,723), whereas Cubans have the highest average sales ($233,660). The largest Latino subgroup, Mexican Americans, have average sales that are very similar to the Latino total. Employment patterns also differ somewhat across Latino subgroups ranging from a low of 0.7 mean employees for Puerto Rican firms to a high of 1.4 mean employees for Cuban firms. Mexican American firms hire an average of one employee.

Overall, there is some variation in business outcomes across Latino subgroups, but these differences are small relative to the difference between Latinos and non-Latino whites. For all Latino subgroups, average sales and employment are substantially lower than for white-owned businesses.

Conclusions

In this chapter, we provide evidence on recent trends in business ownership and business outcomes by race from the CPS, SBO/SMOBE, and CBO. The CPS microdata provide the most up-to-date estimates of the rate of business ownership in the United States, and the SBO/SMOBE provide the most up-to-date national estimates of business outcomes by race. The 1992 CBO microdata, which are used in following chapters, provide evidence for additional business outcomes and allow for the exclusion of businesses in which the owner provides only a minimal work effort. We generate and collect estimates from several sources to create a comprehensive picture of the state of minority businesses in the United States over the past two and a half decades.

A clear ordering of business success exists across racial groups in the United States. Whites and Asians have the highest rates of business ownership and own the most successful businesses. Among all businesses, white firms generally outperform Asian firms slightly; however, after removing small-scale and side businesses, Asian firms outperform white firms. Estimates from 1992 CBO microdata indicate that Asian-owned firms are 16.9 percent less likely to close, 20.6 percent more likely to have profits of at least $10,000, and 27.2 percent more likely to hire employees than white-owned firms. Furthermore, they have mean annual sales that are roughly 60 percent higher than the mean sales of white-owned firms.

African American firms have the lowest rates of business ownership and the worst outcomes of all major ethnic and racial groups. The low rate of business ownership among blacks relative to whites—approximately one third the rate—held for most of the twentieth century. In the past few years, however, there is some evidence of rising black self-employment rates. Estimates from the SBO, SMOBE, and CBO also indicate that black-owned firms have substantially worse outcomes than white- and Asian-owned firms. Black-owned firms have lower revenues and profits, hire fewer employees, and are more likely to close than white- and Asian-owned businesses.

Finally, Latinos have the second lowest rate of business ownership of the four major ethnic and racial groups. Their rate of business ownership is only two thirds the rate of business ownership among white non-Latinos. Estimates from the SBO/SMOBE data also indicate substantially worse outcomes among Latino-owned firms than white- or Asian-owned firms. Latino-owned businesses have lower average sales, are less likely to hire employees, and hire fewer employees than white-owned businesses. Unexpectedly, however, estimates from our CBO sample do not reveal large disparities in business outcomes for Latino-owned firms. We find very similar rates of closure, profits, employment, and mean log sales. The lack of large disparities between white and Latino firms, however, appears to be peculiar to the CBO. Estimates from other sources, such as the SSBF and U.S. Census, in addition to the SBO/SMOBE indicate that Latino-owned businesses have worse average outcomes than white-owned businesses.

3   The Determinants of Small Business Success

In the previous chapter, we reviewed the main findings from the rapidly growing literature on minority business ownership. The findings from this literature indicate that racial differences in access to financial capital, human capital, and parental self-employment contribute to racial disparities in business-ownership rates. A much smaller literature, however, focuses on the related question of why there are such large racial differences in business outcomes, especially using business-level datasets. The lack of research is unfortunate given that racial disparities in many business outcomes are much larger than disparities in business-ownership rates. For example, the average sales of white-owned businesses is more than five times the average sales of black-owned businesses, whereas white rates of business ownership are two to three times larger than black business-ownership rates. We know relatively little about what factors explain the substantial disparities in survival prospects, profits, sales, and employment across businesses owned by different racial groups.

Before examining the causes of racial disparities in business outcomes, however, we first need to identify the determinants of business success. Once these factors are identified, we can make comparisons across racial groups. Of particular interest is determining which owner and firm characteristics are important inputs in the production process and thus are associated with success in business. How important are human capital and financial capital in creating successful businesses? Is the owner's family-business background an important determinant of success, relative to these more well-known factors? How important are prior work experience in a family business, similar type of business, and managerial capacity for business success? We investigate these questions and examine whether additional characteristics of the owner and firm are linked to operating successful businesses using the confidential and restricted-access Characteristics of Business Owners (CBO) microdata.

The owner's education level is likely to be one of the most important determinants of business success. Education is generally found to increase the likelihood of owning a business in the United States even though the returns to education in the labor market are substantial.[1] Perhaps even more important to the success of the business is adequate access to financial capital. As noted in the previous chapter, a large literature finds that an owner's personal wealth is positively associated with business ownership, which has often been interpreted as evidence of liquidity constraints. If some entrepreneurs can obtain only limited amounts of startup capital because they do not have collateral for loans or because they experience lending discrimination, then their newly created businesses may grow more slowly or not perform as well as firms started by entrepreneurs who have access to the optimal levels of startup capital. Thus, access to startup capital is likely to be critical to business success.

The owner's family-business background may also be an important factor in creating and operating successful businesses. The children of business owners are much more likely to own businesses than are the children of nonbusiness owners (Lentz and Laband 1990; Fairlie 1999; Dunn and Holtz-Eakin 2000; Hout and Rosen 2000). Although the intergenerational transmission of business ownership is strong, the effects on small business outcomes *conditioning* on ownership are essentially unknown. An interesting question is whether children of business owners also start more successful firms than children of nonbusiness owners. Furthermore, the underlying causes of intergenerational links in business ownership have not been identified in the literature. These links may be due to the acquisition of general business or managerial experience from working in family-owned businesses, the acquisition of industry- or firm-specific business experience working in family-owned businesses, inheritances of businesses, or a correlation among family members in preferences for entrepreneurial activities.

The previous literature has not analyzed the owner and firm characteristics that are associated with business success in detail because only a few datasets contain sufficient information to thoroughly investigate this issue. Individual-level datasets, such as the U.S. Census or the Current Population Survey (CPS), contain detailed information on the demographic characteristics of self-employed business owners but contain very little information on the characteristics of the business. On the other hand, business-level datasets contain detailed information on the business but generally have few, if any, measures of owner characteristics (see the book's data appendix for more details). Furthermore, only a few nationally representative datasets contain information on parental and family self-employment and business inheritances. To our knowledge, the CBO is the only nationally representative dataset that contains information on prior work experience in businesses owned by family members and prior work experience in businesses providing similar goods and services. The confidential and restricted-access CBO data are ideally suited for examining the effects of family background, human capital, business human capital, and other factors on business outcomes because they include detailed characteristics of both the owner and the firm. The CBO data also include information on several business outcomes.

We first identify some of the key factors and discuss why they might be important determinants of business success. We provide evidence on the simple relationships between several owner and firm characteristics and two measures of business success—sales and employment. Next, we estimate the effects of owner and business characteristics on several business outcomes using multivariate regression models. The use of multivariate regressions allows us to identify the separate and independent effects of these characteristics on the success of the business. Many owner and business characteristics (such as education, family-business ownership, and startup capital) are likely to be correlated. As measures of business success, we use closure rates, profits, employment, and sales. Although none of these is a perfect measure of business success, the results from all four outcomes provide a decent overall picture of business performance.

Education

The success of a business is likely to be linked to the education level of the owner. One reason is that the general and specific knowledge and skills acquired through formal education may be useful for running a successful business. For example, general skills (such as learning how to read, write, and communicate through coursework) or specific skills (such as learning accounting and marketing) increase the ability of the owner to find customers, create new products, and manage the firm. The owner's level of education may also serve as a proxy for his or her

Table 3.1
Small business outcomes by owner's education level, Characteristics of Business Owners (1992)

	Percentage			
	Sales of $50,000+	Sales of $100,000+	Paid Employees	All Firms
High school dropout	21.3%	13.2%	14.1%	10.0%
High school graduate	24.3	15.0	16.8	24.1
Some college	23.6	15.0	16.8	28.9
College graduate	28.0	18.0	18.7	21.5
Graduate school	35.2	23.8	23.7	15.7
All firms	26.4	17.1	18.2	

Source: U.S. Bureau of the Census (1997).
Note: The sample includes businesses that are classified by the IRS as individual proprietorships or self-employed persons, partnerships, and subchapter S corporations and that have sales of $500 or more.

overall ability or as a positive signal to potential customers, lenders, and business suppliers. For all of these reasons, we expect to find that more educated owners have more successful firms.

Published estimates from the 1992 CBO reveal a clear positive relationship between owner's education and business outcomes (U.S. Census Bureau 1997).[2] Table 3.1 reports estimates of the percentage of business owners in five major education levels who have sales of $50,000 and $100,000 or more and hire employees. The percentage of owners who have high average sales generally increases with each education level and the differences are large. For example, 28.0 percent of firms with owners who are college graduates have sales of $50,000 or more compared with 21.3 percent of firms with owners that are high school dropouts. The difference is even larger for firms with owners who have graduate degrees. These firms are 13.9 percentage points (or 65 percent) more likely to have sales of $50,000 or more than are firms owned by high school dropouts. These patterns are consistent across education groups for sales of $100,000 or more as well. The owner's education level is also related to the employment level of the firm. We find that firms with more educated owners are generally more likely to hire employees. Nearly 19 percent of firms owned by college graduates have paid employees compared with 14.1 percent of firms owned by high school dropouts. Overall, the owner's education level is clearly associated with better business outcomes. A multivariate regression analysis is used later to examine the statistical strength of the relationship and its presence after controlling for additional factors that might be correlated with education, such as management experience and startup capital.

Family-Business Background

Another potentially important determinant of business success is the owner's family-business background. The owner's family-business background can be characterized by whether he or she has a parent who was a self-employed business owner, worked for a family business, or inherited a business. All of these factors may influence the likelihood that an individual becomes a business owner and that the business is successful. Indeed, an important finding in the previous literature is that an individual who had a self-employed parent is roughly two to three times more likely to be self-employed than someone who did not have a self-employed parent (Lentz and Laband 1990; Fairlie 1999; Dunn and Holtz-Eakin 2000; Hout and Rosen 2000).[3]

Before exploring whether family-business backgrounds are also important for business success, we review the potential explanations for intergenerational links in business ownership. Several explanations for the intergenerational transmission of business ownership have been offered in the previous literature. First, the informal learning or apprenticeship-type training that occurs in growing up in the context of a family business may provide an important opportunity for future owners to acquire human capital related to operating a successful business (Lentz and Laband 1990). Family-business experience can be classified into two types, which we term *general business human capital* and *specific business human capital*. General business human capital includes "general administrative and personnel management skills" and "general managerial expertise" (Lentz and Laband 1990; Dunn and Holtz-Eakin 2000). Specific business human capital includes "enterprise-specific skills, "information specific to the firm's production," and "job- or industry-specific knowledge." Dunn and Holtz-Eakin (2000) find that self-employed sons follow their father's occupation in only 32 percent of cases, suggesting that the business expertise being passed within families is not only specific to the types of business chosen by these sons.

Another explanation is that intergenerational links in self-employment may be caused by a correlation among family members in preferences or ability for entrepreneurial activities. The correlation may be due simply to similarities among family members in preferences for being one's own boss or entrepreneurship or similarities in other personal characteristics that are associated with self-employment, such as entrepreneurial ability and attitudes towards risk (Fairlie 2002).[4] Using the National Longitudinal Surveys (NLS), however, Dunn and Holtz-Eakin (2000) find that the intergenerational correlation in self-employment is strongest for successfully self-employed parents, suggesting that it is the transmission of business skills rather than similarities in tastes for the self-employed lifestyle that drives the relationship between parents' and children's self-employment propensities. Related to the issue of correlated preferences and ability, intergenerational links may also be created by self-employed parents by creating role models for their children to become business owners. Observing a successfully self-employed parent may improve a child's assessment of his or her own entrepreneurial ability.

Intergenerational links may also be created directly when the children of self-employed business owners become partners with their parents or directly inherit businesses. Forming a partnership with a child may represent a less expensive method of helping a child to become a business owner. Also, partnerships and inheritances may represent an efficient form of transmitting reputation capital or an established clientele from one generation to the next. Related to this issue, successful business owners may be more likely to transfer financial wealth to their children, potentially making it easier for them to become self-employed. Dunn and Holtz-Eakin (2000), however, provide estimates suggesting that wealth transfers play only a modest role. We also find that financial transfers from parents to children are not a common source of startup capital among small business owners. Only 6.4 percent of owners borrowed capital from their families.

Evidence from the CBO on Intergenerational Links in Business Ownership

The CBO contains information on having a self-employed family member, prior work experience in that family member's business, and business inheritances, which allows us to disentangle some of the potential explanations offered in the previous literature. If most business owners have self-employed family members but do not have prior work experience in these family businesses, then we can infer that the correlation in entrepreneurial preferences or ability is more important than

Table 3.2
Family business background measures, Characteristics of Business Owners (1992)

	All Firms (percent)	Sample Size
Had a self-employed family member prior to starting the firm	51.6%	37,740
Worked in that family member's business (conditional)	43.6	36,575
Worked in a family member's business (unconditional)	22.5	36,575
Worked at a business with similar goods or services	50.1	37,238
Inherited their businesses	1.6	37,619
Received their businesses as a transfer of ownership or a gift	6.6	37,707

Notes: (1) The sample includes businesses that are classified by the IRS as individual proprietorships or self-employed persons, partnerships, and subchapter S corporations, have sales of $500 or more, and have at least one owner who worked at least twelve weeks and ten hours per week in the business. (2) All estimates are calculated using sample weights provided by the Characteristics of Business Owners.

acquiring general and specific business human capital in creating the intergenerational link in self-employment. In addition, if very few businesses are inherited, then we can infer that business inheritances play only a minor role in establishing the intergenerational link in business ownership.

Table 3.2 reports the percentage of small business owners who had a family member who was a business owner, the percentage of owners who worked for that family member, and other measures related to family-business background.[5] More than half of all business owners had a self-employed family member prior to starting their business. Conditional on having a self-employed family member, nearly 45 percent of all small business owners worked in that family member's business. Overall, 22.5 percent of small business owners worked in a family business prior to starting or acquiring their business.[6]

The finding that more than 50 percent of all small business owners had a family member who was a self-employed business owner is nearly identical to a National Federation of Independent Business (NFIB) survey that found that 52.2 percent of independent businessmen had parents who were business owners (Lentz and Laband 1990). Although we do not have a comparison group of nonbusiness owners and family members may include spouses and siblings in addition to parents, the finding that half of business owners have a self-employed family member suggests a high level of intergenerational transmission of business ownership. Under reasonable assumptions, it is easy to show that these estimates imply that the children of self-employed parents are three times more likely to be self-employed than are the children of non-self-employed parents, which is consistent with previous findings in the literature (see the appendix to this chapter for more details). Another interesting finding is that more than half of all business owners who have a self-employed family member did not work for that family member's business. This finding suggests that intergenerational links in self-employment are not due solely to the acquisition of general and specific business capital. Thus, part of the reason that the children of business owners are more likely to own businesses appears to be similarities between family members in entrepreneurial preferences and ability.

Work Experience in Family Businesses

The CBO also contains information on whether the owner previously worked in a similar business prior to starting this business.[7] An example of this type of work experience would be a restaurant owner who works in a restaurant prior to starting his or her business. Similar business work experience undoubtedly provides opportunities for acquiring job- or industry-specific business human capital in addition to more general business human capital. About half of all small business owners report working in a similar business prior to starting their business.

Among owners who worked in a family member's business, 55.8 percent report working in a business that provided similar goods and services. Unfortunately, however, we cannot identify whether the family member's business is the same as the business providing similar goods and services. Therefore, our estimate provides only an "upper bound" estimate of the percentage of owners who acquired specific business human capital from working in a family member's business. Nevertheless, the estimate of roughly 50 percent suggests that family businesses are providing opportunities to acquire general business human capital and not just specific business human capital. This finding is consistent with the finding in Dunn and Holtz-Eakin (2000) that self-employed sons follow their father's occupation in only 32 percent of cases.

Business Inheritances

Another explanation is that the children of self-employed business owners become partners with their parents or directly inherit businesses. In contrast to the large percentage of owners who have a self-employed family member and prior work experience in that family business, very few small businesses are inherited. Estimates from the CBO indicate that only 1.6 percent of all small businesses are inherited. This finding suggests that the role of business inheritances in determining intergenerational links in self-employment is limited at best.

For comparison, the Federal Reserve's Survey of Small Business Finances (SSBF) includes information on business inheritances and gifts. Estimates from the SSBF indicate that 4.0 percent of firms are inherited or acquired as gifts. Estimates of the percentage of firms that are inherited from the Federal Reserve's Survey of Consumer Finances (SCF) indicate that 3.5 percent of businesses are inherited or acquired as gifts. Unfortunately, both the SSBF and SCF questionnaires do not distinguish between inheritances and gifts.

Lentz and Laband (1990) also provide estimates of business inheritances from a sample of independent businessmen from the NFIB. They find a much higher rate of business inheritances in their sample (14.2 percent). The discrepancy may be due to the much larger scale of businesses included in the NFIB. These firms had average sales of approximately $2 million in 1979, compared with slightly more than $200,000 in the CBO sample.

The CBO also includes information on whether the owner acquired the business through a "transfer of ownership/gift." This form of receipt of ownership may capture parents who give firms to their children. It may also contain many other forms of business transfers and is not limited to family members. Even with this concern, we find that only 6.6 percent of owners received their business through a transfer of ownership or gift, suggesting that direct parent-to-child transfers of businesses cannot represent a large percentage of all small businesses. In fact, if we remove owners who did not have a self-employed family member prior to starting the business, only 4.0 percent of owners received a transfer of ownership or gift. Thus, the maximum number of owners in the CBO inheriting a business or receiving one as a gift is 5.6 percent. This probably greatly overstates the total, however, as only 4.0 percent of business owners in the SSBF (which includes larger, more established businesses than the CBO) inherited or received their business as a gift. If large corporations other than S corporations are removed, the percentage of businesses that are inherited or acquired as a gift drops to 3.5 percent in the SSBF. There is the possibility, however, that businesses are sold at below-market prices from parents to children. Unfortunately, there is no information available on this type of transfer.

Related to business inheritances, we also find that financial transfers from parents to children are not a common source of startup capital among small business owners. Only 6.4 percent of owners borrowed capital from their family. This finding is consistent with the finding in Dunn and Holtz-Eakin (2000) that financial transfers from parents to children do not appear to be responsible for the intergenerational transmission of business ownership.

Intergenerational Links, Family-Business Backgrounds, and Business Success

Although there is uncertainty over the correspondence between family members and parents on the CBO questionnaire, the estimates reported in table 3.2 provide some suggestive evidence on the causes of intergenerational links in self-employment. These links appear to be partly but not entirely driven by opportunities to acquire both general and specific business human capital from working in family members' businesses. Business inheritances and partnerships with family members appear to play only a minor role. We next examine whether these factors are important in determining small business outcomes.

We first examine the relationship between two family-business background measures and success in small business using published estimates from the CBO. Table 3.3 reports estimates of the percentage of business owners with and without a family-business background who have sales of $50,000 and $100,000 or more and hire employees. The percentage of business owners who have high average sales and hire employees is higher for those who had a self-employed family member. We also find that owners who have prior work experience in a family member's business have better outcomes than owners who do not have this work experience. The differences in outcomes, however, are much larger for having prior work experience. For example, firms with owners who have prior work experience in family member's business are 7.2 percentage points more likely to have sales of $50,000 or more, whereas firms with owners who have a self-employed family member prior to starting the firm are 3.9 percentage points more likely to have sales of $50,000 or more. These findings suggest that the general and specific business human capital acquired from working in a family member's business may have a strong effect on business suc-

Table 3.3
Small business outcomes by family business background measures, Characteristics of Business Owners (1992)

	Percentage			
	Sales of $50,000+	Sales of $100,000+	Paid Employees	All Firms
Had a self-employed family member prior to starting the firm	28.7%	18.9%	20.0%	52.5%
Did not have a self-employed family member prior to starting the firm	24.8	15.5	16.6	47.5
Previously worked in a family member's business	32.2	22.4	23.5	22.9
Did not previously work in a family member's business	25.0	15.5	16.7	77.1
Inherited the business	43.3	36.4	41.7	2.9
Did not inherit the business	26.5	16.8	17.8	97.1
All firms	26.4	17.1	18.2	

Source: U.S. Bureau of the Census (1997).
Note: The sample includes businesses that are classified by the IRS as individual proprietorships or self-employed persons, partnerships, and subchapter S corporations and that have sales of $500 or more.

cess. Having a family member who was a business owner may also be important, but the evidence here suggests that it is less important. We explore this further in the multivariate analysis below.

Table 3.3 also reports estimates of the relationship between business inheritances and business success. As expected, we find that inherited businesses have higher sales and hire more employees than noninherited businesses. These businesses are likely to be larger and more established than noninherited businesses because they are older. Inheriting an already established business apparently represents one route to owning a successful business.

Other Forms of Business Human Capital

As noted above, the CBO contains information on an additional form of acquiring business human capital for the owner—prior work experience in a business whose goods and services were similar to those provided by the owner's business. Another method of acquiring business human capital is prior work experience in a managerial capacity. Both of these types of work experience may be useful for running a

Table 3.4
Small business outcomes by types of prior work experience, Characteristics of Business
Owners (1992)

	Percentage			
	Sales of $50,000+	Sales of $100,000+	Paid Employees	All Firms
Had previous work experience in a managerial capacity	30.5%	20.3%	21.2%	54.8%
Did not have previous work experience in a managerial capacity	22.3	13.6	14.9	45.2
Previously worked in a business with similar goods or services	30.9	19.8	21.8	44.7
Did not previously work in a business with similar goods or services	23.5	15.2	15.6	55.3
All firms	26.4	17.1	18.2	

Source: U.S. Bureau of the Census (1997).
Note: The sample includes businesses that are classified by the IRS as individual proprietorships or self-employed persons, partnerships, and subchapter S corporations and that
have sales of $500 or more.

successful business, but they differ in the types of skills that they are likely to provide the owner. Prior managerial experience is likely to provide the owner with general business human capital. By working in a managerial capacity, the owner may have acquired very useful administrative, management, and human resources skills. These management skills may also be useful for the owner in securing financing.[8]

Prior work experience at a firm providing similar goods and services, on the other hand, is likely to provide the owner with specific business human capital. The owner may have acquired skills that are specific to a type of work or industry that are useful for starting and running a successful business. For example, previous work experience at a restaurant is likely to provide an owner with valuable skills for operating a successful restaurant, and working in a construction trade is likely to impart skills useful for operating a business in that trade.

In both cases, the relationship between these forms of acquiring business human capital and business outcomes are strong (see table 3.4). Small businesses with owners who have prior managerial experience and prior work experience in a similar business have higher sales and are more likely to hire employees. These two types of work experience may provide future business owners with business human capital that is valuable for running successful businesses.

Identifying the Determinants of Business Outcomes: Regression Results

We now turn to estimating the effects of human capital, business human capital, family-business background, and additional owner and business characteristics on several business outcomes. To identify the independent effects of these factors, we conduct a multivariate regression analysis. We are particularly interested in identifying the independent effects on small business outcomes of education, a self-employed family member, prior work experience in that family member's business, and prior work experience in a similar business. The results will have implications for the roles played by general and specific business human capital and by the correlation across family members in entrepreneurial preferences in determining business success. We also examine the relationships between financial capital, industry, and business outcomes.

As mentioned previously, the CBO data contain information on four major business outcomes—closure, profits, employment, and sales. Although none of these measures alone represents a perfect, universally agreed on measure of business success, taken together they provide a fairly comprehensive picture of what it means to be successful in business. We estimate regressions for these probabilities—that a business closes over the period from 1992 to 1996, that it has profits of at least $10,000 per year, and that it has employees.[9] For all of these regressions, we use logit models because the dependent variable takes on only two values—yes = 1 or no = 0. We estimate a linear regression for log sales.[10] Estimates from our CBO sample of businesses indicate that nearly one quarter of small businesses existing in 1992 were not operating by 1996 and that slightly less than 30 percent of businesses report a net profit of at least $10,000. Approximately 20 percent of firms hire any employees, and businesses have average log sales of 10.07.

In addition to the human-capital and family-business-background variables noted above, we include the race, sex, region, and urban status of the firm and the marital status and previous work experience of the owner in the regressions (mean values are reported in table 3.A). The specific family-business background and related business human-capital variables included are dummy variables (that is, equal to 0 or 1) for whether the owner had a family member who was a business owner, worked for that family member's business, had previous work experience in a managerial capacity, worked in a business providing similar goods and services, and inherited the business.

Because of concerns regarding potential endogeneity, we follow the approach taken in many previous studies of self-employment reporting estimates from separate sets of regression models that exclude and include startup capital and industry controls. The concern is that the level of startup capital and industry do not *cause* business success and instead capture the effects of something else. Even with these added variables, we estimate relatively parsimonious specifications to focus on more exogenous owner and firm characteristics that predict business success. We do not include, for example, the owner's hours worked in the business as an additional variable because we are concerned that owners who work less than full-time may not be doing so because they choose to. Instead, they may work less than full-time because of a lack of demand for their products and services or because they had to remain employed at a wage and salary job.[11] For similar reasons, we are also concerned about using hours worked to create adjusted outcome measures such as firm profits or sales per hour.[12] If we control for or adjust outcomes by hours worked, then we are implicitly assuming that all business owners work their desired amount of hours, which is unlikely to be the case. We wanted to err on the conservative side by excluding this variable, which partly captures business success, from the regressions. As an alternative, we experiment with tighter hours-worked restrictions for the sample and note these results below.

Specifications that do not include controls for startup capital and industry are estimated first. Table 3.5 reports results from regression models for each of the business outcomes. To ease the interpretation of coefficient estimates, we report marginal effects and their standard errors for the logit regressions. The marginal effects provide an estimate of the effect of a one-unit change in a variable on the probability of a business closure, large profits, or employment.[13]

Race and ethnicity are important determinants of small business outcomes. In the regressions, white is the excluded race category, and the included dummy variables are black, Hispanic, Native American, and Asian. Thus, the interpretation of the coefficient on each variable is the remaining difference between whites and that minority group in the business outcome. For example, the coefficient on the black-owned business variable in specification 3 implies that black-owned firms are 9.51 percentage points less likely to hire an employee than are

Table 3.5
Logit, linear, and ordered probit regressions for small business outcomes, Characteristics of Business Owners (1992)

	Specification				
	(1)	(2)	(3)	(4)	(5)
Dependent variable	Closure (1992–1996)	Profits $10,000+	Employer Firm	Ln Sales	Profits Ordered
Black-owned business	0.0212 (0.0130)	−0.1786 (0.0207)	−0.0951 (0.0166)	−0.4636 (0.0554)	−0.4160 (0.0376)
Latino-owned business	−0.0138 (0.0121)	−0.0443 (0.0144)	0.0231 (0.0116)	0.0660 (0.0490)	−0.0966 (0.0318)
Native American-owned business	−0.1176 (0.0554)	0.0422 (0.0530)	0.0717 (0.0415)	0.3991 (0.1879)	0.0654 (0.1207)
Asian-owned business	−0.0457 (0.0145)	0.0259 (0.0145)	0.0728 (0.0115)	0.4709 (0.0539)	0.0004 (0.0340)
Female-owned business	0.0247 (0.0050)	−0.2107 (0.0066)	−0.0616 (0.0051)	−0.6941 (0.0206)	−0.3968 (0.0135)
Married	−0.0313 (0.0068)	0.1013 (0.0091)	0.0659 (0.0074)	0.2251 (0.0286)	0.1445 (0.0189)
Never married	0.0429 (0.0081)	−0.0363 (0.0101)	−0.0379 (0.0085)	−0.3563 (0.0338)	−0.0492 (0.0220)
High school graduate	−0.0209 (0.0085)	0.0624 (0.0112)	0.0447 (0.0092)	0.1534 (0.0351)	0.0209 (0.0234)
Some college	−0.0101 (0.0084)	0.0724 (0.0111)	0.0471 (0.0091)	0.0570 (0.0351)	0.1038 (0.0232)
College graduate	−0.0553 (0.0093)	0.1133 (0.0118)	0.0606 (0.0097)	0.2397 (0.0383)	0.1632 (0.0252)
Graduate school	−0.1491 (0.0107)	0.2127 (0.0122)	0.1650 (0.0097)	0.6115 (0.0404)	0.5130 (0.0267)
Urban	0.0164 (0.0058)	0.0447 (0.0069)	−0.0343 (0.0055)	0.1008 (0.0234)	0.1134 (0.0150)
Prior work experience in a managerial capacity	0.0655 (0.0054)	0.0265 (0.0063)	0.0513 (0.0052)	0.2089 (0.0217)	−0.0055 (0.0141)
Prior work experience in a similar business	−0.0425 (0.0049)	0.1024 (0.0059)	0.0432 (0.0048)	0.4087 (0.0202)	0.2484 (0.0131)
Have a self-employed family member	−0.0200 (0.0055)	0.0113 (0.0067)	−0.0022 (0.0055)	−0.0356 (0.0227)	0.0092 (0.0148)
Prior work experience in a family member's business	−0.0419 (0.0069)	0.0322 (0.0079)	0.0552 (0.0063)	0.3784 (0.0273)	0.0471 (0.0178)
Inherited business	−0.1007 (0.0237)	0.1097 (0.0217)	0.2006 (0.0157)	1.3144 (0.0800)	0.3524 (0.0506)
Mean of dependent variable	0.2280	0.2980	0.2070	10.0725	1.2391
Log likelihood/R-square	−17,466.46	−16,957.14	−16,542.74	0.1119	−40,045.16
Sample size	33,485	30,500	34,179	34,179	30,500

Notes: (1) See notes to table 3.2. (2) Logit models are used for specifications 1 to 3, OLS is used for specification 4, and an ordered probit is used for specification 5. The log likelihood value is reported for the logit and ordered probit regressions and R-squared is reported for the OLS model. (3) Marginal effects and their standard errors (in parentheses) are reported for the logit regressions. (4) All specifications also include a constant and dummy variables for region and work experience of the primary owner.

white-owned firms, even after controlling for differences in other variables included in the regressions. After controlling for numerous owner
and business characteristics, black-owned businesses continue to lag
behind white-owned businesses. In all specifications except the closure-
probability equation, the coefficient estimate on the black-owned business dummy variable is large, positive, and statistically significant. In
the closure-probability equation, the coefficient estimate is positive but
statistically insignificant. The results are more mixed for Latino-owned
firms. They have a lower probability of having large profits but have a
higher probability of hiring employees than white-owned firms. The
coefficient estimates in the other two specifications are statistically insignificant. On the other hand, Asian- and Native American-owned
businesses generally have better outcomes than white-owned businesses after controlling for the included variables. However, in the
next set of regressions, which include startup capital and industry controls, the positive Asian coefficients essentially disappear. The black
coefficients also become noticeably smaller after the inclusion of these
additional variables.

The finding of relatively large and statistically significant coefficients
on some of the race variables indicates that the included controls for
education, family background, work experience, and other owner and
firm characteristics cannot entirely explain racial differences in business outcomes. By comparing these to the original racial differences in
business outcomes reported in chapter 2, we can get a sense of how
much of the racial disparities in business outcomes are explained by
racial differences in all of the included owner and business characteristics. However, these comparisons are difficult to make because of
differences in the samples, and we are interested primarily in the explanatory power of individual variables. In other words, the current
estimates do not reveal the relative importance of each of the owner
and business characteristics in explaining racial differences in business
outcomes. For example, do differences in education explain more of the
racial disparities in business outcomes than differences in startup capital? For now, we continue the general discussion of identifying the
determinants of business outcomes and explore this other question further in the next two chapters.

In investigating differences in business outcomes by gender, we find
that female-owned businesses have lower measures of business outcomes than male-owned businesses after controlling for the included
owner and business characteristics. This finding is consistent with the

previous literature. For example, Srinivasan, Woo, and Cooper (1994) use data from the NFIB and find that female-owned firms have a higher probability of closure and a lower probability of growth than male-owned firms. Using 1992 SMOBE and CBO data, Robb (2000) finds that women own just over one quarter of businesses with employees and generate less than 20 percent of employer firm receipts. Female-owned firms are also found to have lower survival rates than male-owned firms. Using earlier CBO data, Boden and Nucci (2000) find that businesses owned by women are less likely to survive than businesses owned by men in both years.[14]

Differences between male- and female-owned businesses in closure rates, profits, employment, and sales may be related to barriers to success for female-owned businesses. For example, Brush et al. (2004) note that female entrepreneurs have access to different business and investment social networks than male entrepreneurs.[15] Differences in business outcomes, however, may also be related to gender differences in the goals and types of businesses and preferences for level of work activity. Previous research indicates that women who are married to self-employed men are more likely to be self-employed or enter self-employment and that the choice of self-employment is partly driven by the desire for flexible schedules and other family-related reasons for women relative to men (Bruce 1999; Robb 2000; Boden 1996, 1999; Carr 1996; Devine 1994; Lombard 2001; Lohmann 2001).[16] Given these alternative explanations, some caution is warranted in interpreting the female coefficient estimates because they may not solely capture differences in business success. Although the disparities in outcomes between male- and female-owned businesses are important, they are beyond the scope of the current analysis. We do, however, investigate whether the determinants of small business success differ between men and women, which is an important issue for our analysis because we include both male and female firms in the sample.

Following previous research, we also include marital status in the regressions. We specifically include indicators for whether the owner is married, is divorced or separated, or has never been married. Married business owners have the best outcomes, whereas never-married owners have the worst outcomes out of the three groups. Spouses may provide financial assistance, paid or unpaid labor for the business, health insurance coverage, and other types of assistance that are useful for running a business. There may also be positive knowledge transfers between married couples that improve business performance (Parker

2005), and businesses owned by married couples may be more successful on average.

Business location affects both the supply of services a firm provides
and the demand it faces, both of which can affect business outcomes.
Robb (2000) found that firm location in a central city or inner suburb
had a negative effect on the probability of firm survival. Because of
possible effects of location, we include a measure of whether the business is located in an urban area. Our results are mixed on whether
urban location matters for business success. Firms located in urban
areas are more likely to close, less likely to have employees, more likely
to have large profits, and more likely to have higher sales than firms
located in nonurban areas. Although not reported, we also include
controls for the region of the country where the business is located.
While there is no consistent pattern of business success by region, we
find some evidence that businesses located in New England and the
Pacific regions generally have better outcomes and that businesses
located in the West South Central region have worse outcomes.

Another variable that is included in the regressions but is not
reported in the table is the number of years of work experience prior
to starting or acquiring ownership of the business. We include several
dummy variables that indicate years of previous work experience. The
estimated effects of prior work experience vary somewhat across outcome measures, although we find some evidence suggesting that individuals with twenty or more years of prior work experience and
owners with very little previous work experience have worse outcomes, on average. Older owners with long prior work experience
may have moved into business ownership as a response to job loss
(Farber 1999; Fairlie and Krashinsky 2005), and younger owners with
very little experience may encounter difficulties identifying good business opportunities.

Educational Effects

We now discuss the results from our main human-capital and family-
background variables. Previous research provides evidence that the
owner's education level increases the chance of survival for the business. For example, estimates from earlier waves of the CBO indicate
that small business closures generally decrease with the education
level of the owner (Bates 1990b, 1997; Astebro and Berhardt 2003).

Using the 1992 CBO linked to the Business Information Tracking Series (BITS), Robb (2000) also finds owner's education to be positively associated with business survival. Furthermore, education is found to be associated with higher entrepreneurial earnings (for a review of the literature, see van der Sluis, van Praag, and Vijverberg 2004).

Estimates from CBO microdata similarly indicate that business survival from 1992 to 1996 is positively associated with the education level of the business owner. We also find that the owner's education level improves the additional business outcomes available in the CBO microdata. For example, compared with businesses that have owners who have dropped out of high school, businesses with college-educated owners are 5.5 percentage points less likely to close, 11.3 percentage points more likely to have profits of $10,000 or more, and 6.1 percentage points more likely to have employees and have approximately 25 percent higher sales.

Owners who have completed graduate school have even more successful businesses. The reported estimates for business outcomes indicate that differences between graduate school owners and high school dropout owners are very large. For example, firms with graduate degree owners are 14.9 percentage points less likely to close than firms with high-school-dropout owners. Owners with a graduate degree are also substantially more likely to have successful firms than are owners with a college degree. For example, they are 10.4 percentage points more likely to hire employees and have sales that are roughly 37 percent higher than businesses owned by college graduates. Looking across education levels, we generally see better business outcomes with each higher level of education. The main exception is that owners with some college do not clearly have better outcomes than owners who are high school graduates. The some-college category includes technical, trade, or vocation school, some college but no degree, and associate degrees. Apparently, the greatest return to a college education is from the four-year degree. Overall, these results suggest that the owner's education is an important factor in determining success in business.

The Effects of Family-Business Background on Outcomes

Having a family-business background is important for business outcomes. The main effect, however, appears to be through the informal learning or apprenticeship-type training that occurs while working at a family business and not from simply having a self-employed family member. The regression results indicate that simply having a family member who owned a business has little or no effect on business outcomes. For all of the business outcomes, except for the closure-probability equation, the regression estimates for this variable are statistically insignificant.

In contrast to these results, prior work experience in a family business increases the likelihood of business success. The regression estimates are large and statistically significant for all four business outcomes. The probability of a business closure is 0.042 lower, the probability of large profits is 0.032 higher, the probability of employment is 0.055 higher, and sales are roughly 40 percent higher if the business owner had worked for one of his or her self-employed family members prior to starting the business. The effects on closures, profits, employment, and sales are large and represent 15.3 to 26.6 percent of the mean values for these outcomes.

Our results for one of the business outcomes, closure, are roughly consistent with the findings from previous studies. Using a sample of white male-owned firms from the 1982 CBO, Bates (1990b) finds that having a close relative who was self-employed has a negative but statistically insignificant (t statistic of 1.41) effect on the probability of a business closure. In the 1982 CBO, however, "close relatives" are defined to include nonfamily members with whom frequent contact was maintained by the owner. Astebro and Berhardt (2003) find a positive but statistically insignificant coefficient estimate on prior work experience in a family business in a survival regression using a sample of 738 newly created firms from the 1987 CBO. Fairlie (1999) provides additional evidence from the Panel Study of Income Dynamics (PSID). Having a self-employed father is found to have a large, negative, and statistically significant effect on the probability of exiting from self-employment for white men. Finally, using German data, Bruderl and Preisendorfer (1998) provide some evidence that network support from "strong ties" (which include spouses, parents, and relatives) improves business outcomes. Unfortunately, these data do not have information on whether these individuals are business owners.

Perhaps not surprisingly, inherited businesses are more successful and larger than noninherited businesses. The regression estimates on inherited businesses are large, positive (negative in the closure equation), and statistically significant in all specifications. Inheritances may

represent a form of transferring successful businesses across generations, but their overall importance in determining small business outcomes is slight at best. Although the coefficient estimates are large in
the small business outcome equations, the relative absence of inherited
businesses (only 1.6 percent of all small businesses) suggests that they
play only a minor role in establishing an intergenerational link in
self-employment.[17]

The strong effect of previous work experience in a family member's
business on small business outcomes suggests that family businesses
provide an important opportunity for family members to acquire
human capital related to operating a business. The general lack of significance of having a self-employed family member may indicate that
correlations across family members in entrepreneurial preferences and
role models are less important in contributing to the intergenerational
link in business success *conditioning* on business ownership than in
contributing to the intergenerational link in business ownership. These
results suggest that it is not enough to have a parent who is a business
owner for children to create successful businesses. Instead, working
in a family business appears to be the more important factor contributing to the success of the firm. Finally, inherited businesses may be
more successful on average than noninherited businesses, but their
limited representation among all small businesses in the United States
suggests that they are only a minor determinant of small business
outcomes.

Other Forms of Business Human Capital

The regression estimates provide evidence of the effects of the two additional methods for owners to acquire business human capital—prior
work experience in a managerial capacity and prior work experience in
a business whose goods and services were similar to those provided by
the owner's business.

The effects of previous work experience in a managerial capacity on
small business outcomes are not consistently strong. Management experience has a large effect in the employer probability equation, but
has a much smaller effect on log sales, and a positive and statistically
significant effect on business closures. Management experience prior to
starting or acquiring a business generally improves business outcomes
but has a less consistent effect than experience working for a close relative. It appears as though acquiring general business human capital

through management experience is somewhat important for business success, but the evidence is not entirely consistent.

The effects of prior work experience in a business whose goods and services were similar to those provided by his or her business are clearer. This method of acquiring specific business human capital appears to be very important. In fact, the coefficient estimates on a dummy variable for whether the owner had work experience in a similar business are comparable in size to the coefficient estimates on prior work experience in a family member's business in the closure-probability and log-sales equations. The coefficient estimate is smaller in the employer-probability equation but larger in the profits equation. In all specifications, the coefficient estimates are large and statistically significant. These findings are consistent with the hypothesis that the acquisition of specific business human capital improves the likelihood of business success. Owners may acquire valuable skills that are specific to starting different types of businesses, which eventually helps them run successful businesses.

Another important point to be taken from these results is that the multivariate regressions control for prior managerial experience and similar business experience. This implies that the large positive estimated effects of working for a self-employed family member are not simply capturing the effects of management experience or specific business human capital on small business outcomes. Instead, prior work experience in a family member's business has an independent effect on small business outcomes, which may in part be due to the acquisition of less specific, general business human capital. But it appears as though the family business might be providing a better opportunity to acquire business human capital or higher-quality business human capital than being a manager at a nonfamily member's business. Family members may impart more trust and give more responsibilities to their workers, which in turn leads to successful future business ventures.

Profits

The CBO does not include a continuous measure of profits in dollars. Instead, a categorical measure of profits is available in which profits are grouped in increments such as $10,000 to $24,999 and $25,000 to $100,000. This makes it difficult to estimate a regression model using profits as a dependent variable. As a baseline, we estimated a standard logit model for profits of $10,000 or more as noted above. Another possibility, however, is to estimate an ordered probit in which all of the categories are taken into account. The model is more complicated as is the interpretation of the resulting coefficients, but this more complex model is useful for checking the sensitivity of our use of profits of $10,000 or more as a dependent variable in addition to the other business outcome measures.

Specification 5 of table 3.5 reports estimates from an ordered probit for the categorical measure of profits available in the CBO.[18] The results are similar to those for the logit model for profits of $10,000 or more. For example, we find a positive and statistically significant relationship between owner's education and profits. We also find that having a self-employed family member has no effect on profits, but prior work experience in a family business and prior work experience in a similar type of business have positive and statistically significant effects on profits. Although not reported, we also estimated a profit equation using $25,000 as the cutoff level and find similar estimates. Apparently, our original use of profits of $10,000 is a reasonable measure of business success in this context.

Gender Issues

Approximately one third of the small businesses analyzed in our study are female-owned. As discussed above, the regression estimates indicate that survival rates, profits, employment, and sales are lower for female-owned firms than male-owned firms after controlling for other factors. Do the determinants of small business outcomes also differ between male- and female-owned businesses, or are they roughly similar? This has implications for the question of whether male- and female-owned businesses should be combined in the same sample used in the regressions.

Before discussing the separate regression estimates, we compare several owner characteristics. Owner's education by sex is shown in figure 3.1. It appears that male and female business owners do not differ substantially in their levels of education. Male owners are slightly more likely to have graduate degrees and not to finish high school. Female owners are slightly more likely to have attended some college or have college degrees. But these differences are relatively small.

Table 3.6 reports estimates of the family-business-background measures by sex. Male and female business owners are similarly likely to

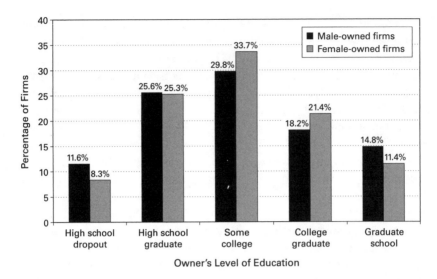

Figure 3.1
Owner's education level by gender, Characteristics of Business Owners (1992)

Table 3.6
Family-business background measures by gender, Characteristics of Business Owners (1992)

	Female	Male	Female Sample Size	Male Sample Size
Had a self-employed family member prior to starting firm	50.6%	52.0%	13,818	23,922
Worked in that family member's business (conditional)	38.3%	46.2%	13,380	23,195
Worked in a family member's business (unconditional)	19.4%	24.0%	13,380	23,195
Worked at a business with similar goods/services	42.5%	53.8%	13,656	23,582
Inherited their businesses	1.4%	1.7%	13,760	23,859

Notes: (1) The sample includes businesses that are classified by the IRS as individual proprietorships or self-employed persons, partnerships, and subchapter S corporations, have sales of $500 or more, and have at least one owner who worked at least twelve weeks and ten hours per week in the business. (2) All estimates are calculated using sample weights provided by the Characteristics of Business Owners.

Table 3.7
Means of analysis variables by gender, Characteristics of Business Owners (1992)

	Male-Owned Firms	Female-Owned Firms
Firm no longer operating in 1996 (closure)	21.6%	24.4%
Net profit of at least $10,000	36.4%	17.3%
One or more paid employees	23.7%	16.4%
Log sales	10.36	9.57
Married	78.1%	73.0%
Never married	10.9%	9.1%
High school graduate	25.6%	25.3%
Some college	29.8%	33.7%
College graduate	18.2%	21.4%
Graduate school	14.8%	11.4%
New England	6.1%	5.3%
Middle Atlantic	14.7%	14.1%
East North Central	15.7%	15.1%
West North Central	8.0%	7.5%
South Atlantic	15.4%	18.3%
East South Central	5.0%	4.9%
West South Central	11.0%	9.9%
Mountain	6.4%	6.9%
Urban	74.7%	77.7%
Prior work experience: 1 year	7.1%	7.7%
Prior work experience: 2 to 5 years	16.6%	16.2%
Prior work experience: 6 to 9 years	15.4%	14.6%
Prior work experience: 10 to 19 years	28.9%	30.3%
Prior work experience: 20 years or more	26.0%	23.9%
Prior work experience in a managerial capacity	56.6%	52.3%
Prior work experience in a similar business	53.8%	42.5%
Have a self-employed family member	52.0%	50.6%
Prior work experience in a family member's business	24.0%	19.4%
Inherited business	1.7%	1.4%
Startup capital: $5,000 to $24,999	25.5%	19.3%
Startup capital: $25,000 to $99,999	12.3%	9.2%
Startup capital: $100,000 and over	5.5%	4.1%
Agricultural services	3.2%	1.7%
Construction	16.3%	3.3%
Manufacturing	3.5%	2.9%
Wholesale	3.8%	3.0%
Finance, insurance, and real estate	9.3%	10.5%

Table 3.7
(continued)

	Male-Owned Firms	Female-Owned Firms
Transportations, communications, and public utilities	5.0%	2.5%
Personal services	24.2%	30.6%
Professional services	17.2%	23.0%
Uncoded industry	4.2%	3.7%
Sample size	13,918	24,102

Notes: (1) The sample includes businesses that are classified by the IRS as individual proprietorships or self-employed persons, partnerships, and subchapter S corporations, have sales of $500 or more, and have at least one owner who worked at least twelve weeks and ten hours per week in the business. (2) All estimates are calculated using sample weights provided by the Characteristics of Business Owners.

have had a self-employed family member prior to starting their firm. Male business owners, however, are more likely to have worked in that family business than female business owners.[19] Male business owners are also more likely to have worked in a similar business before starting their businesses. Differences in these types of work experience by sex, however, are not very large. Finally, both male and female business owners have similarly low rates of inheriting businesses. Table 3.8 reports mean values for all outcomes and explanatory variables separately for male- and female-owned businesses.

Estimates from separate sets of business outcome regressions for male- and female-owned businesses are reported in tables 3.8 and 3.9, respectively. Overall, the results do not differ substantially between men and women. For example, the black coefficients have the same sign and are statistically significant. We find a strong positive relationship between business outcomes and the owner's education level for both male and female firms. Having a self-employed family member has no effect on business outcomes, but prior work experience in a family business has large effects on business outcomes for both men and women. We also find that prior work experience in a similar business improves outcomes for both sexes, whereas prior management experience has inconsistent effects. Thus, the determinants of business outcomes do not differ substantially between male- and female-owned businesses. We continue to include both male and female owners in the remaining analyses.

Table 3.8
Logit and linear regressions for small business outcomes for men, Characteristics of Business Owners (1992)

	Specification			
	(1)	(2)	(3)	(4)
Dependent variable	Closure (1992–1996)	Profits $10,000+	Employer Firm	Ln Sales
Black-owned business	0.0161	−0.2036	−0.1057	−0.5322
	(0.0174)	(0.0274)	(0.0227)	(0.0746)
Latino-owned business	−0.0347	−0.0568	0.0115	0.0013
	(0.0146)	(0.0181)	(0.0150)	(0.0588)
Native American-owned business	−0.1674	−0.0042	0.0467	0.3201
	(0.0795)	(0.0692)	(0.0575)	(0.2397)
Asian-owned business	−0.0512	0.0070	0.0509	0.3240
	(0.0177)	(0.0189)	(0.0154)	(0.0665)
Married	−0.0201	0.1238	0.0658	0.2215
	(0.0091)	(0.0123)	(0.0101)	(0.0381)
Never married	0.0185	−0.0390	−0.0530	−0.4333
	(0.0105)	(0.0132)	(0.0111)	(0.0427)
High school graduate	−0.0313	0.0805	0.0469	0.1686
	(0.0101)	(0.0139)	(0.0118)	(0.0430)
Some college	−0.0149	0.0835	0.0567	0.0437
	(0.0099)	(0.0139)	(0.0116)	(0.0426)
College graduate	−0.0882	0.1341	0.0846	0.2692
	(0.0113)	(0.0148)	(0.0124)	(0.0467)
Graduate school	−0.1433	0.2419	0.2122	0.6930
	(0.0124)	(0.0154)	(0.0123)	(0.0484)
Urban	0.0229	0.0457	−0.0390	0.0934
	(0.0071)	(0.0088)	(0.0071)	(0.0288)
Prior work experience in a managerial capacity	0.0896	0.0226	0.0478	0.2218
	(0.0069)	(0.0082)	(0.0068)	(0.0272)
Prior work experience in a similar business	−0.0532	0.1126	0.0395	0.4381
	(0.0061)	(0.0077)	(0.0063)	(0.0252)
Have a self-employed family member	−0.0012	0.0100	−0.0006	−0.0558
	(0.0069)	(0.0088)	(0.0073)	(0.0288)
Prior work experience in a family member's business	−0.0523	0.0158	0.0513	0.3709
	(0.0085)	(0.0103)	(0.0083)	(0.0340)
Inherited business	−0.0461	0.1004	0.2182	1.1793
	(0.0263)	(0.0279)	(0.0205)	(0.0972)
Mean of dependent variable	0.2170	0.3617	0.2299	10.3239
Log likelihood/R-square	−10,761.38	−11,978.54	−11,107.46	0.0892
Sample size	21,316	19,439	21,753	21,753

Notes: (1) See notes to table 3.5. (2) The sample includes only male-owned firms.

Table 3.9
Logit and linear regressions for small business outcomes for women, Characteristics of Business Owners (1992)

	Specification			
	(1)	(2)	(3)	(4)
Dependent variable	Closure (1992–1996)	Profits $10,000+	Employer Firm	Ln Sales
Black-owned business	0.0261	−0.1155	−0.0737	−0.3708
	(0.0199)	(0.0259)	(0.0219)	(0.0794)
Latino-owned business	0.0466	−0.0113	0.0503	0.2478
	(0.0218)	(0.0214)	(0.0178)	(0.0877)
Native American-owned business	−0.0458	0.1167	0.1003	0.5322
	(0.0798)	(0.0628)	(0.0533)	(0.2925)
Asian-owned business	−0.0333	0.0509	0.1048	0.7822
	(0.0255)	(0.0181)	(0.0161)	(0.0899)
Married	−0.0494	0.0448	0.0618	0.2243
	(0.0107)	(0.0109)	(0.0101)	(0.0420)
Never married	0.1078	−0.0208	−0.0052	−0.1785
	(0.0134)	(0.0139)	(0.0131)	(0.0550)
High school graduate	0.0233	0.0129	0.0321	0.1106
	(0.0162)	(0.0176)	(0.0145)	(0.0627)
Some college	0.0130	0.0355	0.0158	0.0725
	(0.0161)	(0.0171)	(0.0143)	(0.0618)
College graduate	0.0092	0.0584	0.0033	0.1672
	(0.0173)	(0.0180)	(0.0154)	(0.0669)
Graduate school	−0.1597	0.1277	0.0414	0.4034
	(0.0213)	(0.0185)	(0.0162)	(0.0730)
Urban	−0.0004	0.0400	−0.0197	0.1272
	(0.0102)	(0.0098)	(0.0083)	(0.0391)
Prior work experience in a managerial capacity	0.0169	0.0282	0.0561	0.1622
	(0.0092)	(0.0084)	(0.0078)	(0.0355)
Prior work experience in a similar business	−0.0195	0.0709	0.0525	0.3539
	(0.0087)	(0.0078)	(0.0071)	(0.0332)
Have a self-employed family member	−0.0631	0.0150	−0.0051	−0.0027
	(0.0095)	(0.0088)	(0.0081)	(0.0361)
Prior work experience in a family member's business	0.0032	0.0565	0.0560	0.3815
	(0.0123)	(0.0102)	(0.0094)	(0.0456)
Inherited business	−0.2746	0.1185	0.1623	1.5391
	(0.0557)	(0.0276)	(0.0233)	(0.1385)
Mean of dependent variable	0.2495	0.1686	0.1589	9.5403
Log likelihood/R-square	−6,548.74	−4,743.32	−5,234.98	0.0593
Sample size	12,169	11,061	12,426	12,426

Notes: (1) See notes to table 3.5. (2) The sample includes only female-owned firms.

Examining the Sensitivity of Results to Alternative Sample Definitions

As noted in chapter 2 and the book's data appendix, the 1992 CBO and the underlying SMOBE/SBO data appear to include a large number of side or casual businesses. One way to address this concern is by excluding businesses in which the owner worked fewer than twelve weeks or fewer than ten hours per week during the year. These cutoffs were chosen to rule out small-scale businesses but not to rule out other part-time business owners. In particular, we are concerned about removing business owners who work less than full time or less than a full year because of a lack of demand for their products or services. Thus, not working full time is a result of lack of business success instead of a choice about how much to work. Similarly, we do not include hours worked as an extra control because it partly captures business success.

In this section, we check the sensitivity of our results to the removal of part-time business owners. In particular, we estimate means and a separate set of regressions that include only businesses with at least one owner who works thirty hours or more per week and thirty-six weeks or more per year. This restriction reduces our sample size by roughly 20 percent. As expected, we find that business outcomes are better for this sample, but we find very similar patterns for family-business-background measures. We also find that the coefficient estimates on prior work experience in a family business are similar in the profits equation and larger in the other specifications. Similar to the original estimates, we find that having a self-employed family member generally does not improve outcomes. We also continue to find that having inherited businesses and having similar business work experience improve outcomes although the relationship is slightly weaker. We also try a specification that includes even tighter hours- and weeks-worked restrictions and find roughly similar results.

We also checked the sensitivity of our results to the inclusion of smaller firms by excluding firms that required little startup capital. We estimate regressions using a sample that excludes firms with less than $5,000 in startup capital. We do not exclude these firms in our main sample because we are concerned that the receipt of startup capital may be related to the potential success of the business and many successful businesses may have required very little or no capital. In fact, published estimates from the CBO indicate that even among businesses with sales of $100,000 to $200,000 per year, approximately

40 percent of firms required less than $5,000 in startup capital (U.S. Census Bureau 1997). Furthermore, 32.5 percent of firms with $1 million or more in sales started with less than $5,000 in startup capital, and 33.1 percent of firms with 100 or more employees had less than $5,000 in startup capital. Removing these firms and many firms in industries that require very little capital (such as construction and high technology) eliminates some very successful firms.

Family-business backgrounds are similar for this more restrictive sample, which excludes 40 percent of the original sample. For example, 54.1 percent of owners have a self-employed family member compared with 51.6 percent in the full sample, and 25.2 percent of owners have prior work experience in a family business compared with 22.5 percent in the full sample. Furthermore, only 1.5 percent of owners inherited their businesses, which is comparable to the 1.6 percent found in the full sample.

In contrast to these results, the mean outcomes among businesses that started with $5,000 or more in startup capital are considerably better than those for all businesses (see table 3.10). Firms with $5,000 or more in startup capital have higher profits and sales, hire more employees, and are less likely to close than firms with less startup capital. Table 3.10 also reports small-business-outcome-regression estimates for this restricted sample. The results are similar for the effects of the family-business-background measures. We find that having a self-employed family member has little effect on outcomes, whereas prior work experience in a family member's business improves outcomes. Prior work experience in a similar business also has a positive effect on business outcomes. One difference in results is that the estimated relationship between owner's education and small business outcomes is now weaker, possibly due to a strong correlation between education and startup capital. Overall, these estimates indicate that the findings regarding the importance of family-business backgrounds in contributing to small business success are not due to the inclusion of smaller, less successful firms that require little or no startup capital.

To summarize, the results for the determinants of small business outcomes are not overly sensitive to the sample definitions that we choose. Although business outcomes improve when we restrict the sample to full-time working owners or businesses with $5,000 or more in startup capital, the coefficient estimates do not change substantially. To avoid problems with excluding less successful firms that have less

Table 3.10
Small business outcomes regressions for firms with $5,000+ startup capital, Characteristics of Business Owners (1992)

	Specification			
	(1)	(2)	(3)	(4)
Dependent variable	Closure (1992–1996)	Profits $10,000+	Employer Firm	Ln Sales
Black-owned business	0.0085	−0.1966	−0.1419	−0.5556
	(0.0170)	(0.0293)	(0.0268)	(0.0946)
Latino-owned business	0.0333	−0.0562	0.0171	0.0737
	(0.0127)	(0.0199)	(0.0181)	(0.0972)
Native American-owned business	−0.0415	−0.0348	−0.0209	−0.0434
	(0.0583)	(0.0742)	(0.0687)	(0.2923)
Asian-owned business	−0.0288	0.0041	0.0367	0.2575
	(0.0129)	(0.0168)	(0.0155)	(0.0897)
Female-owned business	0.0301	−0.2154	−0.0465	−0.5880
	(0.0057)	(0.0091)	(0.0080)	(0.0924)
Married	0.0455	0.1181	0.1353	0.2979
	(0.0090)	(0.0122)	(0.0118)	(0.1411)
Never married	−0.0214	0.0424	0.0318	−0.2778
	(0.0112)	(0.0144)	(0.0137)	(0.1861)
High school graduate	0.0147	0.0177	0.0334	0.0750
	(0.0102)	(0.0156)	(0.0146)	(0.1589)
Some college	0.0109	0.0477	0.1003	0.1502
	(0.0102)	(0.0155)	(0.0144)	(0.1552)
College graduate	−0.0456	0.0269	0.0971	0.3380
	(0.0113)	(0.0165)	(0.0152)	(0.1759)
Graduate school	−0.0516	0.1603	0.1838	0.5028
	(0.0114)	(0.0168)	(0.0152)	(0.1674)
Urban	0.0333	0.0707	−0.0036	0.1033
	(0.0063)	(0.0089)	(0.0082)	(0.0983)
Prior work experience in a managerial capacity	0.0376	0.0078	0.0634	0.1764
	(0.0061)	(0.0088)	(0.0081)	(0.0900)
Prior work experience in a similar business	−0.0285	0.0910	0.0268	0.2573
	(0.0055)	(0.0080)	(0.0073)	(0.0937)
Have a self-employed family member	−0.0046	0.0105	−0.0173	−0.0517
	(0.0061)	(0.0092)	(0.0084)	(0.1032)
Prior work experience in a family member's business	−0.0490	0.0142	0.0870	0.4342
	(0.0077)	(0.0105)	(0.0096)	(0.1125)
Inherited business	−0.0471	0.0644	0.2980	1.6740
	(0.0261)	(0.0309)	(0.0300)	(0.2486)
Mean of dependent variable	0.1564	0.4117	0.3540	10.8625
Log likelihood/R-square	−8,536.59	−11,959.81	−12,831.09	0.0891
Sample size	20,212	18,886	20,485	20,485

Notes: (1) See notes to table 3.5. (2) The sample includes only firms with at least $5,000 in startup capital.

than full-time working owners because of limited demand and potentially very successful firms that started with less than $5,000 in capital, we continue using our main sample of active firms in which we include all owners with twelve or more weeks and ten or more hours worked per week for the remaining analyses.

Correcting for Missing Data: Multiple Imputation

Another concern with the estimates reported in table 3.5 is missing data for some of the independent variables in the CBO. Approximately 10 percent of the observations for each of the specifications reported in table 3.5 are excluded because of missing values for one or more of the independent variables. Although these levels of missing data are not extremely high, we examine the sensitivity of our results to two alternative methods of correcting for missing data. First, we estimate regressions in which dummy variables are included for missing values of specific independent variables.[20] For example, if the education level of the business owner is missing, then the four education-level dummy variables would be equal to zero, and a special missing education dummy variable would be equal to one. Thus, the missing observation for owner's education would not contribute to the coefficient estimates on the main education-level dummies but would contribute to coefficient estimates on other variables. This technique is becoming increasingly common in the literature because it is easy to implement and provides more precise estimates for the other variables. Although not reported, we find estimates that are similar to the ones reported in table 3.5 for all four specifications.

We also address the missing data problem by using multiple imputation (Rubin 1987; Schafer and Olsen 1998; Schafer 1999; Brownstone and Valetta 2001).[21] The multiple-imputation technique essentially replaces each missing value in the data with a set of plausible values resulting in separate datasets that include the true values for nonmissing observations and the imputed variables for missing observations. The imputations are made by examining correlations between all available independent variables and placing restrictions on minimum and maximum values and rounding.[22] The variables are assumed to have a multivariate normal distribution. Logit or linear regressions are then run on five separately imputed datasets.[23] The results from the five runs are combined for inference, and adjustments are made for sampling variance. The resulting coefficient estimates summarize this information, and their standard errors capture the variability of estimates across the five runs, which differs from the typical overstatement of the statistical precision of estimates from single imputation methods. We report the multiple imputation coefficient estimates and their standard errors in table 3.11. Despite the large increase in sample size, the estimates are similar to those reported in table 3.5. Thus, the removal of observations with missing data does not appear to overly affect our results.

Startup Capital

As noted in the previous chapter, a large literature finds that owners' personal wealth is positively associated with business ownership. A substantial amount of attention in the literature is devoted to credibly determining whether the positive relationship is due to the inability of would-be entrepreneurs to acquire adequate levels of startup capital because of the presence of liquidity constraints. The main concerns with this interpretation are that business ownership may be an effective method of acquiring wealth and that individuals who are adept at accumulating wealth perhaps through wage and salary work may be the same individuals who are the most successful at starting businesses. In both cases, the positive relationship between wealth and business ownership is not caused by the inability to obtain financial capital due to liquidity constraints. Because of these concerns, we first reported estimates of the determinants of business outcomes without controls for startup capital. We now turn to a detailed discussion of the potential effects of startup capital, which is likely to be an important determinant of small business success.

Although we do not present new evidence on the liquidity-constraint debate, we note the possibility that the owner's level of wealth may affect business success. In particular, if liquidity constraints are binding, then this may affect the scale or success of the entrepreneurial venture. Liquidity-constrained entrepreneurs might start smaller undercapitalized businesses than they would have otherwise. In this case, the businesses created by liquidity-constrained entrepreneurs are likely to have worse outcomes than those created in the absence of liquidity constraints. The personal wealth of the entrepreneur then becomes a key factor in the success of the firm because this wealth can be invested directly in the business or used as collateral to obtain business loans.

Table 3.11
Multiple imputation regressions for small business outcomes, Characteristics of Business Owners (1992)

	Specification			
	(1)	(2)	(3)	(4)
Dependent variable	Closure by 1996	Profits $10,000+	Employer Firm	Ln Sales
Black-owned business	0.0213	−0.1866	−0.1038	−0.4883
	(0.0121)	(0.0197)	(0.0157)	(0.0522)
Latino-owned business	−0.0190	−0.0340	0.0167	0.0552
	(0.0113)	(0.0135)	(0.0111)	(0.0463)
Native American-owned business	−0.1220	0.0338	0.0650	0.3944
	(0.0522)	(0.0502)	(0.0396)	(0.1783)
Asian-owned business	−0.0473	0.0198	0.0696	0.4549
	(0.0135)	(0.0137)	(0.0110)	(0.0508)
Female-owned business	0.0199	−0.2066	−0.0640	−0.6942
	(0.0047)	(0.0063)	(0.0049)	(0.0197)
Married	−0.0259	0.1007	0.0675	0.2349
	(0.0065)	(0.0090)	(0.0073)	(0.0275)
Never married	0.0415	−0.0443	−0.0414	−0.3552
	(0.0077)	(0.0099)	(0.0083)	(0.0324)
High school graduate	−0.0280	0.0634	0.0390	0.1620
	(0.0080)	(0.0108)	(0.0090)	(0.0346)
Some college	−0.0188	0.0734	0.0419	0.0781
	(0.0080)	(0.0105)	(0.0088)	(0.0342)
College graduate	−0.0619	0.1141	0.0542	0.2428
	(0.0089)	(0.0112)	(0.0097)	(0.0373)
Graduate school	−0.1596	0.2187	0.1581	0.6181
	(0.0102)	(0.0119)	(0.0098)	(0.0396)
Urban	0.0171	0.0476	−0.0291	0.1260
	(0.0055)	(0.0066)	(0.0053)	(0.0225)
Prior work experience in a managerial capacity	0.0617	0.0247	0.0529	0.2395
	(0.0053)	(0.0062)	(0.0052)	(0.0228)
Prior work experience in a similar business	−0.0423	0.1014	0.0414	0.3862
	(0.0049)	(0.0057)	(0.0049)	(0.0208)
Have a self-employed family member	−0.0241	0.0174	0.0011	−0.0138
	(0.0059)	(0.0065)	(0.0056)	(0.0231)
Prior work experience in a family member's business	−0.0389	0.0311	0.0535	0.3607
	(0.0083)	(0.0077)	(0.0074)	(0.0327)
Inherited business	−0.1266	0.1378	0.1987	1.2058
	(0.0225)	(0.0200)	(0.0145)	(0.0736)
Mean of dependent variable	0.2253	0.3009	0.2131	10.0995
Sample size	37,156	33,804	38,020	38,020

Note: (1) See notes to table 3.5. (2) Missing values for all independent variables are imputed. See the text for more details.

Surprisingly, however, the relationship between owner's wealth and business success has not been examined extensively in the literature. Holtz-Eakin, Joulfaian, and Rosen (1994b) examine whether current changes in asset levels through inheritances affect survival probabilities and sales growth. They find that a $150,000 inheritance increases the probability of remaining a business owner by 1.3 percentage points, and if the firm survives, receipts increase by 20 percent. Fairlie and Krashinsky (2005) also find evidence of a positive effect of initial owner-asset levels on entrepreneurial survival.

Unfortunately, the CBO does not contain a measure of the owner's net worth prior to starting the business.[24] Instead, the CBO contains categorical information on "the total amount of capital required to start/acquire the business" (U.S. Census Bureau 1997, p. C-15). Some caution is warranted when exploring the relationship between this measure of startup capital and business outcomes (Bates 1990b). The problem is that potentially successful business ventures are likely to generate more startup capital than business ventures that are viewed as being potentially less successful. Thus, we cannot determine with certainty that lower levels of startup capital are primarily driven by constraints in obtaining financing. In support of the use of this measure, however, there is evidence suggesting that the size of inheritances received by individuals increases the amount of capital invested in the business (Holtz-Eakin, Joulfaian, and Rosen 1994a). This finding suggests that the receipt of inheritances might relieve liquidity constraints and that lower levels of startup capital at least partly reflect barriers to access to financial capital.

Additional evidence on the link between startup capital and owner's wealth is provided by examining the relationship between business loans and personal commitments, such as using personal assets for collateral for business liabilities and guarantees that make owners personally liable for business debts. Using data from the SSBF and Survey of Consumer Finances (SCF), Avery, Bostic, and Samolyk (1998) find that the majority of all small business loans have personal commitments. The common use of personal commitments to obtain business loans suggests that wealthier entrepreneurs may be able to negotiate better credit terms and obtain larger loans for their new businesses, possibly leading to more successful firms.[25] Cavalluzzo and Wolken (2005) find that personal wealth, primarily through home ownership, decreases the probability of loan denials among existing business owners. If personal wealth is important for existing business owners in acquiring

Table 3.12
Small business outcomes by firm's startup capital, Characteristics of Business Owners (1992)

Total Capital Needed by Firm to Start to Acquire the Business	Percentage			
	Sales of $50,000+	Sales of $100,000+	Paid Employees	All Firms
Less than $5,000	17.6%	10.3%	11.1%	61.2%
$5,000 to $24,999	35.0%	20.9%	23.1%	22.5%
$25,000 to $99,999	49.1%	36.0%	38.1%	11.1%
$100,000 or more	55.1%	46.1%	44.5%	5.3%
All firms	26.4%	17.1%	18.2%	

Source: U.S. Bureau of the Census (1997).
Note: The sample includes businesses that are classified by the IRS as individual proprietorships or self-employed persons, partnerships, and subchapter S corporations and that have sales of $500 or more.

business loans, then it may be even more important for entrepreneurs in acquiring startup loans. Avery, Bostic, and Samolyk (1998), however, do not find evidence of a consistent relationship between personal commitments and owner's wealth across specifications.

We now turn to examining the relationship between startup capital and business outcomes. We first examine published estimates from the CBO (U.S. Census Bureau 1997), which reveal a very strong positive correlation between startup capital and outcomes. Table 3.12 reports estimates of sales and employment by startup-capital level. Firms with higher levels of startup capital are much more likely to have high sales levels and hire employees. These results are consistent with liquidity constraints limiting access to financial capital leading to less successful businesses. This simple analysis of the relationships between startup capital and business outcomes, however, does not account for the effects of other correlated owner and business characteristics. The regression results allow us to investigate this issue further.

Industry

The industry of the business is also likely to be associated with the size and success of the business. Some industries have higher business-turnover rates than others, most notably retail and services (Robb 2000; Reynolds and White 1997). Published estimates from the CBO also indicate large industry differences in survival rates (see table 3.13).

Table 3.13

Small business outcomes by major industry, Survey of Minority-Owned Business Enterprises (1992) and Characteristics of Business Owners (1992)

	Average Sales	Mean Number of Employees	Percentage Closing between 1992 and 1996	Percentage with Profits of $10,000+	Percentage of All Firms
Agricultural services, forestry, fishing, and mining	$106,859	0.9	23.7%	31.0%	3.4%
Construction	$167,862	1.2	29.8%	38.5%	10.6%
Manufacturing	$872,526	7.1	19.6%	41.2%	3.0%
Transportation, communications, and utilities	$186,053	1.7	30.4%	44.8%	4.1%
Wholesale Trade	$1,190,794	3.2	24.0%	54.0%	3.1%
Retail Trade	$291,646	2.8	24.2%	33.6%	14.4%
Finance, insurance, and real estate	$166,021	0.9	19.5%	42.1%	11.3%
Services	$84,954	1.2	27.0%	27.1%	45.1%
Professional	$103,455	1.2			19.1%
Personal	$71,344	1.2			26.0%
Industries not classified	$29,130	0.1	33.6%	15.6%	5.1%
All firms	$192,672	1.6	26.0%	32.5%	

Source: U.S. Census Bureau, Economic Census, Survey of Minority-Owned Business Enterprises (1992) and U.S. Bureau of the Census (1997).

Note: The sample includes businesses that are classified by the IRS as individual proprietorships or self-employed persons, partnerships, and subchapter S corporations and that have sales of $500 or more.

The highest closure rates are found for businesses in construction (29.8 percent) and transportation, communications, and utilities (30.4 percent). In contrast, fewer than 20 percent of manufacturing firms and finance, insurance, and real estate firms closed from 1992 to 1996.

Additional business outcomes from published CBO data and the 1992 SMOBE are reported in table 3.13. Wholesale trade and manufacturing firms have substantially higher sales than firms in other industries. Firms in these two industries and in retail trade hire more employees than other industries. The most profitable industry appears to be wholesale trade followed by transportation, communications, and utilities; finance, insurance, and real estate; and manufacturing. Businesses in personal services have the lowest average sales of all industries and have one of the lowest levels of average employees. The patterns in outcomes across industries are somewhat difficult to summarize, but wholesale trade and manufacturing generally have the best outcomes, and personal services have the worst outcomes.

Although we find large differences in business outcomes across industries, it is difficult to interpret the results. The main issue is that the choice of industry, starting, and size of business may be simultaneously determined. For example, consider the decision of a worker at manufacturing plant who is considering starting a business. The decision for this worker is likely to be between remaining a manufacturing worker or starting a business in a different industry in which business ownership is more common, such as retail trade. The simultaneity of the decision suggests that there exist several potential explanations for finding a relationship between industry and business success. First, it is possible that some entrepreneurs are constrained in their choice of industries because of capital requirements, lack of relevant skills, or discrimination (Boden 1996; Bates 1997; Boden and Nucci 2000; Robb 2000). Discrimination from certain industry sectors, such as construction, may occur directly through limited opportunities to penetrate networks (Bates 1993a; Feagin and Imani 1994; Bates and Howell 1997). Industry differences may also result from differences in the preferences of owners for types of work. All of these explanations support the idea that industry choice is a determinant of business success.

On the other hand, industry differences may result from differences in the preferences of entrepreneurs for the goals of the business. Entrepreneurs seeking to "make it rich" instead of simply providing a steady income may choose certain high-growth, high-risk industries instead of other industries. Differences in entrepreneurial ability may also lead to different choices of industries. The most able entrepreneurs are likely to choose the industries that provide them with the highest potential returns, whereas less able entrepreneurs are likely to be limited in their choice of industries in which they can start businesses. High-ability entrepreneurs may also have higher levels of human capital and more access to financial capital, enabling them to start businesses in "better" industries. In these cases, the potential success of the business (or ability of the entrepreneur) is causing the industry choice. For these reasons, we did not include industry controls in the previous specifications. Previous studies also take this approach of reporting results with and without industry controls (see Bates 1997, for example).

Startup Capital and Industry Estimates

We estimate a second set of small-business-outcome regressions that include dummy variables for different levels of startup capital and major industry categories in addition to the independent variables included in the previous regressions. Estimates are reported in table 3.14.[26] In addition to providing evidence on the importance of these factors in determining business outcomes, controlling for them will provide more confidence in our estimates of the effects of business human-capital and family-background variables on business outcomes. If startup capital and industry are correlated with human capital, business human capital, and family-business background, then the earlier results may not accurately capture the effects of these variables.

As expected, small business outcomes are positively associated with the amount of capital used to start the business. The coefficients on the startup-capital dummies are large, positive (negative for the closure probability), and statistically significant in all specifications. In almost every specification, outcomes improve with each higher level of startup capital. The strength of the relationship between startup capital and business success is also strong for each type of business outcome. For example, firms with $100,000 or more in startup capital are 23.0 percentage points less likely to close than are firms with less than $5,000 in startup capital and are 9.9 percentage points less likely to close than are firms with $25,000 to $99,999 in startup capital. These results hold even after controlling for detailed owner and firm characteristics, including business human capital and the industry of the firm. Owners who use lower levels of startup capital appear to start less successful businesses.

Previous studies using the 1992 CBO and earlier waves of the CBO also find a strong relationship between firm survival and startup capital. For example, Bates (1990b) uses the 1982 CBO and finds that firm survival increases with the amount of financial capital invested at startup for a sample of white, male-owned firms that started between 1976 and 1982. Using the 1987 CBO and several different samples and specifications, he consistently finds a strong positive relationship between startup capital and firm survival (Bates 1997). Robb (2000), using the 1992 CBO linked to the 1992 to 1996 Business Information Tracking Series, finds that higher levels of startup capital are positively correlated with business survival among employer firms. Headd (2003), using the 1992 CBO for a sample of firms started between 1989

Table 3.14
Logit and linear regressions for small business outcomes, Characteristics of Business Owners (1992)

	Specification			
	(1)	(2)	(3)	(4)
Dependent variable	Closure by 1996	Profits $10,000+	Employer Firm	Ln Sales
Black-owned business	0.0077	−0.1684	−0.0703	−0.3215
	(0.0133)	(0.0213)	(0.0176)	(0.0506)
Latino-owned business	−0.0143	−0.0444	0.0277	0.0735
	(0.0123)	(0.0149)	(0.0126)	(0.0447)
Native American-owned business	−0.1270	0.0322	0.0696	0.3468
	(0.0564)	(0.0548)	(0.0454)	(0.1706)
Asian-owned business	−0.0091	−0.0176	−0.0164	0.0216
	(0.0149)	(0.0150)	(0.0128)	(0.0495)
Female-owned business	0.0150	−0.1943	−0.0498	−0.5708
	(0.0053)	(0.0069)	(0.0057)	(0.0193)
Married	−0.0286	0.1068	0.0594	0.1539
	(0.0070)	(0.0094)	(0.0081)	(0.0261)
Never married	0.0344	−0.0080	−0.0316	−0.2853
	(0.0083)	(0.0105)	(0.0093)	(0.0309)
High school graduate	−0.0065	0.0428	0.0251	0.0324
	(0.0087)	(0.0116)	(0.0099)	(0.0325)
Some college	0.0095	0.0637	0.0398	0.0011
	(0.0086)	(0.0115)	(0.0098)	(0.0322)
College graduate	−0.0433	0.0855	0.0470	0.1441
	(0.0096)	(0.0123)	(0.0106)	(0.0355)
Graduate school	−0.1617	0.1573	0.1674	0.5567
	(0.0117)	(0.0137)	(0.0115)	(0.0397)
Urban	0.0079	0.0610	−0.0144	0.1831
	(0.0059)	(0.0071)	(0.0059)	(0.0214)
Prior work experience in a managerial capacity	0.0826	0.0075	0.0212	0.0401
	(0.0056)	(0.0066)	(0.0057)	(0.0200)
Prior work experience in a similar business	−0.0505	0.0962	0.0426	0.4081
	(0.0052)	(0.0061)	(0.0053)	(0.0187)
Have a self-employed family member	−0.0181	0.0004	−0.0057	−0.0651
	(0.0057)	(0.0069)	(0.0060)	(0.0207)
Prior work experience in a family member's business	−0.0323	0.0210	0.0344	0.2300
	(0.0071)	(0.0081)	(0.0069)	(0.0250)
Inherited business	−0.0761	0.1351	0.2267	1.3143
	(0.0246)	(0.0238)	(0.0182)	(0.0764)
Startup capital: $5,000 to $24,999	−0.0871	0.1505	0.1487	0.7156
	(0.0061)	(0.0068)	(0.0059)	(0.0214)
Startup capital: $25,000 to $99,999	−0.1308	0.2312	0.3077	1.4676
	(0.0090)	(0.0088)	(0.0070)	(0.0291)

Table 3.14
(continued)

	Specification			
	(1)	(2)	(3)	(4)
Startup capital: $100,000 or more	−0.2295 (0.0166)	0.1791 (0.0125)	0.3735 (0.0099)	2.1520 (0.0422)
Agricultural services	0.0112 (0.0164)	−0.0111 (0.0184)	−0.1586 (0.0167)	−0.9204 (0.0574)
Construction	0.0438 (0.0096)	0.0528 (0.0111)	−0.0353 (0.0090)	−0.2546 (0.0350)
Manufacturing	−0.0625 (0.0171)	0.0358 (0.0166)	0.0035 (0.0129)	−0.1055 (0.0532)
Wholesale	0.0057 (0.0148)	0.1305 (0.0153)	−0.0006 (0.0127)	0.6082 (0.0518)
Finance, insurance, and real estate	−0.0609 (0.0109)	0.0771 (0.0122)	−0.1856 (0.0109)	−0.4926 (0.0367)
Transportation, communications, and public utilities	0.0600 (0.0130)	0.1205 (0.0147)	−0.1523 (0.0139)	−0.3300 (0.0486)
Personal services	0.0195 (0.0079)	−0.0488 (0.0096)	−0.1161 (0.0077)	−0.7430 (0.0286)
Professional services	0.0973 (0.0089)	0.0650 (0.0110)	−0.1191 (0.0092)	−0.7021 (0.0328)
Uncoded industry	0.0198 (0.0132)	−0.1020 (0.0183)	−0.5054 (0.0334)	−0.9842 (0.0490)
Mean of dependent variable	0.2280	0.2975	0.2066	10.0668
Sample size	33,116	30,271	33,701	33,701

Note: See notes to table 3.5.

and 1992, also finds that startup capital is negatively associated with closure of the firm between 1992 and 1996.

Industry is also linked to business success as many of the dummy variables for industries are large in magnitude and statistically significant. The left-out category in the regressions is retail trade. Thus, the reported regression estimates capture the difference between the average business outcome in that industry and the average business outcome in retail trade, after controlling for other owner and business characteristics. The estimates vary across specifications, however, making it difficult to summarize the association between industries and business outcomes.

It is also important to note that the addition of startup capital and industry do not overly influence the estimated effects of the human capital, family-business background, and business human-capital variables. The estimated effects of owner's education do not change substantially after including startup capital and industry. The coefficient estimates on having a self-employed family member and inheriting the business also do not change substantially. The coefficient estimates on previous work experience in a family member's business are generally smaller in absolute value (although still statistically significant) in the new specifications. The coefficients on prior work experience in a similar business are very similar. These findings suggest that the interrelatedness of human-capital and financial-capital inputs is not problematic for our regression estimates.

Age of the Business

The CBO also includes information on when the business was established. We estimate a set of regressions that control for the age of the business. As expected, we find that the age of the business is a strong predictor of business success. For each specification, we find that business outcomes improve with business age. This finding is not surprising as older firms have had more time to grow, and as time progresses, weaker firms have discontinued operations. Thus, the age of the business is better viewed as another business outcome instead of as a determinant of business success. Most important, however, we find that the inclusion of the age of the business does not substantially alter the estimates of the effects of our main explanatory variables on business outcomes. The main exception is that the coefficient estimate on whether the business was inherited is smaller in absolute value in each of the specifications.

We also estimate specifications that exclude older firms to make sure that our results hold for more recently created firms. In particular, we find that our estimates are not overly sensitive to the exclusion of firms started before 1980. The exclusion of these firms reduces our sample size by roughly one third.

Overall, these findings indicate that our estimates are not overly sensitive to controlling for the age of the business or the inclusion of much older businesses. We do not investigate the relationship between our business outcomes and age of the business further because of endogeneity concerns. This is especially important when we later investigate the causes of racial differences in business outcomes. A finding, for example, that black firms are less successful because they are younger than white firms does not identify the underlying cause of the lack of success.

Conclusions

What makes a business successful? Do the owner's education level and types of prior work experience matter? Is the amount of capital invested at startup key to the eventual success of the firm? We answer these questions in this chapter using confidential and restricted-access microdata from the CBO. Using the detailed information available in the CBO on both the characteristics of the owner and the business, we examine the potential determinants of business success measured by closure rates, profits, employment, and sales. We explore the effects of human and financial capital on business outcomes as well as less-studied determinants, such as family-business backgrounds and types of prior work experience.

The owner's education level is an important determinant of business success. For example, businesses owned by college graduates have approximately 25 percent higher sales on average than businesses owned by high school dropouts. Furthermore, firms with owners who have a graduate degree have nearly 40 percent higher sales than firms with owners who are college graduates. The general and specific knowledge and skills acquired through formal education, especially at the college and graduate-school levels, may be useful for running a successful business. The owner's level of education may also serve as a proxy for his or her overall ability or as a positive signal to potential customers, lenders, or other businesses.

We also find a strong positive relationship between startup capital and business outcomes. Firms with higher levels of startup capital are more likely to have higher profits and sales and to hire employees and are less likely to close. The estimates are large and consistent across outcomes. This positive relationship is consistent with the inability of some entrepreneurs to obtain the optimal level of startup capital because of borrowing constraints. In this case, differences in startup capital may be due to differences in the personal wealth of the entrepreneur because this wealth can be invested directly in the business or used as collateral to obtain business loans. Because these entrepreneurs are constrained in the amount of startup capital that could be used to purchase buildings, equipment, and other investments, their businesses are less successful than if they could have invested the optimal amount of capital. As noted in the previous literature, however, the positive relationship may alternatively be due to the ability of potentially successful business ventures to generate startup capital. Although we cannot rule out this possibility, we provide evidence from the literature suggesting that at least part of the relationship is likely due to limited access to capital. Lack of access to capital because of low levels of personal wealth and lending discrimination may be especially important for minority business owners, which we discuss further in the next chapter.

Using rare or unique information contained in the CBO on family-business backgrounds, we also provide new evidence on the underlying causes of intergenerational links in self-employment and the related issue of how having a family-business background affects small business outcomes. Estimates from the CBO indicate that more than half of all business owners had a self-employed family member prior to starting their business. Conditional on having a self-employed family member, less than half of small business owners worked in that family member's business. This suggests that it is unlikely that intergenerational links in self-employment are due solely to the acquisition of general and specific business capital. Similarities across family members in entrepreneurial preferences may explain part of the relationship.

In contrast, estimates from regression models for small business outcomes *conditioning* on business ownership indicate that having a self-employed family member plays only a minor role relative to prior work experience in that family member's business. For most business outcomes, having a family member who owns a business has no effect on the success of the business. Working in a family member's business, however, has a large, positive, and statistically significant effect for all business outcomes. The inclusion of controls for similar business work experience and management experience in the multivariate regressions suggests that the positive estimated effects of working for a self-employed family member are not simply capturing the effects of management experience or specific business human capital on small business outcomes. Instead, prior work experience in a family member's business has an independent effect on small business outcomes, which may in part be due to the acquisition of less formal or more general business human capital. Business owners who worked in family businesses may simply learn how to run a successful business instead of how to run just a particular kind of business.

Although many owners had a self-employed family member and previous work experience in a family member's business, estimates from the CBO indicate that only 1.6 percent of all small businesses are inherited. Inherited businesses are more successful on average than noninherited businesses, but their limited representation among the population of small businesses suggests that business inheritance is only a minor determinant of small business outcomes.

Business owners can also acquire business human capital through two additional methods—prior work experience in a managerial capacity and prior work experience in a business whose goods and services were similar to those provided by the owner's business. Our regression results provide mixed evidence on whether acquiring general business human capital through management experience is important for business success. On the other hand, we find consistent evidence that prior work experience in a similar type of business improves business outcomes. Acquiring skills that are specific to a type of work or industry—specific business human capital—through prior work experience appear to be useful for starting and running successful businesses.

Several important determinants of business outcomes are identified from analyzing the CBO microdata. Business success is related to the financial capital, human capital, and family-business backgrounds of owners. The next step is to determine whether racial differences in these factors explain the large disparities in business outcomes discussed in chapter 2.

Appendixes

Estimating the Intergenerational Transmission in Business Ownership
Business ownership rates for the children of business owners and the children of nonbusiness owners are estimated from our CBO sample. To estimate these rates, we need to make two key assumptions. The difficulty in estimating business ownership rates arises because we do not have a comparison group of nonbusiness owners in the CBO data. We first make the conservative assumption that 25 percent of small business owners have a self-employed parent, which is derived from our estimate that 51.6 percent of business owners had a self-employed family member prior to starting their firms. We also have to make the assumption that the self-employment rate is not changing rapidly over time and is in a steady state of roughly 10 percent. Making these two assumptions, we find that the children of self-employed parents are three times more likely to be self-employed than are the children of non-self-employed parents.

To see this, we express the joint probability of having a self-employed parent $(S_{t-1} = 1)$ and a self-employed child when they are adults $(S_t = 1)$ as

$$P(S_{t-1} = 1, S_t = 1) = P(S_{t-1} = 1 \mid S_t = 1)P(S_t = 1)$$

$$= P(S_t = 1 \mid S_{t-1} = 1)P(S_{t-1} = 1). \tag{3.1}$$

$P(S_{t-1} = 1 \mid S_t = 1)$ is the probability that the parent of a self-employed child is self-employed, and $P(S_t = 1 \mid S_{t-1} = 1)$ is the probability that the child of a self-employed parent is self-employed. Equation (3.1) must hold because of the laws of probability.

We first assume a steady-state relationship in which the total self-employment rate of parents is the same as the total self-employment rate of adult children, $P(S_t) = P(S_{t-1}) = 0.10$. If we also assume a one-to-one matching of parents to children, the probability that the child is self-employed given that his or her parent was self-employed or the "intergenerational pickup rate" (Hout and Rosen 2000) equals the probability that a business owner has a self-employed parent. This can be expressed as

$$P(S_{t-1} = 1 \mid S_t = 1) = P(S_t = 1 \mid S_{t-1} = 1). \tag{3.2}$$

Thus, the self-employment rate among the children of the self-employed is 0.25. To find the self-employment rate among children on the non-self-employed, we can work with the joint probability of having a non-self-employed parent and a self-employed child, which can be expressed as

$$P(S_{t-1} = 0, S_t = 1) = P(S_{t-1} = 0 \mid S_t = 1)P(S_t = 1)$$

$$= P(S_t = 1 \mid S_{t-1} = 0)P(S_{t-1} = 0). \tag{3.3}$$

Substituting $P(S_t = 1) = 0.10$, $P(S_{t-1} = 0) = 0.90$ and $P(S_{t-1} = 0 \mid S_t = 1) = 0.75$, we can solve for $P(S_{t-1} = 0 \mid S_t = 1)$, which is the probability of self-employment among the children of non-business owners. Thus, the self-employment rate of the children of the non-self-employed is 0.08 indicating that the children of self-employed parents are roughly three times more likely to be self-employed than the children of non-self-employed parents, which is consistent with previous findings in the literature.

The percentage of owners who had a self-employed family member prior to business startup certainly overstates the percentage of owners who had a self-employed parent, but the discrepancy may not be that large. The strong positive influence of parental self-employment is common to brothers, suggesting that a propensity for business ownership runs in families (Dunn and Holtz-Eakin 2000), and the question on the CBO asks whether the owner had a self-employed family member *prior* to starting his or her business limiting the likelihood that older siblings are referring to younger self-employed siblings. Furthermore, estimates from the 2002 Current Population Survey indicate that the average probability of having a self-employed spouse among all self-employed business owners is only 24 percent. We suspect that a large percentage of affirmative responses to the CBO question on whether the owner had a self-employed family member prior to starting his or her business refer to the owner's parents.

Finally, the assumption that the self-employment rate of parents and adult children is essentially the same appears to be reasonable. Estimates of long-term trends indicate that business ownership rates have not changed that much over time. As discussed in chapter 2, self-employment rates did not change substantially from the middle to near the end of the twentieth century, and estimates from the CPS indicate relatively constant business ownership rates over the past two and a half decades.

Table 3.A
Means of analysis variables, Characteristics of Business Owners (1992)

	All Firms (percent)	Sample Size
Firm no longer operating in 1996 (closure)	22.5%	37,156
Net profit of at least $10,000	30.1	33,804
One or more paid employees	21.3	38,020
Log sales	10.1	38,020
Female-owned business	32.9	38,020
Married	76.4	36,906
Never married	10.3	36,906
High school graduate	25.5	36,782
Some college	31.1	36,782
College graduate	19.2	36,782
Graduate school	13.7	36,782
Northeast	5.8	38,020
Middle Atlantic	14.5	38,020
East North Central	15.5	38,020

Table 3.A
(continued)

	All Firms (percent)	Sample Size
West North Central	7.8	38,020
South Atlantic	16.3	38,020
East South Central	4.9	38,020
West South Central	10.6	38,020
Mountain	6.6	38,020
Urban	75.7	38,020
Prior work experience: 1 year	7.3	37,503
Prior work experience: 2 to 5 years	16.5	37,503
Prior work experience: 6 to 9 years	15.1	37,503
Prior work experience: 10 to 19 years	29.3	37,503
Prior work experience: 20 years or more	25.3	37,503
Prior work experience in a managerial capacity	55.2	37,417
Prior work experience in a similar business	50.1	37,238
Have a self-employed family member	51.6	37,740
Prior work experience in a family member's business	22.5	36,575
Inherited business	1.6	37,619
Startup capital: $5,000 to $24,999	23.5	37,388
Startup capital: $25,000 to $99,999	11.3	37,388
Startup capital: $100,000 and over	5.0	37,388
Agricultural services	2.7	38,020
Construction	12.1	38,020
Manufacturing	3.3	38,020
Wholesale	3.5	38,020
Finance, insurance, and real estate	9.7	38,020
Transportation, communications, and public utilities	4.2	38,020
Personal services	26.3	38,020
Professional services	19.1	38,020
Uncoded industry	4.1	38,020

Notes: (1) The sample includes businesses that are classified by the IRS as individual proprietorships or self-employed persons, partnerships, and subchapter S corporations, have sales of $500 or more, and have at least one owner who worked at least twelve weeks and ten hours per week in the business. (2) All estimates are calculated using sample weights provided by the Characteristics of Business Owners.

4   Why Are African American-Owned Businesses Less Successful?

African Americans are less likely to own businesses than whites, and their businesses are less successful on average than are white-owned businesses. The evidence presented in chapter 2 indicates that black businesses have lower revenues and profits, hire fewer employees, and are more likely to close than white-owned businesses. In most cases, the disparities are large. For example, average sales among black firms are roughly one fourth that of white firms, and black firms hire one third the number of employees on average as white firms. The relative underperformance of black-owned businesses is alarming because of the implications of successful business ownership for economic advancement, job creation, and income equality.

In the previous chapter's exploration of the determinants of business outcomes, several owner and firm characteristics are identified as predictors of success. Human capital, financial capital, and family-business backgrounds are found to improve business outcomes. Do black business owners have lower levels of education, less access to startup capital, and more disadvantaged family backgrounds than white business owners? Can these factors explain why black-owned businesses have lower survival rates, profits, employment, and sales than white-owned businesses?

The single most important factor determining business success is startup capital. We find that higher levels of startup capital are associated with lower closure probabilities, higher profits and sales, and more employment. Therefore, less access to capital for black business owners compared with white owners may partly explain why black-owned businesses have worse outcomes than white-owned firms, on average. Previous research indicates that low levels of wealth limit business creation among blacks (Fairlie 1999, 2006) and low levels of startup capital increase closure rates among black-owned businesses

(Bates 1997; Robb 2000). There is also a large body of evidence indicating that black businesses face lending discrimination (Blanchflower, Levine, and Zimmerman 2003; Cavalluzzo, Cavalluzzo, and Wolken 2002). Given these findings, we suspect that racial differences in wealth and startup capital contribute substantially to differences in business outcomes, but we do not know the extent of their contribution.

Another determinant of success in small business is the owner's education level. After controlling for other factors, firms with more highly educated owners have lower closure probabilities, higher profits and sales, and more employment. Therefore, if black business owners have lower education levels than white business owners, disparities in education levels could explain why black-owned businesses underperform relative to white-owned firms, on average.

Building on the finding in the previous literature that the children of business owners are more likely than the children of nonbusiness owners to become business owners, we examine whether the businesses created by the children of business owners are also more successful. In the previous chapter, we find that previous work experience in a family member's business and previous work experience in a business providing similar goods and services have large positive effects on business outcomes. These findings suggest that the lack of opportunities for black owners to acquire important general and specific business human capital may limit their ability to create successful businesses. In fact, there is evidence in the previous literature indicating that current differences between blacks and whites in business ownership rates are partly determined by racial differences in business ownership in the previous generation (Fairlie 1999; Hout and Rosen 2000). Although the intergenerational transmission of business ownership is important in creating racial disparities in rates of business ownership, we do not know if it also contributes to racial disparities in business outcomes conditioning on ownership. In particular, can these disparities explain why black-owned businesses lag behind white-owned businesses in survival rates, profits, employment, and sales?

Several recent studies have examined the reasons behind the lack of black-owned businesses and find that relatively low levels of education, assets, and parental self-employment are partly responsible (see Bates 1997, Fairlie 1999, and Hout and Rosen 2000 for a few examples reviewed in chapter 2). Although these results are informative, they do not shed light on why the average performance of black-owned firms lags behind that of white-owned firms. We know much less about why black-owned firms have lower outcomes relative to white-owned businesses. This is partly due to the small number of datasets that identify the race of the owner, additional owner characteristics, and business outcomes.

We use data from the Characteristics of Business Owners (CBO) to examine the role that financial capital and human capital play in contributing to racial disparities in business outcomes, such as closures, profits, employment size, and sales. We also examine the role that intergenerational links in self-employment play in contributing to racial differences in business outcomes. Do black business owners have limited opportunities for the acquisition of general and specific business human capital from working in family-owned businesses and the receipt of business inheritances, in addition to less education and access to financial capital? We build on findings from the previous chapter on the determinants of business success and use a special decomposition technique to identify the underlying causes of differences in outcomes between black and white firms. The decomposition technique identifies whether a particular factor is important and identifies how much it explains of the gap in a particular outcome. This allows the relative strengths of the factors to be compared.

The confidential and restricted-access CBO microdata are useful for this analysis because they are one of the only nationally representative datasets containing a large enough sample of black firms and detailed information on family-business backgrounds. For example, the CBO appears to be the only nationally representative dataset containing information on previous work experience in businesses owned by family members. Overall, the detailed information on both the characteristics of the owner and the business available in the CBO is important for exploring additional potential causes of the racial differences in business outcomes.

Racial Differences in Education

Over the twentieth century, blacks made considerable progress in educational attainment. Figure 4.1 displays estimates of the percentage of black and white adults age twenty-five and over who have completed four or more years of high school. In 1940, only 7.7 percent of blacks completed four years of high school or more. By 2004, more than 80 percent of blacks had high school educations. The percentage of blacks who completed at least four years of college also increased markedly

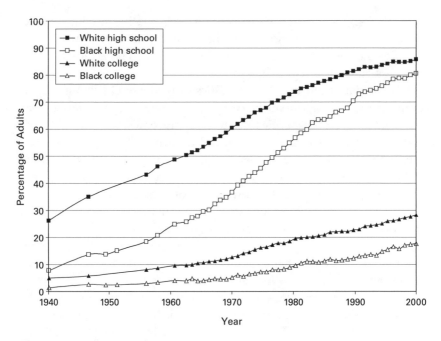

Figure 4.1
Educational attainment by race, U.S. Census Bureau estimates (1940 to 2004)

over the period. Only 1.3 percent of blacks were college educated in 1940, but nearly 20 percent were college educated by 2004. Although blacks have made considerable progress both in absolute terms and relative to whites, large disparities in educational attainment remain. In 2004, 85.8 percent of whites had at least four years of high school, and 28.2 percent had at least four years of college. Racial parity in educational attainment has not yet occurred.

Racial disparities in educational attainment are smaller for business owners than the general population but remain large. Figure 4.2 displays estimates of educational attainment by race from CBO microdata. Black business owners are more likely to be high school dropouts and are less likely to be college graduates. Black business owners, however, are equally likely to have graduate school degrees as white business owners. Overall, 26.2 percent of black business owners have at least a college education compared with 33.3 percent of white business owners.

In the previous chapter, we find that the education level of the owner is an important predictor of business success. Therefore, the

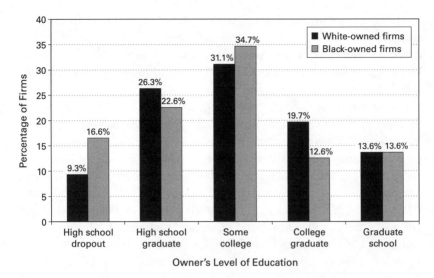

Figure 4.2
Owner's education level by race, Characteristics of Business Owners (1992)

racial disparities in education levels displayed here suggest that differences between black and white owners in education levels may contribute to racial differences in business outcomes. Boyd (1991) finds that close to one third of the gap in the earnings between self-employed Asian Americans and blacks is explained by disparities in education levels. Blacks may have less of the general and specific knowledge and skills that are useful for running a successful business because of lower levels of formal education. Lower levels of education among blacks may also limit business opportunities because they provide less of a positive signal to potential customers, lenders, or other businesses. The decomposition technique employed below will allow us to examine whether and how much racial differences in education can explain of racial disparities in the business outcomes available in the CBO.

Family-Business Background

Regression estimates from the CBO indicate that family-business backgrounds are important for small business success. In particular, working in a family member's business, perhaps through the acquisition of general and specific business human capital, improves the future success of businesses owned by these individuals. The estimated effects are large in magnitude: they increase outcomes anywhere from 15 to 40 percent. Given these results and the extensive literature addressing concerns with the African American family (Wilson 1987; Tucker and Mitchell-Kernan 1995; Wilson 2002), it is useful to explore the relationship between race, families, and business success.

Recent estimates indicate that blacks are 40 percent less likely to be married than are whites and that black women are nearly 80 percent more likely to have a nonmarital birth than are white women (U.S. Census Bureau 2001; National Center for Health Statistics 2003). As a result, 53.3 percent of black children live with only one of their parents compared with 21.5 percent of white children (U.S. Census Bureau 2001). The high incidence of single black parents is likely to have adverse educational, economic, and emotional outcomes for this group of children (McLanahan and Sandefur 1994; Seltzer 1994; Amato 2000). The loss of resources associated with having one parent missing from the household may be especially detrimental to the future outcomes of black children.

One area in which the lack of exposure to both parents may be limiting is in business ownership. As noted above, previous research indicates that the probability of self-employment is substantially higher among the children of the self-employed than among the children of the non-self-employed (Lentz and Laband 1990; Fairlie 1999; Dunn and Holtz-Eakin 2000; Hout and Rosen 2000). These studies generally find that an individual who had a self-employed parent is roughly two to three times as likely to be self-employed as someone who did not have a self-employed parent. The high incidence of growing up in a single-parent family and the strong intergenerational link in self-employment may limit business ownership opportunities for blacks. If black children are less likely to live with both parents, they will have a lower likelihood of being exposed to a self-employed parent and fewer chances to work in a family business.

Although the high rates of black children currently growing up in single-parent families may have a detrimental effect on future business ownership rates and business outcomes, historical estimates of single-parent family rates contribute to current differences in business outcomes. The earliest reported data from the U.S. Census Bureau, which are for 1960, indicate that black children were more than twice as likely to live in single-parent families as white children. In 1960, 21.9 percent of black children lived in single-parent families compared with 7.1 percent of white children (U.S. Census Bureau 2005b). On average, these children would be forty-two years old at the time of the CBO survey. Nearly half of the sample of black business owners in the CBO is under the age of forty-five, suggesting that historically high levels of single-parent households may be contributing to the lower outcomes of the current generation of business owners. Marriage rates among current black business owners are also lower than marriage rates among white business owners: 77 percent of white owners are married compared with 68 percent of black owners.

Concerns about the negative consequences of weak family ties on business opportunities among blacks are not new. In fact, nearly forty years ago, Nathan Glazer and Daniel Patrick Moynihan made the argument that the black family "was not strong enough to create those extended clans that elsewhere were most helpful for businessmen and professionals" (Glazer and Moynihan 1970, p. 33). More recently, Hout and Rosen (2000) note a "triple disadvantage" faced by black men in terms of business ownership. They are less likely than white men to have self-employed fathers, to become self-employed if their fathers were not self-employed, and to follow their father in self-employment. Furthermore, Fairlie (1999) provides evidence from the Panel Study of Income Dynamices (PSID) that current racial patterns of self-employment are in part determined by racial patterns of self-employment in the previous generation. Thus, there is some concern that the lack of a strong family-business background may limit opportunities for black business success.

Racial Differences in Family-Business Experience

Previous research indicates that the relatively low likelihood of having a self-employed parent limits blacks' chances of becoming a self-employed business owner. We know less, however, about whether blacks and whites differ in prior work experience in family businesses and their likelihood of receiving business inheritances and whether these patterns contribute to the lower outcomes by black firms relative to white firms, on average. Black and white business owners indeed have different family-business backgrounds. Table 4.1 reports the percentage of owners who had a family member who was a business owner and the percentage of owners who worked for that family member.[1] More than half of all white business owners had a self-employed family member owner prior to starting their business. In contrast, approximately one third of black business owners had a self-employed

Table 4.1
Family business background by race, Characteristics of Business Owners (1992)

	All Firms	White- Owned Firms	Black- Owned Firms
Had a self-employed family member prior to starting firm	51.6%	53.1%	33.6%
Previously worked in that family member's business (conditional)	43.6%	43.9%	37.4%
Previously worked in a family member's business (unconditional)	22.5%	23.3%	12.6%
Inherited their businesses	1.6%	1.7%	1.4%
Sample size	38,020	15,872	7,565

Notes: (1) The sample includes businesses that are classified by the IRS as individual proprietorships or self-employed persons, partnerships, and subchapter S corporations, have sales of $500 or more, and have at least one owner who worked at least twelve weeks and ten hours per week in the business. (2) All estimates are calculated using sample weights provided by the Characteristics of Business Owners.

family member. Black business owners are much less likely to be part of a family with business experience.

Although family members may include spouses and siblings in addition to parents, these results are consistent with Hout and Rosen's (2000) finding of a lower probability of self-employment among the children of self-employed parents (the "intergenerational pickup rate with respect to self-employment") for blacks than for whites. As mentioned previously, this represents one of the three disadvantages in business ownership faced by blacks, according to Hout and Rosen.

To see the similarity with Hout and Rosen's finding, we can use equations (3.1) and (3.2) from this chapter's appendix and evidence on long-term trends in black and white self-employment rates. As displayed in figure 2.2, business-ownership rates have not changed substantially over time and thus across generations for either whites or blacks. This implies that self-employment rates are roughly in a long-term steady-state relationship in which the current generation's self-employment rate is similar to the previous generation's self-employment rate. If we also assume that there exists a one-to-one matching of parents to children, the intergenerational pickup rate equals the probability of a business owner having a self-employed parent as indicated in equation (3.2). Using this equation, we find that the intergenerational pickup rate for blacks is approximately 0.330, whereas the intergenerational pickup rate is 0.531 for whites and 0.516 for all firms. The black/total ratio for the probability of having a self-employed family member is 0.632, which is in the range of Hout and Rosen's (2000) estimates. Therefore, the CBO data provide support for the hypothesis that blacks are less likely to become business owners than whites, even for those individuals who have self-employed parents.

Family businesses may provide important opportunities for acquiring general and specific business human capital (Lentz and Leband 1990). Estimates from the CBO indicate that conditional on having a self-employed family member, black business owners were also less likely to have worked for that person than were white business owners. As shown in table 4.1, 37.4 percent of black business owners who had a self-employed family member worked for that person's business, whereas 43.9 percent of white business owners who had a self-employed family member worked for that person's business.[2] Finally, black business owners overall were much less likely than white business owners to work for a family member's business. The unconditional rate of working in a family member's business was 12.6 percent for blacks and 23.3 percent for whites.

Black business owners were slightly less likely to inherit their businesses than were white owners: 1.4 percent of black owners inherited their firms compared with 1.7 percent of white owners. All rates of inheritance are very low and suggest that racial differences in inheritances cannot explain much of the gaps in small business outcomes. We also find that only 4.3 percent of white owners and 2.0 percent of black owners acquired the business through a "transfer of ownership/gift" and had a self-employed family member prior to starting their business. These upper-bound estimates of direct parent-to-child transfers or gifts of businesses that are not inheritances combined with the estimates of business inheritances suggests that only a small percentage of all existing businesses are acquired from parents. They are also confirmed by estimates from the 1998 Survey of Small Business Finances (SSBF), which indicate that 4.2 percent of whites and 4.0 percent of blacks inherited or received their business as a gift.

Overall, black business owners have a relatively disadvantaged family-business background compared with white business owners. The lack of family-business experience may contribute substantially to the relative lack of success of black-owned businesses because of limited opportunities to receive the informal learning or apprenticeship-type training that occurs in working in a family business. Family businesses provide an opportunity for family members to acquire general business human capital and in many cases also provide the opportunity for acquiring specific business human capital. The impact of racial differences in these opportunities on racial differences in small business outcomes will be explored using a special decomposition technique shown later in the chapter.

Racial Differences in Business Human Capital

Having prior work experience in businesses whose goods and services were similar to those provided by the owner's business is found to be an important determinant of business success. If blacks have less prior work experience in a similar business, then they may have had less of a chance to acquire the skills that are specific to a type of work or industry that are useful for running a successful business. Black business owners may also have less prior management experience than white business owners. The results from our regression analysis, however, do not provide clear evidence on the effects of having prior work experience in a managerial capacity on business outcomes.

Table 4.2 reports estimates of the percentage of black and white firms with owners who previously worked in a business with similar goods and services and who have previous work experience in a managerial capacity. Black business owners have less work experience in a similar business prior to starting or acquiring their businesses than whites. Half of all white business owners have this type of work experience, compared with 43.1 percent of black business owners. The dif-

Table 4.2
Types of prior work experience by race, Characteristics of Business Owners (1992)

	All Firms	White- Owned Firms	Black- Owned Firms
Previously worked in a business with similar goods/ services	50.1%	50.4%	43.1%
Previous work experience in a managerial capacity	55.2%	55.6%	47.1%
Sample size	38,020	15,872	7,565

Notes: (1) The sample includes businesses that are classified by the IRS as individual proprietorships or self-employed persons, partnerships, and subchapter S corporations, have sales of $500 or more, and have at least one owner who worked at least twelve weeks and ten hours per week in the business. (2) All estimates are calculated using sample weights provided by the Characteristics of Business Owners.

ference in prior work experience at a business with similar goods and services may translate into black owners having less specific business human capital than white owners on average.

Black business owners are also less likely to have prior work experience in a managerial capacity than are white business owners. The percentage of black business owners with prior managerial experience is 47.1 percent compared with 55.6 percent for whites. Although there is a racial difference in managerial experience, the findings from our regression analysis in chapter 3 are mixed on the importance of this type of experience in predicting business success. Thus, it is difficult to predict whether lower levels of prior managerial experience among black business owners lead to worse outcomes relative to white businesses.

Financial Capital

An important limiting factor for the performance of black firms may be access to financial capital. Relatively low levels of wealth among blacks and the existence of liquidity constraints in U.S. financial markets may limit the ability of black entrepreneurs to raise the optimal levels of capital needed to start businesses. As discussed in chapter 2, there is evidence in the literature that low levels of assets among blacks are one of the major causes of low rates of business creation. Estimates from both the CPS and PSID indicate that roughly 15 percent of the white/black gap in business entry rates is due to wealth disparities (Fairlie 1999, 2006).

Very little previous research focuses on the related question of whether low levels of personal wealth and liquidity constraints also limit the ability of black entrepreneurs to raise startup capital. Undercapitalization likely leads to lower survivability, profits, employment, and sales. Indeed, we find in the previous chapter that the level of startup capital is a strong predictor of business success. If startup capital levels are influenced by entrepreneurial wealth, then a strong link between racial inequality in wealth and racial disparities in business outcomes is expected. Related to this issue and potentially exacerbating the problem is that black entrepreneurs may face discrimination in the lending market, which would also limit their ability to invest in their businesses.

Racial inequality in wealth may also have an effect on the continuing success of businesses. If business owners cannot freely borrow to offset periods of low sales, then those owners with fewer financial resources may be more likely to close. In addition, access to personal or family wealth may allow owners to avoid potential liquidity constraints in expanding existing businesses. Even if black business owners are able to obtain adequate startup capital, future limitations in accessing financial capital may result in less successful businesses.

Some suggestive evidence on racial differences in access to financial capital is provided by published estimates from the CBO (U.S. Census Bureau 1997). The CBO questionnaire asks owners with unsuccessful businesses from 1992 to 1996 why their businesses were unsuccessful. Black business owners are twice as likely as all business owners to report "lack of access to business loans/credit" as a reason for closure (16.2 percent compared with 8.3 percent). They are also nearly three times more likely than all business owners to report "lack of access to personal loans/credit" as a reason for closure (8.8 percent compared with 3.3 percent). Capital constraints appear to be more relevant for black entrepreneurs than for white entrepreneurs.

To further explore this hypothesis, we first document and discuss the causes of racial differences in wealth in the United States. We next review the findings from the literature on lending discrimination against black-owned businesses. Finally, we present estimates of black/white differences in startup capital from the CBO. We argue that racial differences in startup capital capture racial differences in access to capital. Low levels of startup capital invested in black-owned businesses partly reflect racial inequality in personal and family wealth and may also result from discrimination in the lending market.

Black/White Differences in Wealth
Racial inequality in the accumulation of wealth in the United States stands in stark contrast to wage and earnings inequality. For example, median weekly earnings for full-time black workers are 80 percent of median weekly earnings of full-time white workers (U.S. Bureau of Labor Statistics 2004). The median net worth of whites, on the other hand, is nearly eleven times higher than the median net worth of blacks (see table 4.3). The median level of net worth, defined as the current value of all assets minus all liabilities on those assets, for black households is only slightly more than $6,000. Remarkably, that estimate implies that if you add home equity, savings, retirement accounts, mutual fund accounts, and other assets, 50 percent of all black households in the United States have less than $6,166 in net worth. The median level of net worth among white households is $67,000. Large racial dif-

Table 4.3
Median value of assets for households by race, U.S. Census Bureau Estimates (1983 to 2000)

	Total	White .	White non-Latino	Black
1983	$32,667	$39,135		$3,397
1988	$35,752	$43,279		$4,169
1991	$36,623	$44,408		$4,604
1993	$37,587	$45,740		$4,418
1995	$40,200	$49,030		$7,073
1998	$41,681	$52,301	$59,700	$5,490
2000	$46,506	$58,716	$67,000	$6,166

Source: U.S. Census Bureau estimates from various years of the Survey of Income and Program Participation.

ferences in net worth are also found using other datasets and within age groups, education levels, and marital statuses (Blau and Graham 1990; Oliver and Shapiro 1995; Scholz and Levine 2004; Altonji and Doraszelski 2001).

Examining the full distribution of wealth reveals a more pronounced inequality than what is revealed by a comparison of medians (figure 4.3). Forty-five percent of blacks have net worth of less than $5,000. Less than one fifth of all whites have net worth below this level. At the top of the distribution, only 2.7 percent of blacks have a value of net worth that is at least $250,000. Among whites, 22.2 percent have values of net worth in this range. Comparing asset distributions makes it strikingly clear: most blacks have very low levels of wealth, and relatively few have high levels of wealth when compared with whites.

The single largest asset held by most households is their home. Estimates of home ownership reported in table 4.4 indicate that only 46.8 percent of all black households own their own homes. For whites, 73.0 percent own their own home. Among home owners, blacks have much less equity in their homes than whites. The median home equity among black homeowners is $35,000, whereas the median home equity among white homeowners is $64,200. Blacks are clearly less likely to own their own homes, and among those who own a home, they have less equity in their homes. This is due to a combination of lower home values and lower equity/debt ratios in their homes.

Estimates from the SIPP indicate that wealth inequality has decreased only slightly in the past two decades. In 1983, the white/

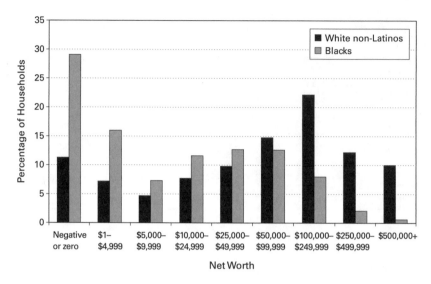

Figure 4.3
Distribution of net worth by race, U.S. Census Bureau Estimates, Survey of Income and
Program Participation (2000)

Table 4.4
Home ownership and median home equity by race, U.S. Census Bureau Estimates from
the Survey of Program and Income Participation (2000)

	Total	White non-Latino	Black
Percentage with own home	67.2%	73.0%	46.8%
Median equity in own home among homeowners	$59,000	$64,200	$35,000

Source: U.S. Census Bureau estimates from various years of the Survey of Income and
Program Participation.

black ratio of median asset levels was 11.5. By 2000, the ratio dropped
to 9.5. However, some of this decrease may have been due to the large
increase in the white Latino population in the 1980s and 1990s. Latinos
have very low levels of net worth, which are only slightly higher than
black levels. If white non-Latinos are used to calculate the white/black
ratio of median net worth, we find a ratio of 10.9. In either case, racial
wealth inequality is extremely large and does not appear to be dis-
appearing quickly.

As expected, a large percentage of the racial gap in wealth accumulation is due to differences in permanent or lifetime income, family
composition, and other demographic characteristics. Income differ-

ences between blacks and whites alone explain a large part of the gap (Scholz and Levine 2004). Racial differences in inheritances and gifts also appear to contribute to the wealth gap measured in mean levels (Menchik and Jianakoplos 1997; Gittleman and Wolff 2004; Avery and Rendall 1997, 2002). The contribution to the racial gap in median levels of net worth is likely to be smaller, however, as most households do not receive inheritances (Scholz and Levine 2004). Other types of inter-generational transfers may also be important in contributing to the racial wealth gap. Racial differences in parental wealth explain part of the wealth gap (Conley 1999). Charles and Hurst (2002) find that 42 percent of white families receive assistance from their family for a down payment on a home compared with only 10 percent of black families.

Lower levels of asset accumulation among blacks may also be due to differences in investment types (Scholz and Levine 2004), lower rates of return on assets within asset types (Menchik and Jianakoplos 1997), and higher participation rates in welfare programs and public housing, which have asset restrictions. Finally, racial differences in self-employment partly explain racial differences in asset accumulation (Menchik and Jianakoplos 1997; Altonji and Doraszelski 2001). This finding, however, begs the question of whether self-employment increases asset accumulation or wealth increases self-employment as discussed in previous chapters.

The consequences of racial wealth inequality are severe. Low asset levels affect the ability of black families to smooth their consumption over fluctuations in income due to job loss and other negative labor-market outcomes. Wealth inequality also translates into political, social, residential, and educational inequality. Current asset levels, and not only current and future income, are important for home purchases and financing education. Through inheritances and intergenerational transfers, black/white wealth inequality is also transmitted to future generations.

Racial inequality in wealth is also likely to have negative consequences for business formation and success through its effects on access to financial capital. Clearly, lower levels of wealth among blacks are likely to translate into less access to startup capital. Business creation is often funded by owner's equity, and investors frequently require a substantial level of owner's investment of his or her own capital as an incentive and as collateral. Racial differences in home equity may be especially important in providing access to startup capital.

Homes provide collateral for business loans, and home equity loans can provide relatively low-cost financing.[3] Thus, lower levels of wealth can lead to inadequate access to financial capital, which in turn can both limit business creation and result in undercapitalized businesses.

Family Wealth

Lower levels of parental wealth may also limit access to financial capital for black entrepreneurs. Black families have less to pass on to their children through inheritances. This in turn will result in lower wealth holdings and access to startup capital among the current generation of blacks. The lower likelihood of receiving inheritances and the smaller amount of inheritances that are received may also have a direct effect on business success for blacks. The receipt of inheritances among business owners is associated with higher survival rates and higher sales among surviving businesses (Holtz-Eakin, Joulfaian, and Rosen 1994a).

Business owners also turn to family members for loans and equity financing. Family members may provide business loans with favorable terms. From the other side, investing in a child's, sibling's, or relative's business may be an attractive option because of the extra information and trust.

The CBO includes information on whether owners receive personal loans from family members to finance their business ventures.[4] Estimates from our CBO sample indicate that family loans are not a common source of startup capital among small business owners. Only 6.4 percent of all owners borrowed capital from their family for starting or acquiring the business. Furthermore, a similar percentage of black and white owners borrowed from their families. Given that startup capital levels are lower for black businesses as noted below, this implies that black owners borrow a smaller total amount from family members than white owners.

Bates (1997) provides estimates of borrowing startup capital from family members from the 1987 CBO. Among firms that borrow startup capital, he finds that 21.2 percent of black firms borrow from family members and that the average amount borrowed is $18,306. A larger percentage of white borrowers obtained loans from family members (26.8 percent) and for a higher average amount ($35,446). However, for capital needs of established firms, evidence from the SSBF paints a different picture. Over 10 percent of firms owned by blacks obtained loans from family and friends, compared with less than 6 percent of white-owned businesses (Bitler, Robb, and Wolken 2001).

Lower levels of family wealth among blacks may limit their ability to obtain sufficient startup capital or ongoing financing. Consequently, blacks may start fewer businesses, and for those black businesses that do start, they may be smaller than what would be optimal.[5] Thus, racial differences in family wealth may contribute to racial differences in business outcomes.

Lending Discrimination
An additional factor that might explain differing rates of startup capital by race is lending discrimination. Much of the recent research on the issue of discrimination in business lending uses data from the Survey of Small Business Finances (SSBF).[6] The main findings from this literature are that minority-owned businesses experience higher loan denial probabilities and pay higher interest rates than white-owned businesses even after controlling for differences in credit-worthiness and other factors (Cavalluzzo, Cavalluzzo, and Wolken 2002; Blanchflower, Levine, and Zimmerman 2003; Coleman 2002, 2003; Blanchard, Yinger, and Zhao 2004; Cavalluzzo and Wolken 2005; Robb and Fairlie 2006).

Using the 1993 National Survey of Small Business Finances (NSSBF), Cavalluzzo, Cavalluzzo, and Wolken (2002) find that black business owners are more likely than whites to have unmet credit needs and more likely to have been denied credit, even after controlling for many factors related to creditworthiness. Blanchflower, Levine, and Zimmerman (2003), using the 1993 SSBF and 1998 SSBF, find that blacks pay a higher interest rate on loans obtained. They also find that concerns over whether a loan application would be denied prevented some prospective borrowers from applying for a loan in the first place. The disparities between the denial rates between whites and blacks are greater when including these individuals with those that actually applied for a loan. Bostic and Lampani (1999) include additional geographic controls but also find a statistically significant difference in approval rates between blacks and whites.

Using the 1998 SSBF, Cavalluzzo and Wolken (2005) find substantial unexplained differences in loan denial rates between African American- and white-owned firms. They also find that while greater personal wealth is associated with a lower probability of denial, a large difference in denial rates between blacks and whites remains, even after controlling for personal wealth. Finally, they find that denial rates for blacks increase with lender-market concentration, which is consistent with Becker's (1971/1957) classic theories of discrimination.

Cavalluzzo and Wolken (2005) estimate the magnitude of contributions from group differences in characteristics to racial gaps in loan denial rates and find that group differences in credit history differences explain most of the difference in denial rates. When examining specific loan types, Mitchell and Pearce (2004) find that black firms faced significantly greater loan-denial probabilities than white-male-owned firms on both relationship bank loans and transaction bank loans.

Using the 1998 SSBF, Robb and Fairlie (2006) focus on more established businesses—those five years and older. They find that established black-owned business are still significantly less likely than white-owned businesses to be approved for loans, to pay a higher rate of interest on approved loans, and not to apply for credit when needed because of fear that the loan application would be denied. They also find that blacks are more likely than whites to be denied trade credit and to rely on credit cards for borrowing purposes. Older, more-established black-owned businesses appear to also face significant barriers in accessing financial capital.

Although it is difficult to prove without a doubt that lending discrimination exists, the evidence from the literature is consistent with the existence of continuing lending discrimination against black-owned firms. Black firms are more likely to be denied loans and pay higher interest rates and are less likely to borrow from banks for startup or continuing capital. Lending discrimination may have a direct effect on business outcomes because it limits access to loans that can help a business "weather a storm" or diversify into new products or markets.

Although most of the evidence from this literature focuses on existing black businesses, lending discrimination may also severely limit access to startup capital, discouraging would-be minority entrepreneurs and jeopardizing the scale and longevity of their businesses.

Differential Types of Financing

Black and white entrepreneurs differ in the types of financing they use for their businesses. Although these differences are likely to be caused by many factors, they may be partly due to differences in personal wealth and lending discrimination. Focusing on startup capital differences, there is evidence of less use of banks by black entrepreneurs for startup capital. Published estimates from the CBO indicate that only 6.6 percent of black firms received business loans from banking or commercial lending institutions (see table 4.5). Nearly twice that

Table 4.5
Sources of borrowed and equity capital by race, Characteristics of Business Owners (1992)

	Percentage		
	All Firms	White-Owned Firms	Black-Owned Firms
Sources of borrowed capital for owner:			
Personal loan using home mortgage/equity line of credit	5.0%	5.0%	3.5%
Personal credit card	3.0	2.9	3.8
Personal loan from spouse	1.2	1.1	1.5
Personal loan from family	6.1	5.8	4.6
Other personal loan	7.1	7.1	5.6
Sources of nonborrowed capital for owner:			
None (100 percent borrowed capital)	6.6	6.8	4.4
Use of owner's personal/family physical assets (building, motor vehicle, equipment, etc.)	18.5	19.1	14.1
Proceeds from the sale of owner's personal assets	2.5	2.4	1.7
Owner's personal/family savings	40.7	40.5	35.1
Other source	3.9	3.7	7.7
Sources of borrowed capital for firm:			
Business loan from banking or commercial lending institution	11.7	12.1	6.6
Government-guaranteed business loan from banking or commercial lending institution	0.4	0.4	0.7
Business loan from federal, state, or local government	0.3	0.3	0.3
Business loan from investment company/profit or nonprofit private source	0.6	0.6	0.5
Business loan from previous owner	1.9	1.9	0.6
Business trade credit from supplier	0.9	0.9	0.6
Other business loan	1.6	1.6	0.9

Source: Characteristics of Business Owners (1992) are reported in U.S. Census Bureau (1997).
Notes: (1) The sample includes businesses that are classified by the IRS as individual proprietorships or self-employed persons, partnerships, and subchapter S corporations and that have sales of $500 or more. (2) White category is equal to the total minus all minority groups. (3) More than one source of capital can be reported for each firm.

percentage of white firms received bank loans for startup capital. Blacks are also less likely to use a home equity line for startup capital than are whites, which may be partly due to the lower rates of home ownership reported above. Blacks are also less likely than whites to use equity or nonborrowed sources of startup capital and to have loans from other sources (except government-backed loans). On the other hand, black business owners are more likely to use credit cards for startup funds than are white business owners.[7]

In studies using the 1987 CBO, Bates (1997, 2005) conducts a thorough comparison of differences between black and white firms in their use of startup capital. Bates finds that black firms were more likely to start with no capital, less likely to borrow startup capital, and more likely to rely solely on equity capital than white-owned firms. In his sample of male-owned firms started in the past ten years, he finds that 29 percent of black firms used borrowed funds for startup capital compared with 37 percent of white firms. Focusing on startup funding from financial institutions, he also finds that black-owned firms receive less in startup capital from banks on average than white-owned firms. Among firms borrowing startup capital, he estimates that the average black firm borrowed $31,958 from financial institutions compared with $56,784 for white firms.

Bates also explores whether disparities in levels of startup capital are partly due to differences in equity startup capital. He finds that black firms receive $2.69 per dollar of equity capital invested in loans from financial institutions. This is lower than the $3.10 per dollar of equity investment for white firms. After controlling for other owner and business characteristics, he finds a roughly similar-sized difference between black and white debt per equity dollar invested. These differences are not large, however, suggesting that an important hurdle to obtaining loans from financial institutions for black entrepreneurs is low levels of equity financing in addition to differential treatment by financial institutions (Bates 2005). In fact, from a pooled sample of black and white firms, Bates (2005) finds that loans received by black firms borrowing startup capital are significantly smaller than those received by white firms even after controlling for equity capital and owner and business characteristics such as education and industry. Racial differences in personal wealth, which are not measured in the CBO, may be a key factor in explaining the remaining black/white differences in business loans.

For older, more established firms, these racial differences in financing patterns continue. Using data from the 1998 SSBF, Robb and Fairlie (2006) find that black firms are less likely than white firms to have credit lines, equipment loans, business mortgages, motor vehicle loans, or trade credit. They are also less likely to use business credit cards, use personal credit cards for business purposes, or hold checking accounts. In fact, the only types of loans that they hold more frequently than white firms are capital leases and a catch-all category of "other" loans. Blacks are more likely than whites to borrow through the use of credit cards and trade credit (carrying balances on those lines of credit and paying interest on those balances), which often have higher interest rates than conventional loans.

Overall, these racial differences in types of financing for startup or continuing capital may be the result of many different factors. For example, we cannot rule out the possibility that the lower likelihood of acquiring capital from financial institutions among black businesses is due to a lower evaluated probability of success for these businesses. However, the patterns are consistent with large racial differences in personal wealth and lending discrimination.

Racial Differences in Startup Capital

Black-owned businesses have very low levels of startup capital relative to white-owned businesses (figure 4.4). Fewer than 2 percent of black firms start with $100,000 or more of capital, and 6.5 percent have between $25,000 and $100,000 in startup capital. Nearly two thirds of black businesses have less than $5,000 in startup capital. Although a large percentage of white firms also start with little capital, a higher percentage of white firms start with large amounts of capital than black firms.

Racial disparities in startup capital may reflect differences in the potential success of firms and thus ability to raise capital by firms. In other words, some black entrepreneurs may have difficulty raising capital because their businesses are predicted to be less likely to succeed. If so, banks and other investors will rationally decline to invest in these businesses. Of course, an alternative explanation is that black business owners invest less startup capital in their businesses because they have less access to capital. This may be due to having lower levels of personal and family wealth to borrow against or use as equity financing but may also be due to lending discrimination. Evidence favoring these

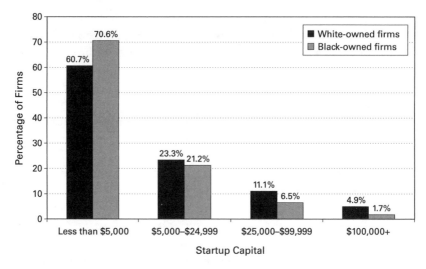

Figure 4.4
Startup capital by race, Characteristics of Business Owners (1992)

explanations is provided by the finding that black-owned firms have lower levels of startup capital across all major industries (U.S. Census Bureau 1997). Thus, racial disparities in startup capital do not simply reflect racial differences in the industries of these firms. In addition, the finding that personal wealth decreases the probability that an existing firm is denied a loan is consistent with racial disparities in wealth contributing to racial differences in startup capital.

What are the likely consequences of these racial disparities in startup capital? The literature on minority business ownership provides evidence that access to financial capital limits opportunities for blacks to start businesses as discussed in chapter 2. A much smaller literature indicates that racial differences in wealth or startup capital affect business success. Using earlier CBO data, Bates (1989, 1994, 1997) finds evidence that black-owned businesses have substantially lower levels of startup capital than white-owned businesses. He also finds that startup capital levels are strongly positively associated with business survival. These two findings indicate that racial disparities in startup capital contribute to racial differences in survival.

Robb (2000) provides additional evidence on the importance of startup capital using employer firms from the 1992 CBO linked to the 1992 to 1996 Business Information Tracking Series (BITS). Estimates from regression models indicate that the level of startup capital has a negative and statistically significant effect on the probability of business closure. Black-employer firms are also found to have substantially lower levels of startup capital than white-employer firms. Thus, racial disparities in the amount of capital used to start the business result in higher closure rates among black-employer firms relative to white-employer firms.

Our estimates also indicate that racial disparities in startup capital contribute to worse outcomes among black-owned businesses. In the multivariate regressions reported in chapter 3, we find a strong positive relationship between startup capital and business success. Higher levels of startup capital are associated with lower closure probabilities, higher profits, more employment, and higher sales. In addition, estimates from the 1992 CBO indicate that blacks have substantially lower levels of startup capital. Thus, black/white differences in startup capital appear to contribute to racial disparities in business outcomes. What we do not know from these findings, however, is how much these racial differences in startup capital contribute to differences in business outcomes relative to racial differences in other factors such as education, business human capital, and family-business backgrounds.

Using individual-level data, Fairlie (1999, 2006) provides some evidence on this question. Focusing on the causes of the higher annual rate of exit from self-employment for blacks than whites, estimates from the CPS indicate that racial differences in personal wealth explain 7.3 percent of the gap. Estimates from the PSID indicate that 1.8 to 11.1 percent of the male black/white gap in exit rates from self-employment is explained by differences in asset levels. The use of individual-level data, the focus on transitions out of self-employment, and the inclusion of personal wealth, however, make it difficult to draw conclusions about whether racial disparities in access to startup capital contribute to racial differences in business outcomes. The decompositions estimated below provide evidence on the relative importance of racial differences in startup capital to racial disparities in business outcomes.

Industry Differences

Racial differences in industry distributions may also contribute to differences between blacks and whites in small business outcomes. Some industries, most notably retail and services, have higher business turnover rates than others (Robb 2000; Reynolds and White 1997). Those

Table 4.6

Industry distribution by race, Characteristics of Business Owners (1992)

	White-Owned Firms	Black-Owned Firms
Agricultural services	2.7%	1.7%
Construction	12.5%	7.1%
Manufacturing	3.4%	1.7%
Wholesale trade	3.6%	1.1%
Retail trade	14.7%	14.5%
Finance, insurance, and real estate	10.1%	6.1%
Transportation, communications, and public utilities	3.9%	8.5%
Personal services	25.9%	32.8%
Professional services	19.3%	20.8%
Uncoded industry	3.9%	5.7%
Sample size	15,872	7,565

Notes: (1) The sample includes businesses that are classified by the IRS as individual proprietorships or self-employed persons, partnerships, and subchapter S corporations, have sales of $500 or more, and have at least one owner who worked at least twelve weeks and ten hours per week in the business. (2) All estimates are calculated using sample weights provided by the Characteristics of Business Owners.

with higher capital requirements for entry, such as manufacturing and wholesale, typically have lower turnover rates. Estimates from the CBO reported in chapter 3 indicate differences in business outcomes across industries, although the differences are somewhat mixed in the regression models that control for other owner and firm characteristics. One consistent result, however, is that firms in personal services have worse outcomes.

Black and white firms concentrate in different industries. Table 4.6 reports estimates of industry distributions by race from CBO microdata. Black firms are underrepresented in construction, manufacturing, wholesale trade, agricultural services and finance, insurance, and real estate relative to white firms. Black firms are more concentrated in transportation, communications and public utilities, and personal services than white firms. These industries generally have worse business outcomes than the previous industries, but as noted above the regression results provide mixed evidence on which industries are associated with worse outcomes.

Black and white firms may concentrate in different industries for several reasons. First, capital constraints may limit which industries an individual can enter due to higher capital requirements of certain industries (Bates 1997). In addition, industry choice may be constrained due to a lack of relevant skills and discrimination (Boden 1996; Boden and Nucci 2002; Robb 2000). Discrimination may occur directly in self-employment through limited opportunities to penetrate networks, such as those in construction (Bates 1993a; Feagin and Imani 1994; Bates and Howell 1997). While differences in entrepreneurial ability may lead to different choices of industries, differences in industry concentrations may simply reflect differences in preferences.

Overall, the estimates presented here suggest that black/white differences in industry distributions may contribute to racial differences in business outcomes. However, these industry differences may result from different constraints, preferences or abilities, which affect the interpretation of our results. A concern is that industry choice may simply be a measure of business success, implying that black firms have limited entry into certain industries because they are less successful and not because the industry concentration of black firms leads to less success.

Identifying the Causes of Black/White Differences in Business Outcomes

The estimates reported above indicate that black business owners have less family-business experience, lower levels of education, and lower levels of startup capital than white business owners and differ along several additional dimensions. These owner and firm characteristics are important determinants of small business outcomes. Taken together, these results suggest that racial differences in family-business background, education, and startup capital contribute to why black-owned businesses have worse outcomes on average than white-owned businesses. The impact of each factor, however, is difficult to summarize. In particular, we want to identify the separate contributions from racial differences in the variables included in the regressions.

The most common approach used to quantify these contributions is the technique of decomposing racial differences in mean levels of an outcome into those due to different observable characteristics or "endowments" between racial groups and those due to different effects of characteristics or "coefficients" of groups. The technique is commonly attributed to Blinder (1973) and Oaxaca (1973). The Blinder-Oaxaca decomposition technique is especially useful for identifying and quantifying the separate contributions of group differences in measurable characteristics, such as education, experience, and geographical location, to racial gaps in outcomes. The technique is easy to apply and requires only coefficient estimates from linear regressions for the outcome of interest and sample means of the independent variables used in the regressions. We use this technique for the log sales specification, which is estimated using a linear regression.

The Blinder-Oaxaca technique, however, cannot be used without modification to decompose racial differences in the three other outcomes—closure, profits, and employment. This is because each of these business outcomes is binary (they take on the values of either 0 or 1), and their specifications are estimated with logit regressions instead of linear regressions. Instead, we use a decomposition technique that takes into account the nonlinearity of the logit regressions used to estimate the other outcomes. This technique is described in the appendix to this chapter and Fairlie (1999, 2005) in more detail.

Table 4.7 reports estimates from this procedure for decomposing the black/white gaps in small business outcomes (see also Fairlie and Robb 2007). We first discuss the results for the more simplified model that does not include startup capital or industry. The underlying regression estimates are taken from table 3.5, and the means for black and white firms are reported in table 4.A. The separate contributions from racial differences in each set of independent variables are reported. As noted above, the black/white gaps in small business outcomes are large. Black firms are more likely to close and have lower profits, employment, and sales than white firms. Racial differences in the male/female ownership of the firm contribute significantly to the gaps in small business outcomes. The large contributions are the result of a higher percentage of black-owned firms than white-owned firms also being female-owned and of female-owned firms having lower business outcomes than male-owned businesses, on average. Similar to the previous chapter, we calculate separate decompositions by gender and discuss the results below.

Lower marriage rates among blacks also contribute to the black/white gaps in small business outcomes. Sixty-eight percent of black owners are married compared with 77 percent of white owners. Spousal income may act as a buffer against downturns in sales for the business and allow the owner to stay in business longer.

Although racial disparities in education are smaller for business owners than for the general population, low levels of education among

Table 4.7
Decompositions of black/white gaps in small business outcomes, Characteristics of Business Owners (1992)

	Specification			
	(1)	(2)	(3)	(4)
Dependent variable	Closure	Profits	Employer	Ln Sales
Black mean	0.2696	0.1410	0.1121	9.4241
White mean	0.2282	0.3004	0.2067	10.0680
Black/white gap	−0.0414	0.1594	0.0946	0.6439
Contributions from racial differences in:				
Sex	−0.0032	0.0253	0.0083	0.0689
	7.7%	15.9%	8.8%	10.7%
Marital status	−0.0037	0.0044	0.0042	0.0166
	8.9%	2.8%	4.4%	2.6%
Education	−0.0027	0.0056	0.0023	0.0156
	6.5%	3.5%	2.4%	2.4%
Region	−0.0033	0.0032	−0.0050	0.0139
	8.0%	2.0%	−5.3%	2.2%
Urban	−0.0026	−0.0060	0.0051	−0.0154
	6.3%	−3.8%	5.4%	−2.4%
Prior work experience	0.0011	−0.0017	−0.0008	−0.0011
	−2.7%	−1.1%	−0.8%	−0.2%
Prior work experience in a managerial capacity	0.0061	0.0016	0.0042	0.0178
	−14.7%	1.0%	4.4%	2.8%
Prior work experience in a similar business	−0.0025	0.0036	0.0017	0.0277
	6.0%	2.3%	1.8%	4.3%
Have a self-employed family member	−0.0037	0.0017	−0.0004	−0.0070
	8.9%	1.1%	−0.4%	−1.1%
Prior work experience in a family member's business	−0.0048	0.0027	0.0053	0.0412
	11.6%	1.7%	5.6%	6.4%
Inherited business	−0.0002	0.0005	0.0002	0.0021
	0.5%	0.3%	0.2%	0.3%
All included variables	−0.0200	0.0409	0.0251	0.1910
	48.3%	25.7%	26.5%	29.7%

Notes: (1) The samples and regression specifications are the same as those used in table 3.5. (2) Contribution estimates are mean values of the decomposition using 1,000 subsamples of whites. See text for more details.

black business owners relative to white business owners appear to have a negative effect on business outcomes. As noted above, the differences are large. For example, 27 percent of black business owners have a college education compared with 33 percent of white business owners. These educational differences, however, do not translate into very large effects: racial differences in the education level of the owner explain from 2.4 to 6.5 percent of the black/white gaps in business outcomes. Black business owners are less educated on average than are white business owners, but these educational differences do not appear to be an extremely large hindrance to operating successful businesses.

Although black-owned businesses have a different regional distribution and are more likely to be located in urban areas than are white-owned businesses, racial differences in geographical locations do not appear to contribute substantially to the gaps in small business outcomes. Racial differences in the amount of prior work experience and management experience have either small effects or mixed effects on gaps in the different business outcomes.

As reported in table 4.1, black business owners are much less likely to have a self-employed family member than are white business owners. This difference, however, does not contribute to racial disparities in profits, employment, and sales. The only exception is that racial differences in having a self-employed family member explain about 9 percent of the black/white gap in closure rates. The contribution of group differences in parental self-employment to racial differences in small business outcomes appears to be smaller than the contribution to rates of self-employment and entry into self-employment. Estimates from the PSID indicate that racial differences in the probability of having a self-employed father explain 8 to 14 percent of the black/white gap in the entry rate into self-employment and 4 to 6 percent of the gap in the self-employment rate (Fairlie 1999).

The explanatory power of racial differences in prior work experience in a family member's business is stronger. With the exception of the profits specification, racial differences in this variable explain 5.6 to 11.6 percent of the black/white gaps in small business outcomes. Apparently, the lack of work experience in family businesses among future black business owners, perhaps by restricting their acquisition of general and specific business human capital, limits the successfulness of their businesses relative to whites.

Racial differences in prior work experience in a business providing similar goods and services consistently explain a small part of the gaps in outcomes. Although the coefficient estimates in the small business outcome regressions are generally similar in magnitude to coefficient estimates on the family-business work-experience variable, the contributions from racial differences are somewhat smaller. The racial disparity in the percentage of owners who worked in a family member's business is larger than the disparity in the percentage of owners who worked in a business with similar goods and services. Black owners appear to acquire less specific business human capital from working in similar business prior to starting their own businesses.

Black-owned businesses are less likely to be inherited than white-owned businesses, and inherited businesses are generally more successful than noninherited businesses, but racial differences in business inheritances explain virtually none of the gaps in small business outcomes. The overall likelihood of business inheritances (1.6 percent) is too small to play a major role in explaining racial differences in business outcomes.

This finding is interesting in light of the finding in the literature that blacks are less likely to receive inheritances and typically receive much smaller inheritances than whites. As noted above, there is recent evidence suggesting that the lack of inheritances among blacks is an important factor explaining why blacks have asset levels that are substantially lower than white levels (Menchik and Jianakoplos 1997; Gittleman and Wolff 2000; Avery and Rendall 1997, 2002). Furthermore, the receipt of inheritances is a major determinant of starting and remaining in business (Holtz-Eakin, Joulfaian, and Rosen 1994a, 1994b; Blanchflower and Oswald 1998), suggesting that lower levels of inheritances among blacks contribute to lower rates of business ownership. With regard to business inheritances, however, they are apparently not very important in explaining differences in business outcomes.

Differences between Male and Female Business Owners

We also investigate whether the causes of racial differences in business outcomes are similar for male- and female-owned businesses. As noted in chapter 3, male firms tend to have lower closure rates, higher profit rates, higher employer rates, and more sales than female firms. In terms of owner characteristics, however, there are many similarities between the sexes. We also found that estimates from separate sets of business outcome regressions that the determinants of business outcomes do not differ substantially between men and women. The remaining question then is whether the explanations for black/white disparities in business outcomes differ between male- and female-owned businesses.

Tables 4.8 and 4.9 report estimates from separate decompositions for racial differences in business outcomes for men and women, respectively. Mean characteristics are reported in table 4.10. Estimates from the CBO indicate that black firms have higher closure rates, have lower profits, are less likely to have employees, and have lower sales than white firms for both male- and female-owned businesses. These disparities in outcomes are large for both sexes.

Turning to the explanatory factors, we find that lower levels of education among blacks explain part of the gaps in business outcomes for men but not for women. In contrast, estimates from the decompositions indicate roughly similar patterns for the family-business-background variables. Racial differences in having a self-employed family member explain very little of the gaps in business outcomes, whereas having prior work experience in a family member's business explains part of the gaps. Racial differences in business inheritances explain virtually none of the gap for either men or women.

For additional explanatory factors, we find that racial differences in management experience continue to have inconsistent explanatory power across specifications. Racial differences in prior work experience in similar businesses contribute to the black/white gaps in business outcomes for men but not to the gaps for women. Racial differences in marital status explain a much larger portion of the disparities in business outcomes for women than for men. Black female business owners are less likely to be married than are white female business owners, and this marital status is associated with better business outcomes. The contribution estimates from racial differences in region and urban status are similarly inconsistent across specifications.

Overall, the decompositions indicate some differences in the results for men and women, but the main findings for the family-business-background variables are similar. Racial differences in prior work experience in family businesses explain part of the gaps in business outcomes, whereas racial differences in having self-employed family members and business inheritances have little explanatory power. We continue to group men and women in the remaining analyses. A more extensive analysis of these patterns, however, is beyond the scope of the current analysis.

Table 4.8
Decompositions of black/white gaps in small business outcomes for men, Characteristics of Business Owners (1992)

	Specification			
	(1)	(2)	(3)	(4)
Dependent variable	Closure	Profits	Employer	Ln Sales
Black mean	0.2496	0.1902	0.1310	9.6709
White mean	0.2189	0.3661	0.2311	10.3259
Black/white gap	−0.0306	0.1759	0.1001	0.6550
Contributions from racial differences in:				
Marital status	−0.0005	0.0007	0.0004	−0.0034
	1.7%	0.4%	0.4%	−0.5%
Education	−0.0065	0.0086	0.0038	0.0315
	21.1%	4.9%	3.8%	4.8%
Region	−0.0009	0.0020	−0.0024	0.0265
	3.0%	1.1%	−2.4%	4.1%
Urban	−0.0032	−0.0067	0.0059	−0.0141
	10.5%	−3.8%	5.9%	−2.1%
Prior work experience	0.0000	−0.0034	−0.0005	−0.0023
	0.0%	−1.9%	−0.5%	−0.4%
Prior work experience in a managerial capacity	0.0094	0.0023	0.0047	0.0206
	−30.7%	1.3%	4.7%	3.2%
Prior work experience in a similar business	−0.0040	0.0067	0.0022	0.0355
	13.2%	3.8%	2.2%	5.4%
Have a self-employed family member	−0.0002	0.0017	−0.0001	−0.0113
	0.7%	1.0%	−0.1%	−1.7%
Prior work experience in a family member's business	−0.0057	0.0016	0.0052	0.0416
	18.5%	0.9%	5.2%	6.4%
Inherited business	−0.0003	0.0006	0.0014	0.0057
	0.8%	0.4%	1.4%	0.9%
All included variables	−0.0119	0.0142	0.0206	0.1304
	38.8%	8.1%	20.5%	19.9%

Notes: (1) The samples and regression specifications are the same as those used in table 3.8. (2) Contribution estimates are mean values of the decomposition using 1,000 sub-samples of whites. See the text for more details.

Table 4.9
Decompositions of black/white gaps in small business outcomes for women, Characteristics of Business Owners (1992)

	Specification			
	(1)	(2)	(3)	(4)
Dependent variable	Closure	Profits	Employer	Ln Sales
Black mean	0.2968	0.0767	0.0865	9.0901
White mean	0.2475	0.1693	0.1563	9.5221
Black/white gap	−0.0494	0.0926	0.0697	0.4321
Contributions from racial differences in:				
Marital status	−0.0120	0.0061	0.0091	0.0364
	24.2%	6.6%	13.0%	8.4%
Education	0.0048	0.0024	−0.0001	0.0183
	−9.8%	2.6%	−0.2%	4.2%
Region	−0.0070	0.0038	0.0007	−0.0040
	14.1%	4.1%	1.0%	−0.9%
Urban	0.0001	−0.0054	0.0030	−0.0189
	−0.2%	−5.8%	4.3%	−4.4%
Prior work experience	0.0016	−0.0016	−0.0022	−0.0047
	−3.2%	−1.7%	−3.2%	−1.1%
Prior work experience in a managerial capacity	0.0012	0.0007	0.0046	0.0103
	−2.5%	0.7%	6.6%	2.4%
Prior work experience in a similar business	0.0002	−0.0003	−0.0002	0.0078
	−0.5%	−0.4%	−0.2%	1.8%
Have a self-employed family member	−0.0122	0.0025	−0.0010	−0.0005
	24.6%	2.7%	−1.4%	−0.1%
Prior work experience in a family member's business	0.0003	0.0045	0.0050	0.0353
	−0.7%	4.8%	7.2%	8.2%
Inherited business	0.0006	0.0002	−0.0017	−0.0050
	−1.2%	0.2%	−2.4%	−1.2%
All included variables	−0.0222	0.0128	0.0171	0.0752
	44.9%	13.9%	24.6%	17.4%

Notes: (1) The samples and regression specifications are the same as those used in table 3.9. (2) Contribution estimates are mean values of the decomposition using 1,000 subsamples of whites. See the text for more details.

Table 4.10
Means of selected variables by gender, Characteristics of Business Owners (1992)

	Male		Female	
	White-Owned Firms	Black-Owned Firms	White-Owned Firms	Black-Owned Firms
Firm no longer operating in 1996 (closure)	0.2189	0.2496	0.2475	0.2968
Net profit of at least $10,000	0.3661	0.1902	0.1693	0.0767
One or more paid employees	0.2311	0.1310	0.1563	0.0865
Log sales	10.3319	9.6719	9.5245	9.09
Female-owned business	0.0000	0.0000	1.0000	1.0000
Married	0.7850	0.7240	0.7540	0.5750
Never married	0.1014	0.0892	0.1040	0.1293
High school graduate	0.2678	0.2135	0.2597	0.2357
Some college	0.3013	0.3384	0.3350	0.3476
College graduate	0.1864	0.1150	0.2165	0.1484
Graduate school	0.1450	0.1490	0.1153	0.1366
Northeast	0.0665	0.0191	0.0597	0.0198
Midatlantic	0.1493	0.1368	0.1420	0.1244
East North Central	0.1699	0.1347	0.1598	0.1479
West North Central	0.0861	0.0353	0.0817	0.0299
South Atlantic	0.1501	0.3215	0.1794	0.3319
East South Central	0.0519	0.0892	0.0517	0.0656
West South Central	0.1031	0.1496	0.0934	0.1371
Mountain	0.0650	0.0168	0.0713	0.0156
Urban	0.7251	0.8756	0.7556	0.9040
Prior work experience: 1 year	0.0673	0.0785	0.0776	0.0539
Prior work experience: 2 to 5 years	0.1651	0.1536	0.1621	0.1451
Prior work experience: 6 to 9 years	0.1525	0.1500	0.1471	0.1372
Prior work experience: 10 to 19 years	0.2936	0.3096	0.3047	0.3206
Prior work experience: 20 years or more	0.2661	0.2396	0.2407	0.2389
Prior work experience in a managerial capacity	0.5707	0.4776	0.5231	0.4594
Prior work experience in a similar business	0.5420	0.4611	0.4226	0.4005
Have a self-employed family member	0.5289	0.3257	0.5113	0.3249
Prior work experience in a family member's business	0.2514	0.1392	0.2019	0.1092
Inherited business	0.0157	0.0109	0.0130	0.0162
Startup capital: $5,000 to $24,999	0.2596	0.2403	0.1919	0.1710
Startup capital: $25,000 to $99,999	0.1188	0.0780	0.0904	0.0463
Startup capital: $100,000 and over	0.0520	0.0187	0.0383	0.0143
Agricultural services	0.0312	0.0250	0.0176	0.0074
Construction	0.1712	0.1116	0.0351	0.0176

Table 4.10
(continued)

	Male		Female	
	White-Owned Firms	Black-Owned Firms	White-Owned Firms	Black-Owned Firms
Manufacturing	0.0352	0.0189	0.0281	0.0142
Wholesale	0.0388	0.0132	0.0302	0.0087
FIRE	0.0949	0.0598	0.1097	0.0616
Trans., communications, and public utilities	0.0459	0.1229	0.0240	0.0309
Personal services	0.2367	0.3287	0.3071	0.3280
Professional services	0.1771	0.1541	0.2269	0.2767
Uncoded industry	0.0407	0.0575	0.0364	0.0569
Sample size	7,425	4,588	6,857	2,243

Notes: (1) The sample includes businesses that are classified by the IRS as individual proprietorships or self-employed persons, partnerships, and subchapter S corporations, have sales of $500 or more, and have at least one owner who worked at least twelve weeks and ten hours per week in the business. (2) All estimates are calculated using sample weights provided by the CBO.

Contributions from Startup Capital and Industry Differences

Table 4.11 reports the results of decompositions that include startup capital and industry. We exclude these variables from the first set of decompositions because of concerns over endogeneity as discussed in chapter 3. The regression estimates are taken from table 3.14.

Black-owned firms clearly have less startup capital than white-owned firms. For example, 8 percent of black-owned businesses had at least $25,000 in startup capital compared with nearly 16 percent of white-owned businesses. These racial differences in startup capital explain a substantial portion of the black/white gaps in small business outcomes. The contribution estimates range from 14.5 to 43.2 percent for the different outcomes. Clearly, lower levels of startup capital among black-owned firms are associated with less successful businesses. These lower levels of startup capital are likely to be related to difficulty in obtaining funding because of low levels of personal wealth and possibly lending discrimination. Black levels of wealth are one eleventh white levels. The result is that black/white differences in startup capital are the single most important factor in explaining racial differences in business outcomes.

Black-owned businesses appear to be overrepresented in less successful industries relative to white-owned businesses. Racial differences

Table 4.11
Decompositions of black/white gaps in small business outcomes, Characteristics of Business Owners (1992)

	Specification			
	(1)	(2)	(3)	(4)
Dependent variable	Closure	Profits	Employer	Ln Sales
Black mean	0.2692	0.1414	0.1116	9.4221
White mean	0.2288	0.3003	0.2065	10.0615
Black/white gap	−0.0404	0.1590	0.0948	0.6394
Contributions from racial differences in:				
Sex	−0.0019	0.0231	0.0060	0.0562
	4.7%	14.6%	6.3%	8.8%
Marital status	−0.0030	0.0055	0.0041	0.0118
	7.5%	3.5%	4.3%	1.8%
Education	−0.0031	0.0045	0.0013	0.0066
	7.8%	2.8%	1.4%	1.0%
Region	−0.0031	0.0035	0.0010	0.0160
	7.6%	2.2%	1.0%	2.5%
Urban	−0.0012	−0.0078	0.0021	−0.0277
	2.9%	−4.9%	2.2%	−4.3%
Prior work experience	0.0014	−0.0021	−0.0010	−0.0032
	−3.5%	−1.3%	−1.1%	−0.5%
Prior work experience in a managerial capacity	0.0065	0.0005	0.0018	0.0035
	−16.1%	0.3%	1.9%	0.5%
Prior work experience in a similar business	−0.0029	0.0042	0.0022	0.0277
	7.1%	2.6%	2.3%	4.3%
Have a self-employed family member	−0.0032	0.0001	0.0009	−0.0128
	7.8%	0.0%	1.0%	−2.0%
Prior work experience in a family member's business	−0.0032	0.0019	0.0033	0.0246
	7.9%	1.2%	3.4%	3.8%
Inherited business	−0.0001	0.0005	0.0000	0.0007
	0.1%	0.3%	0.0%	0.1%
Startup capital	−0.0175	0.0231	0.0350	0.1512
	43.2%	14.5%	36.9%	23.6%
Industry	−0.0083	0.0112	0.0092	0.0633
	20.5%	7.0%	9.7%	9.9%
All included variables	−0.0395	0.0683	0.0658	0.3179
	97.7%	42.9%	69.4%	49.7%

Notes: (1) The sample and regression specifications are the same as those used in table 3.14. (2) Contribution estimates are mean values of the decomposition using 1,000 subsamples of whites. See the text for more details.

in industry composition explain from 7.0 to 20.5 percent of the black/ white gaps in small business outcomes. In particular, black-owned firms are more likely to be located in personal services, which have worse outcomes on average than other industries. These findings are consistent with Robb (2000). The results are difficult to interpret, however, because of the joint decision between business ownership and industry.

Overall, racial differences in the explanatory variables explain a large percentage of the total black/white gaps in small business outcomes. They explain nearly 50 percent of the racial gap in profits and employment and nearly 70 percent of the total gap in log sales. Nearly 100 percent of the black/white gap in business closure rates is explained by racial differences in the explanatory variables. Although we employed relatively parsimonious specifications focusing on well measured and less endogenous owner and firm characteristics, our models performed quite well in explaining racial disparities in business outcomes. These factors are likely to be several of the most important inputs into the production process of the firm.

Although the decompositions explain most of the black/white gaps in business outcomes, it is useful to consider the remaining or "unexplained" portion of the gaps. The "unexplained" portion of the racial gaps may be due to lending discrimination and consumer discrimination against black-owned firms, the omission of important unmeasurable factors such as risk aversion, or the inability to accurately measure racial differences in access to capital. We now briefly discuss some of these factors.

Other Potential Explanations: Consumer Discrimination

Although the decomposition technique reveals several explanations for black/white differences in business outcomes, we discuss a few additional explanations, which are difficult to identify using the technique or cannot be measured with the CBO. One potential explanation for the remaining racial differences in business outcomes is consumer discrimination against black-owned firms. Black firms may have difficulty selling certain products and services to nonblack customers limiting the size of their markets and resulting success. Discriminating customers could be individuals, other firms or the government. Using microdata from the 1980 Census, Borjas and Bronars (1989) explore whether the large variance in self-employment rates across racial groups are partly due to consumer discrimination. They find that blacks negatively select into self-employment, with the most able blacks remaining in the wage and salary sector, whereas whites positively select into self-employment and negatively select into wage and salary work. These findings are consistent with the most-able minorities avoiding potential discrimination by white consumers by working in wage and salary jobs instead of starting businesses. Kawaguchi (2004) finds that among African Americans, low wage and salary earners are the most likely to enter into business ownership, whereas both low-and high-earning whites are the most likely to enter self-employment. He notes that this finding is consistent with the theoretical predictions of consumer and credit-market discrimination against blacks. However, in contrast to these results, Meyer (1990) does not find evidence supporting the consumer discrimination hypothesis. Using data from the 1987 Characteristics of Business Owners (CBO), he finds that black businesses are relatively more common in industries in which white customers more frequently patronize black businesses.

More generally, black-owned firms may face limited market access for the goods and services that they produce (Bates 1997). This may be partly due to consumer discrimination by customers, other firms, or the government in addition to redlining. But it may also be due to the types, scale, and locations of black firms. Published estimates from the CBO indicate that black-owned businesses serve smaller geographical areas than white-owned businesses on average (table 4.12). Black firms are more likely than white firms to report that their neighborhood is the geographic area that best describes where the business's goods and services are sold. Black owners are less likely to report larger geographical areas as markets for their goods and services. Furthermore, they are much more likely to sell to a minority clientele than are white businesses (figure 4.5), which may reflect more limited market access. As expected, market access or penetration is both a cause and consequence of success in business making it difficult to interpret racial differences in these measures. More successful black firms are likely to expand to larger market areas.

Networks

Racial differences in networks may also contribute to the lack of success among black businesses. Previous research indicates that the size and composition of social networks is associated with self-employment

Table 4.12
Market area of small businesses by race, Characteristics of Business Owners (1992)

	Percentage		
	All Firms	White-Owned Firms	Black-Owned Firms
Geographic area that best describes marketplace:			
Neighborhood	32.8%	31.6%	45.2%
City/county	53.8	54.1	51.9
Regional (adjoining counties or states)	24.5	25.7	14.7
National	6.8	7.0	4.7
International	2.0	1.8	1.3

Source: Characteristics of Business Owners (1992) as reported in U.S. Census Bureau (1997).
Notes: (1) The sample includes businesses that are classified by the IRS as individual proprietorships or self-employed persons, partnerships, and subchapter S corporations and that have sales of $500 or more. (2) White category is equal to the total minus all minority groups.

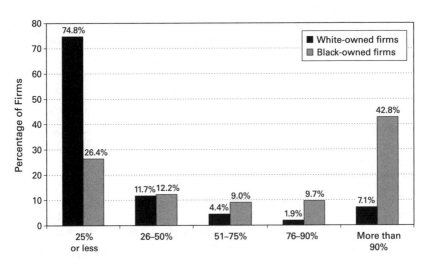

Figure 4.5
Minority customers served by the business (percentage), Characteristics of Business Owners (1992)

(Allen 2000) and that having close friends and neighbors in business and being a member of a business network are positively associated with outcomes among nascent entrepreneurs (Davidsson and Honig 2002). If minority firms have limited access to business, social, or family networks or have smaller networks then they may be less likely to enter business and create successful businesses. These networks may be especially important in providing financing, customers, technical assistance, role models, and contracts.[8] These same networks, however, are likely to also be useful for finding employment in the wage and salary sector creating a dampening effect on self-employment.

In an earlier study, Fratoe (1988) finds that black business owners are less likely to have business role models, obtain loans from other family members, and use family members as unpaid labor. Social networks may be especially important in industries such as construction, where deals are often made in informal settings (Feagin and Imani 1994). If minorities are blocked from these industries perhaps due to discrimination, then their business networks may be restricted (Bates 1993b; Feagin and Imani 1994; Bates and Howell 1997). Examining the retail industry in New York, Rauch (2001) finds evidence that African American businesses were less able to organize "mutual self-help" than immigrant businesses.

Ethnic and racial groups may differ not only in the size of their networks but also in their ability to transfer information related to running a business among coethnics. There is evidence that experience as an employee of a small business and transfers of information are important (Meyer 1990). Strong patterns of industry concentrations for businesses owned by many ethnic groups are consistent with this explanation (Fairlie and Meyer 1996). The industry concentration of black businesses has become more similar to white businesses over time, however, while the there has been no convergence in rates of business ownership (Fairlie and Meyer 2000).

A major limitation of these explanations is that they are difficult to analyze empirically. The problem is that success in business for some groups may simply create larger and more efficient business and social networks. Thus, it is difficult to identify the direction of causation between networks and success. Coethnic networks may also create a multiplier effect whereby small differences in initial business success between groups may lead to large differences in future business success. This point is related to the argument noted above that the lack of black traditions in business enterprise is a major cause of current low levels of black business ownership (Du Bois 1899; Myrdal 1944; Cayton and Drake 1946; Frazier 1957).

Conclusions

African Americans have levels of wealth that are one eleventh those of whites. The median level of net worth, defined as the current value of all assets minus all liabilities on those assets, for black households is only $6,166. This disparity in personal wealth appears to have two major consequences for business success. First, low levels of wealth limit business formation among blacks. In fact, roughly 15 percent of the black/white gap in business creation rates is due to racial differences in assets (Fairlie 1999, 2006). Second, black entrepreneurs who do start businesses invest much less capital at startup on average than white entrepreneurs. For example, estimates from the CBO microdata indicate that the percentage of black-owned firms starting with at least $25,000 in capital is roughly half the percentage of white-owned firms starting with at least $25,000 in capital.

Lower levels of startup capital among black businesses limit their ability to grow and succeed. Specifically, we find that racial disparities in startup capital contribute to higher failure rates, lower sales and profits, and less employment among black-owned businesses. Estimates from nonlinear decompositions indicate that racial differences in startup capital explain from 14.5 to 43.2 percent of the gaps in small business outcomes. Startup capital disparities are the most important explanatory factor in contributing to racial differences in business outcomes. Limited access to financial capital among black entrepreneurs, which appears to be caused by wealth inequality and possibly lending discrimination, is a major reason for less successful black businesses.

Racial differences in family-business backgrounds are also an important factor. Previous research indicates that the probability of business ownership is substantially higher among the children of business owners than among the children of nonbusiness owners and that current racial patterns of self-employment are in part determined by racial patterns of self-employment in the previous generation (Lentz and Laband 1990; Fairlie 1999; Dunn and Holtz-Eakin 2000; Hout and Rosen 2000). The CBO microdata allow us to build on these findings by exploring whether the intergenerational transmission of business ownership is also important in creating racial disparities in business outcomes *conditioning* on ownership.

Estimates from the CBO indicate that black business owners have a relatively disadvantaged family-business background compared with white business owners. Black business owners are much less likely than white business owners to have had a self-employed family-member owner prior to starting their business and are less likely to have worked in that family member's business. Only 12.6 percent of black business owners had prior work experience in a family member's business compared with 23.3 percent of white business owners. Racial differences and overall rates of business inheritances are much smaller. The percentage of business owners inheriting their firms was 1.4 percent for blacks and 1.7 percent for whites.

Estimates from linear and nonlinear decompositions indicate that the lower likelihood of having a self-employed family member prior to business startup among blacks than among whites does not generally contribute to racial differences in small business outcomes. Instead, the lack of prior work experience in family businesses among future black business owners, perhaps by restricting their acquisition of general and specific business human capital, limits the successfulness of their businesses relative to whites. With the exception of the profits specification, racial differences in this variable explain 5.6 to 11.6 percent of the gaps in small business outcomes. Providing some additional evidence on the importance of limited opportunities for acquiring business human capital, racial differences in prior work experience in similar businesses also consistently explain part of the gaps in small business outcomes. Furthermore, the combination of these two factors suggests that racial differences in opportunities to acquire business human capital in general contribute substantially to the differential success of black- and white-owned businesses.

Inherited businesses are generally more successful than noninherited businesses, but racial differences in business inheritances explain virtually none of the gaps in small business outcomes. The likelihood of business inheritances among black and white owners (under 2 percent) is just too small to play a major role in explaining racial differences in business outcomes.

We also examine the contributions of other factors to racial differences in small business outcomes. Lower levels of education among black business owners relative to white business owners explain a modest but nontrivial portion (2.4 to 6.5 percent) of the black/white gaps in business outcomes. Although black-owned businesses have a different regional distribution and are more likely to be located in urban areas than are white-owned businesses, racial differences in geo-graphical locations do not appear to contribute substantially to the gaps in small business outcomes. Racial differences in the amount of prior work experience and management experience have either small effects or mixed effects across specifications. Finally, racial differences in industry composition explain part of the gaps in business outcomes, but these results are difficult to interpret because industry differences may reflect different preferences or constraints on entry into more prof-itable industries.

Overall, the relatively simple empirical models of business outcomes do quite well in explaining the black/white gaps in business outcomes. Although there are many unmeasurable factors that may explain out-come disparities as discussed above, we explain 50 to 100 percent of the differences in business outcomes using the human capital, financial capital, family business background, and other owner and firm charac-teristics available in the CBO. In comparison, decompositions of earn-ings differences between blacks and whites typically explain no more than half of the gap unless a measure of ability is included (Altonji and Blank 1999).

Our estimates indicate that blacks are less likely than whites to have previous work experience in a family member's business and are less likely to have previous work experience in a similar business. The rela-tive lack of opportunities for acquiring general and specific business human capital apparently has a negative effect on the outcomes of black-owned firms. This finding has important policy implications. Most minority-business-development policies currently in place, such as set-asides and loan-assistance programs, are targeted toward allevi-ating financial constraints not toward providing opportunities for work experience in small businesses. To break the cycle of low rates of business ownership and relatively worse business outcomes being passed from one generation of blacks to the next, programs that di-rectly address deficiencies in family-business experience, possibly through an expansion of apprenticeship-type entrepreneurial training programs, may be needed in addition to programs focused on improv-ing access to financial capital.

Appendixes

Nonlinear Decomposition Method
In this appendix, we describe the decomposition techniques used in this chapter to identify the causes of black/white differences in busi-

ness outcomes. These techniques decompose intergroup differences in mean levels of an outcome into those due to different observable characteristics or "endowments" across groups and those due to different effects of characteristics or "coefficients" of groups. We describe the standard Blinder-Oaxaca technique, which is used for dependent variables that are estimated with linear regressions, such as log sales. An alternative nonlinear decomposition technique due to Fairlie (1999, 2005a) is also described. The technique is useful for decomposing racial differences in binary outcomes, such as closure, having profits of $10,000 or more, and having employees. Logit regressions are estimated to identify the determinants of these business outcomes. This nonlinear technique has broader applications for identifying the causes of racial, gender, geographical, or other categorical differences in any binary dependent variable in which a logit or probit model is used. SAS programs are available at ⟨people.ucsc.edu/~rfairlie/decomposition⟩, and Stata programs are available by entering "ssc install fairlie" in Stata.

For a linear regression, the standard Blinder-Oaxaca decomposition of the white/black gap in the average value of the dependent variable, Y, can be expressed as

$$\bar{Y}^W - \bar{Y}^B = [(\bar{X}^W - \bar{X}^B)\hat{\beta}^W] + [\bar{X}^B(\hat{\beta}^W - \hat{\beta}^B)], \tag{4.1}$$

where $\bar{X}^j$ is a row vector of average values of the independent variables and $\hat{\beta}^j$ is a vector of coefficient estimates for race j. Following Fairlie (1999), the decomposition for a nonlinear equation, such as $Y = F(X\hat{\beta})$, can be written as

$$\bar{Y}^W - \bar{Y}^B = \left[\sum_{i=1}^{N^W} \frac{F(X_i^W \hat{\beta}^W)}{N^W} - \sum_{i=1}^{N^B} \frac{F(X_i^B \hat{\beta}^W)}{N^B}\right]$$

$$+ \left[\sum_{i=1}^{N^B} \frac{F(X_i^B \hat{\beta}^W)}{N^B} - \sum_{i=1}^{N^B} \frac{F(X_i^B \hat{\beta}^B)}{N^B}\right], \tag{4.2}$$

where N^j is the sample size for race j. This alternative expression for the decomposition is used because $\bar{Y}$ does not necessarily equal $F(\bar{X}\hat{\beta})$.[9] In both (4.1) and (4.2), the first term in brackets represents the part of the racial gap that is due to group differences in distributions of X, and the second term represents the part due to differences in the group processes determining levels of Y. The second term also captures the portion of the racial gap due to group differences in unmeasurable or unobserved endowments. Similar to most previous studies applying the decomposition technique, we do not focus on this "unexplained" portion of the gap because of the difficulty in interpreting results (for more discussion, see Jones 1983 and Cain 1986).

To calculate the decomposition, define $\bar{Y}^j$ as the average probability of the binary outcome of interest for race j and F as the cumulative distribution function from the logistic distribution.[10] Alternatively, for a probit model F would be defined as the cumulative distribution function from the standard normal distribution.

An equally valid method of calculating the decomposition is to use the minority coefficient estimates, $\hat{\beta}^M$, as weights for the first term and the white distributions of the independent variables, $\bar{X}^W$, as weights for the second term. This alternative method of calculating the decomposition often provides different estimates, which is the familiar index problem with the Blinder-Oaxaca decomposition technique. A third alternative is to weight the first term of the decomposition expression using coefficient estimates from a pooled sample of the two groups (see Oaxaca and Ransom 1994, for example). We follow this approach to calculate the decompositions. In particular, we use coefficient estimates from a logit regression that includes a sample of all racial groups.

Using the pooled coefficients from a sample of all racial groups has the advantage over using the white coefficients because it captures the determinants for all groups and are more precisely estimated (because of the larger sample and more heterogeneity of firms). They are also preferred over the minority coefficients because they are less likely to be influenced by discrimination. The goal of the decomposition is to estimate how much differences in owner or firm characteristics explain of the racial gap in business outcomes given a nondiscriminatory environment.

The first term in (4.2) provides an estimate of the contribution of racial differences in the entire set of independent variables to the racial gap in the dependent variable. Estimation of the total contribution is relatively simple as one needs only to calculate two sets of predicted probabilities and take the difference between the average values of the two. Identifying the contribution of group differences in specific variables to the racial gap, however, is not as straightforward. To simplify, first assume that $N_B = N_W$ and that there exists a natural one-to-one matching of black and white observations. Using coefficient estimates from a logit regression for a pooled sample, $\hat{\beta}^*$, the independent contribution of X_1 to the racial gap can then be expressed as

$$\frac{1}{N^B} \sum_{i=1}^{N^B} F(\hat{\alpha}^* + X_{1i}^W \hat{\beta}_1^* + X_{2i}^W \hat{\beta}_2^*) - F(\hat{\alpha}^* + X_{1i}^B \hat{\beta}_1^* + X_{2i}^W \hat{\beta}_2^*).^{11} \tag{4.3}$$

Similarly, the contribution of X_2 can be expressed as

$$\frac{1}{N^B} \sum_{i=1}^{N^B} F(\hat{\alpha}^* + X_{1i}^B \hat{\beta}_1^* + X_{2i}^W \hat{\beta}_2^*) - F(\hat{\alpha}^* + X_{1i}^B \hat{\beta}_1^* + X_{2i}^B \hat{\beta}_2^*). \tag{4.4}$$

The contribution of each variable to the gap is thus equal to the change in the average predicted probability resulting from sequentially switching the white characteristics to black characteristics one variable or set of variables at a time.[12] A useful property of this technique is that the sum of the contributions from individual variables will be equal to the total contribution from all of the variables evaluated with the full sample.

In practice, the sample sizes of the two groups are rarely the same and a one-to-one matching of observations from the two samples is needed to calculate (4.3) and (4.4). In this example, it is likely that the black sample size is substantially smaller than the white sample size. To address this problem, first use the pooled coefficient estimates to calculate predicted probabilities, $\hat{Y}_i$, for each black and white observation in the sample. Next, draw a random subsample of whites with a sample size equal to N_B and randomly match it to the full black sample. The decomposition estimates obtained from this procedure depend on the randomly chosen subsample of whites. Ideally, the results from the decomposition should approximate those from matching the entire white sample to the black sample. A simple method of approximating this hypothetical decomposition is to draw a large number of random subsamples of whites, match each of these random subsamples of whites to the black sample, and calculate separate decomposition estimates. The mean value of estimates from the separate decompositions is calculated and used to approximate the results for the entire white sample. All of the decompositions reported in this chapter use 1,000 random subsamples of whites to calculate these means.

Table 4.A
Means of selected variables, Characteristics of Business Owners (1992)

	White-Owned Firms	Black-Owned Firms
Firm no longer operating in 1996 (closure)	0.2282	0.2696
Net profit of at least $10,000	0.3004	0.1410
One or more paid employees	0.2067	0.1121
Log sales	10.07	9.42
Female-owned business	0.3268	0.4261
Married	0.7650	0.6780
Never married	0.1020	0.1200
High school graduate	0.2651	0.2230
Some college	0.3123	0.3423
College graduate	0.1962	0.1292
Graduate school	0.1353	0.1437
Northeast	0.0643	0.0194
Midatlantic	0.1469	0.1315
East North Central	0.1666	0.1403
West North Central	0.0847	0.0330
South Atlantic	0.1597	0.3259
East South Central	0.0518	0.0792
West South Central	0.0999	0.1443
Mountain	0.0670	0.0163
Urban	0.7351	0.8877
Prior work experience: 1 year	0.0707	0.0680
Prior work experience: 2 to 5 years	0.1641	0.1500
Prior work experience: 6 to 9 years	0.1507	0.1445
Prior work experience: 10 to 19 years	0.2973	0.3143
Prior work experience: 20 years or more	0.2578	0.2393
Prior work experience in a managerial capacity	0.5552	0.4699
Prior work experience in a similar business	0.5030	0.4353
Have a self-employed family member	0.5231	0.3254
Prior work experience in a family member's business	0.2352	0.1264
Inherited business	0.0148	0.0132
Startup capital: $5,000 to $24,999	0.2374	0.2107
Startup capital: $25,000 to $99,999	0.1095	0.0645
Startup capital: $100,000 and over	0.0475	0.0168
Agricultural services	0.0269	0.0175
Construction	0.1261	0.0718
Manufacturing	0.0330	0.0168
Wholesale	0.0360	0.0112

Table 4.A
(continued)

	White-Owned Firms	Black-Owned Firms
Finance, insurance, and real estate	0.0987	0.0609
Transportation, communications, and public utilities	0.0389	0.0834
Personal services	0.2616	0.3287
Professional services	0.1937	0.2060
Uncoded industry	0.0391	0.0572
Sample size	14,282	6,831

Notes: (1) The sample includes businesses that are classified by the IRS as individual proprietorships or self-employed persons, partnerships and subchapter S corporations, have sales of $500 or more, and have at least one owner who worked at least twelve weeks and ten hours per week in the business. (2) All estimates are calculated using sample weights provided by the CBO.

5   Why Are Asian-Owned Businesses More Successful?

In this chapter, we explore potential explanations for the relative success of Asian American-owned businesses in the United States. Asian Americans differ from other minority groups in that they have high rates of business ownership. In the past few years, more than 11 percent of Asian workers in the United States were self-employed business owners. This is comparable to the white rate of business ownership. In addition to having relatively high rates of self-employment, Asians have better business outcomes on average than other racial groups. For example, Asian-owned businesses are 16.9 percent less likely to close, 20.6 percent more likely to have profits of at least $10,000, and 27.2 percent more likely to hire employees than businesses owned by whites.

The success of Asians in business ownership in the United States is well documented and has been used as an example of how disadvantaged groups utilize business ownership as a route for economic advancement. It has been argued, for example, that the economic success of Chinese and Japanese immigrants is in part due to their ownership of small businesses (Loewen 1971; Light 1972; Bonacich and Modell 1980). More recently, Koreans have also purportedly used business ownership for economic mobility (Min 1989, 1993).

Most prior research on Asian business ownership relies on household survey data, such as the Census of Population, and focuses on explaining the relatively high rates of self-employment among Asians (Min 1986–1987; Bonacich and Light 1988; Kim, Hurh, and Fernandez 1989; Hout and Rosen 2000; Mar 2005). These studies find that Asian Americans, especially immigrants, have self-employment rates that are higher than other minority groups and typically on par with that of whites in the United States. Evidence from Canada and the United

Kingdom also indicates that Asians have relatively high rates of business ownership (Clark and Drinkwater 1998, 2000; Fairlie 2006). Previous research also finds that self-employed Asians have relatively high earnings.[1]

Although research on Asian business ownership is extensive, only a handful of previous studies use business-level data to study the outcomes of Asian-owned firms. The few studies using business-level data to explore why Asian-owned businesses are more likely to survive and are more profitable than businesses owned by other racial groups, find that high levels of investment of human and financial capital are the most important factors (Bates 1989, 1997; Robb 2000). The lack of research on the outcomes of Asian firms is due primarily to the limited availability of data with large enough samples of Asian-owned businesses and detailed information on business outcomes. This lack of research is especially unfortunate given such dramatic differences in outcomes across racial groups.

In this chapter, we use CBO microdata to explore the causes of why Asian-owned firms are less likely to close and have higher profits, employment, and sales than white-owned firms. The confidential and restricted-access CBO microdata are useful for studying this question because of the large oversample of Asian-owned businesses and detailed information on the characteristics of both owners and firms. Although the CBO microdata contain information on immigrant status and country of origin, in most analyses we combine the various Asian subgroups. The estimates presented in chapter 2 and later in this chapter indicate that business outcomes are roughly similar for immigrant and U.S.-born Asians and across major Asian subgroups. Also, roughly 80 percent of Asian-owned businesses in the United States are owned by immigrants, suggesting that the results presented below are being driven primarily by businesses owned by Asian immigrants.

The analysis also focuses mainly on the effects of measurable inputs in the firm's production process. We are particularly interested in exploring the role that financial capital and human capital play in contributing to the relative success of Asian businesses. Are Asian businesses more successful because of higher levels of startup capital and owner's human capital? We also examine the role that intergenerational links in self-employment play in contributing to racial differences in small business outcomes. Do Asian business owners have greater opportunities for the acquisition of general and specific business human capital from working in family-owned businesses?

We build on findings from previous chapters on the determinants of business success to identify the underlying causes of differences in business performance between Asian and white firms. The decomposition technique used for this analysis not only identifies whether a particular factor is important but also identifies how much of the gap it explains for a particular outcome. This allows the relative contributions of racial differences in startup capital, human capital, and family-business backgrounds to be compared to try to explain why Asian firms have better outcomes on average than white firms. Although this approach might not reveal all of the reasons that Asian firms have better average outcomes than white firms, the results are easily interpreted and have clear policy implications.

Social Capital and Ethnic Resources

The previous literature offers various explanations for high rates of Asian self-employment, including high levels of human and financial capital (sometimes referred to as *class resources*) and extensive social or ethnic resources (such networks, rotating credit associations, and access to coethnic labor and customers).[2] Several studies focus on the importance of social resources, especially for Asian immigrants.[3] Networks of coethnics may provide valuable resources such as customers, labor, and technical assistance to assist in starting and running businesses (Light 1972; Waldinger, Aldrich, and Ward 1990; Saxenian 2002; Zhou 2004; Kalnins and Cheung 2006; Gil and Hartmann 2007). Coethnic networks may also be useful for providing access to financial capital for entrepreneurs through rotating credit associations, direct loans, and equity investments in the business.

Ethnic enclaves facilitate the transmission of social and ethnic resources. In particular, enclaves create opportunities for would-be entrepreneurs by providing access to markets, labor, and information (Aldrich et al. 1985; Borjas 1990). For example, the protected-market hypothesis maintains that ethnic enterprises often better serve the market of ethnic minorities by offering transactions in their own language and more efficiently responding to a group's tastes and demands (Light 1972; Aldrich et al. 1985; Waldinger et al. 1990). Ethnic groups often concentrate in a given area, which can result in the decision of nonminority business owners to leave and correspondingly open up opportunities that can be taken advantage of by minority groups (Aldrich et al. 1985). Niche markets arise in some areas due to underserved markets, especially in inner cities (Porter 1995; Yoon 1991, 1997).

Ethnic entrepreneurs often get their start in business by serving a predominantly minority clientele, which typically populate the area where the ethnic businesses are located. While enclaves offer opportunities for market access to ethnic entrepreneurs, relying on the ethnic enclave as the sole source of demand can limit growth potential because of the limited market size (Bates 1997; Waldinger et al. 1990). Enclaves may also reduce a business's survival prospects because many individuals from the same enclave could opt for business ownership for the same reasons and result in excess competition, causing some of the locations to go out of business (Bates 1997; Waldinger et al. 1990; Yoon 1991). Consistent with these arguments, Boyd (1991) finds no benefit of a concentrated ethnic population on ethnic immigrant entrepreneurs.

Some ethnic minorities have a comparative advantage in attracting cheap labor from within their own network (Waldinger 1986; Bonacich and Light 1988). Asians can access coethnics and family members, which may provide an edge in hiring low-paid and trusted workers (Fratoe 1988; Min 1986–1987; Boyd 1991). Ethnic immigrant workers may have restricted job opportunities because of limited English skills but fit in well working for ethnic business owners who understand their own language and culture (Yoon 1991, 1993; Min 1988). However, the vast majority of the self-employed do not have any employees, so this argument alone may not be able to explain much of the large racial differences in self-employment rates and outcomes.

Relying heavily on social or ethnic resources may be necessary for those with lower levels of class resources but could result in worse outcomes. Chaganti and Greene (2002) find that entrepreneurs with higher levels of involvement in their ethnic community have lower levels of personal resources and are more reliant on their communities. Yoon (1991) finds that Korean immigrant businesses that are more reliant on ethnic resources have lower levels of start up capital and lower levels of gross sales. Bates (1997) finds that Asian Indian businesses are the least oriented to serving a minority clientele, least likely to employ a predominantly minority labor force, and hence least likely to utilize resources of ethic enclaves, yet they have the best average performance of all Asian-owned firms. The Asian subgroup that he examined with the lowest average outcomes, the Vietnamese, is very active and reliant on ethnic enclaves to start and operate businesses.

Human, Financial, and Other Types of Capital

For the purpose of this chapter, we focus on the factors that we can measure with CBO microdata, such as human capital, business human capital, and financial capital. The standard economic model predicts that these factors are important inputs in the firm's production process. In the ethnic-entrepreneurship literature, these owner characteristics are often referred to as *class resources*. The models we estimate are relatively parsimonious specifications that focus on the more exogenous owner and firm characteristics that predict business success. A detailed analysis of the effects of social resources is not possible with the CBO data and is very difficult with any dataset because of measurement issues and identification problems (such as whether the social network causes business success or whether successful entrepreneurs create larger social networks). But many of the factors that we examine may result from ethnic resources (such as startup capital and prior similar industry work experience) or are related to them (such as family-business backgrounds). We now examine each of the factors that can be measured using the Characteristics of Business Owners (CBO) data.

Educational Differences

The education level of the owner is an important determinant of business success. From the early works of Knight (1921) and Schumpeter (1934) to the more contemporary works of Lucas (1978) and Jovanovic (1982), human capital or "ability" has always played a role in theoretical discussions of determinants of the successful formation and operation of businesses. Previous empirical research also provides evidence of a positive relationship between owner's education and business survival (Bates 1997; Astebro and Bernhardt 2003; Robb 2000; Headd 2003). Estimates from our CBO sample similarly indicate that survival, profits, employment, and sales are positively associated with the education level of the business owner.

Low levels of education are found to limit business creation and outcomes among African Americans. Does the converse hold true? Are Asian firms more successful than white-owned firms in part because they have higher levels of education? In comparing self-employed Asian Americans and blacks, Boyd (1991) finds that close to one third of the gap in self-employment earnings between these two groups is explained by disparities in education levels.

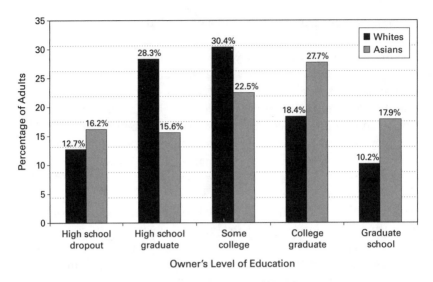

Figure 5.1
Educational attainment distribution for Asian and white population, 2000 U.S. Census
5% PUMS Microdata

Asians are the most educated racial group in the United States. As
figure 5.1 illustrates, Asians are much more likely than whites to graduate from college or graduate school. Estimates from 2000 U.S. Census
microdata indicate that nearly half of all Asian adults have at least a
college degree. This compares with less than 30 percent of whites. The
pattern of higher education levels among Asians is also observed when
we look at our sample of active business owners. As illustrated in figure 5.2, 47 percent of Asian business owners have at least a college degree, and 22 percent have gone beyond an undergraduate degree to
pursue graduate school. Roughly one third of whites have at least a
college degree, and 14 percent have a graduate degree.

Research on blocked mobility for minorities and especially immigrants indicates that some groups are "pushed" into self-employment
(Kassoudji 1988; Waldinger, Aldrich, and Ward 1990; Boyd 1990; Kim,
Hurh, and Fernandez 1989; Min 1984). Potential employers may under-
value educational accomplishments by Asians in the wage and salary
sector because the education was usually obtained in their home country: about 80 percent of Asians in our sample are immigrants. Bates
(1997) finds that those Asians that are pushed into self-employment
due to undervalued education or limited English-language skills typically locate in the lowest-yielding industries—retailing and personal

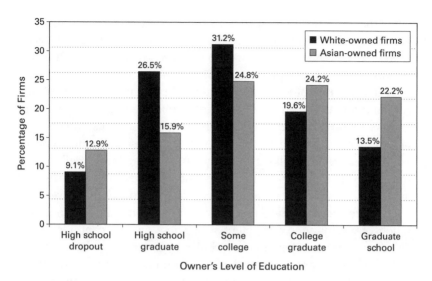

Figure 5.2
Owner's education level by race, Characteristics of Business Owners (1992)

services—while those "pulled" into self-employment are drawn into self-employment in skill-intensive industries such as professional services, finance, insurance, and real estate. Published estimates from the 1992 CBO indicate that the most educated Asians locate in high human-capital-intensive industries such as finance, insurance, and real estate (FIRE) rather than in low human-capital-intensive industries, such as retail trade (U.S. Census Bureau 1997).

The importance of education in our business outcome regressions from chapter 3 indicates that higher education levels are potentially one explanation for the superior outcomes of Asian-owned businesses, a finding consistent with previous research on fewer outcome measures (Bates 1997; Robb 2000). Our decompositions expand on these findings by providing an estimate of how much observed racial differences in education explain the Asian/white differences in business outcomes.

Family-Business Experience

Comparisons of family backgrounds between Asians and whites are difficult to make because of the large share of Asians who are immigrants and the lack of information on family formation in their home countries. The current snapshot in the United States indicates that Asian marriage rates and single-parent household rates are not overly different than white rates. More than 60 percent of Asian adults are currently married, compared with 57 percent of whites. Asians have about half the rate of nonmarital births (22 percent) as whites (40 percent), and about 14 percent of Asian children live with single parents, compared with 20 percent of white children (U.S. Census Bureau 2001; National Center for Health Statistics 2003). These estimates indicate that Asians are more likely to grow up in two-parent families than whites, which differs from the experience for blacks as described in chapter 4. However, it is important to keep in mind that these estimates are relevant for current Asian children and not the previous generation of Asians who are potential business owners captured in the CBO data. Unfortunately, published historical data on Asians living in the United States are not available. In addition, we do not have information on the family backgrounds of Asian immigrants in their home countries. Nevertheless, the combination of relatively high rates of self-employment and low rates of growing up in single-parent families, at least for the current generation of Asians, implies that Asians may be more likely to have parents who are self-employed business owners.

The owner's family-business background and type of prior work experience are important factors in successfully running a business. Family businesses appear to provide an important opportunity for family members to acquire human capital related to operating a business. In addition, prior work experience in a similar business may provide the owner with valuable specific business human capital. If Asians have plentiful opportunities to acquire important general and specific business human capital through these avenues, then it could partly explain why they tend to have more successful businesses.

Focusing on current business owners, however, we do not find evidence that Asian owners have more advantaged family-business backgrounds than whites. Estimates of having a self-employed family member, working in family businesses, and having business inheritances are reported in table 5.1. About 44 percent of Asian business owners indicate that they had a self-employed family member prior to starting their firm. This compares with 53 percent of white-owned firms. About 41 percent of Asian owners with a self-employed family member previously worked in that family member's business compared with 44 percent of white business owners. Additionally, about 18 percent of Asian business owners previously worked in a family

Table 5.1
Family business background by race, Characteristics of Business Owners (1992)

	All Firms	White-Owned Firms	Asian-Owned Firms
Had a self-employed family member prior to starting firm	51.6%	53.1%	44.3%
Previously worked in that family member's business (conditional)	43.6%	43.9%	40.5%
Previously worked in a family member's business (unconditional)	22.5%	23.3%	18.0%
Inherited their businesses	1.6%	1.7%	1.3%
Sample size	38,020	15,872	6,321

Notes: (1) The sample includes businesses that are classified by the IRS as individual proprietorships or self-employed persons, partnerships, and subchapter S corporations, have sales of $500 or more, and have at least one owner who worked at least twelve weeks and ten hours per week in the business. (2) All estimates are calculated using sample weights provided by the Characteristics of Business Owners.

member's business before starting their own, compared with about 23 percent of white business owners. Inheritance was an infrequent source of business ownership, with only 1.3 percent and 1.7 percent of Asian and white business owners, respectively, citing this as a source of their businesses. These estimates indicate that the current generation of Asian business owners does not have an advantaged family-business background relative to white business owners. Instead, Asian owners appear to have less experience, on average, than white owners in working for family businesses prior to starting their own businesses.

Related to the family-business background of the owner, marriage is associated with business success. Spouses may provide financial assistance, paid or unpaid labor for the business, health insurance coverage, and other types of assistance useful for running a business. Estimates from the CBO indicate that 82 percent of Asian owners are married compared with 77 percent of white owners (see the appendix to this chapter). The difference is not that large, however, suggesting that differences between Asians and whites in marital status cannot have a large explanatory effect on racial differences in business outcomes.

Differences in Business Human Capital

As noted in previous chapters, prior work experience also plays a role in business performance. Our data show that white and Asian business

Table 5.2
Types of prior work experience by race, Characteristics of Business Owners (1992)

	All Firms	White-Owned Firms	Asian-Owned Firms
Previously worked in a business with similar goods/services	50.1%	50.4%	46.8%
Previous work experience in a managerial capacity	55.2%	55.6%	56.4%
Sample size	38,020	15,872	6,321

Notes: (1) The sample includes businesses that are classified by the IRS as individual proprietorships or self-employed persons, partnerships and subchapter S corporations, have sales of $500 or more, and have at least one owner who worked at least twelve weeks and ten hours per week in the business. (2) All estimates are calculated using sample weights provided by the Characteristics of Business Owners.

owners have similar business and management experience. As indicated in table 5.2, 50 percent of white business owners and 47 percent of Asian business owners previously worked in a business that provided similar goods or services as the businesses they currently own. This type of work experience undoubtedly provides opportunities for acquiring job- or industry-specific business human capital in addition to more general business human capital. In addition, about 56 percent of both white and Asian owners have previous work experience in a managerial capacity prior to owning their current business, which provides an opportunity to gain professional and management experience useful in running future business ventures. The similarity of these factors across white and Asian owners implies that they cannot explain much, if any, of the observed differences in business outcomes.

As noted in chapter 3, the number of years of work experience prior to starting the business had mixed effects across outcome measures, although we find some evidence that individuals with twenty or more years or very few years of prior work experience have worse outcomes, on average. A larger share of Asian business owners had less than six years of work experience than white owners before starting their business. The opposite is true at the other end of the distribution. More than one quarter of white business owners had twenty or more years of work experience, prior to opening their businesses, compared with 13 percent of Asian business owners. The racial differences in previous work experience are large between the two groups, indicating that this may play a role in the differences in business outcomes.

Wealth Differences

The owner's wealth may be an important determinant of business success because it affects access to financial capital at startup and over the life of the firm. Personal wealth can be invested directly in the business or used as collateral to obtain loans. We provide evidence in the previous chapter that low levels of wealth are found to limit business creation and outcomes for black-owned businesses. Are Asians more successful in business partly because they have better access to financial capital? We first examine wealth differences between Asians and whites and then, using the CBO data, explore whether financial capital differences explain why Asian-owned businesses outperform white-owned businesses on average.

Estimates from pooling the 1984 to 2001 Survey of Income and Program Participation (SIPP) Panels indicate that Asians and whites have similar wealth levels.[4] Using households headed by individuals twenty-five to sixty-four years old, the median total net worth in 2000 dollars is about $59,400 for whites and $49,300 for Asians. Asians have a slightly higher mean total net worth of about $129,300, compared with $123,600 for whites. In earlier work, Bates (1997) also finds that Asians had a slightly higher mean value of wealth ($73,222) than whites ($68,768) using the 1984 SIPP. Separate estimates by immigrant status indicate that Asian immigrants and U.S.-born Asians have similar average levels of wealth (Hao 2007).

These estimates indicate that, unlike blacks as shown in the previous chapter, Asians have wealth levels that are comparable to whites. Do these similar wealth levels translate into similar levels of startup capital, or do Asians and whites differ in the types of financing used, potentially resulting in different levels of startup capital? We investigate these questions next.

Types of Financing

Asian and other minority owners differ from white business owners in the types of financing they used to start their businesses. Table 5.3 reports published estimates of sources of capital from the CBO for whites and the combined group of Asians and other minority-owned firms (Pacific Islanders, American Indians, and Alaska natives) (U.S. Census Bureau 1997). Thus, when examining sources of borrowed and equity capital, we are limited to presenting estimates for Asians and

Table 5.3
Sources of borrowed and equity capital by race, Characteristics of Business Owners (1992)

	Percentage		
	All Firms	White-Owned Firms	Asian-and Other Minority-Owned Firms
Sources of borrowed capital for owner:			
Personal loan using home mortgage/equity line of credit	5.0%	5.0%	7.8%
Personal credit card	3.0	2.9	4.7
Personal loan from spouse	1.2	1.1	1.6
Personal loan from family	6.1	5.8	13.8
Other personal loan	7.1	7.1	10.8
Sources of nonborrowed capital for owner:			
None (100 percent borrowed capital)	6.6	6.8	5.0
Use of owner's personal/family physical assets (building, motor vehicle, equipment, etc.)	18.5	19.1	14.4
Proceeds from the sale of owner's personal assets	2.5	2.4	3.4
Owner's personal or family savings	40.7	40.5	53.2
Other source	3.9	3.7	3.8
Sources of borrowed capital for firm:			
Business loan from banking or commercial lending institution	11.7	12.1	12.3
Government-guaranteed business loan from banking or commercial lending institution	0.4	0.4	0.7
Business loan from federal, state, or local government	0.3	0.3	0.4
Business loan from investment company/profit or nonprofit private source	0.6	0.6	1.1
Business loan from previous owner	1.9	1.9	4.8
Business trade credit from supplier	0.9	0.9	1.4
Other business loan	1.6	1.6	2.7

Source: Characteristics of Business Owners (1992) are reported in U.S. Census Bureau (1997).
Notes: (1) The sample includes businesses that are classified by the IRS as individual proprietorships or self-employed persons, partnerships, and subchapter S corporations and that have sales of $500 or more. (2) White category is equal to the total minus all minority groups. (3) More than one source of capital can be reported for each firm.

Native Americans combined. However, nearly 85 percent of this group is in fact Asians and Pacific Islanders. Nearly 8 percent of Asian and other minority owners used a personal loan through a home mortgage or equity line of credit for startup capital, compared with 5 percent of whites. Asian firms were also more likely than white firms to use a personal credit card or a personal loan from a spouse. More significantly however, 13.8 percent of Asians and other minorities used a personal loan from a family member and 10.8 percent used some other type of personal loan. These compare with 5.8 percent and 7.1 percent for whites, respectively.[5] Thus, Asian owners are much more likely than white owners to rely on family sources for borrowed startup capital for their businesses.[6]

The story is mixed for nonborrowed startup capital. Published CBO estimates show that white firms were more likely to use an owner's personal or family physical assets for the business startup (19.1 percent) than were Asians (14.4 percent). Bates (1997) finds that the majority of Asian startup capital on the equity side comes from family wealth. Asians were slightly more likely to use proceeds from the sale of owner's assets to finance a business venture, but only 3 percent of Asians did so. Finally, Asians were much more likely to invest personal or family savings in the business (53.2 percent) than were whites (40.5 percent).

In examining the sources of borrowed startup capital for the firm, the story was similar. Asian-owned businesses were more likely to have borrowed capital from each of the different sources than were whites. Business loans from banking or commercial lending institutions were the most common, followed by business loans from a previous owner and other business loans. Very few businesses used loans from the federal, state, or local governments.

Estimates from the 1998 Survey of Small Business Finances (SSBF) for more established businesses indicate that less than 47 percent of Asian-owned firms have an outstanding loan compared with nearly 56 percent of white-owned firms. Asians are less likely to have credit lines, mortgages, vehicle loans, equipment loans, or capital leases. Asians are more likely than whites to have owner loans and to borrow through the use of credit cards (Bitler, Robb, and Wolken 2001). These findings could mean that Asian owners are necessarily more reliant on friends and family or on owner equity than are white owners.

One line of research in the sociological literature examines rotating credit associations and other types of financing, which emerge out of

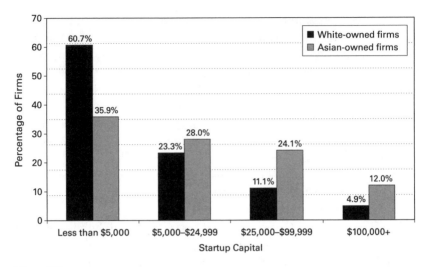

Figure 5.3
Startup capital by race, Characteristics of Business Owners (1992)

ethnic networks. Rotating credit associations allow people in the network to pool their savings and lend to individuals, many of whom start up businesses with the borrowed capital. Previous research has noted the role of rotating credit associations in providing financial capital for Asian businesses (Light, Kwuon, and Zhong 1990; Yoon 1991). Yet estimates from the CBO indicate that, at most, 14.6 percent of Asian and other minority business owners report having a personal or business loan from "other" sources, which is lower than the total incidence for bank loans and credit cards. It appears that many rotating credit associations generally provide very short-term capital and that their role as a saving mechanism may be more important than their role in providing loans.[7]

Startup Capital

Estimates from the CBO indicate that Asians start their businesses with far more capital than whites and other groups. Figure 5.3 indicates that 12 percent of Asian-owned businesses started with more than $100,000 in capital, compared with just 5 percent of white-owned firms. Nearly a quarter of Asian-owned businesses started with $25,000 to $100,000, compared with just 11 percent of white-owned firms. More than 60 percent of white owned firms were started with less than $5,000, whereas just 36 percent of Asian-owned firms were started with comparable levels of startup capital.

Bates (1997) finds similar patterns using the 1987 CBO. The total financial capital at startup was about $14,000 on average for blacks and $32,000 on average for nonminorities, whereas it was nearly $54,000 for Asian immigrants. He also finds that nearly half of Asians used borrowed funds to finance the business startup (compared with 29 percent of blacks and 34 percent of nonminorities). Bates compares active versus discontinued firms owned by Asian immigrants and finds that those that remained active over a five-year period averaged more than $62,000 in startup capital, compared with less than $16,000 for discontinued firms.

High levels of capitalization among Asian firms may be related to differential selection into business ownership, family and coethnic resources, and the types of firms that they create. Differences in types of firms, however, do not appear to explain much of the differences. Higher levels of startup capital among Asian and other minority firms than among white firms are consistent across most industry sectors (U.S. Census Bureau 1997). Even in services and retail, where Asians are disproportionately located, Asians use higher-than-average levels of startup capital. Asians are more reliant on personal and family equity and borrowed capital than whites. While Asians have similar wealth levels as whites, they turn that wealth into higher levels of start up capital, both equity (nonborrowed) and debt capital (borrowed). Furthermore, they leverage their wealth into higher levels of borrowing by both the owner (for example, through personal loans and credit cards) and the firm (such as business loans). The next question then is how much higher levels of startup capital explain better average outcomes among Asian-owned businesses than white-owned businesses.

Industry Differences

As mentioned in chapter 3, firms located in certain industries tend to have higher turnover rates than firms located in other industries (most notably retail and services). And those with higher capital requirements for entry, such as manufacturing and wholesale trade, typically have lower turnover rates and higher average sales. Table 5.4 shows the industry distribution of white- and Asian-owned firms. Asian firms are much less frequently found in the construction industry than white firms, even though their wealth and capital access appear to be on

Table 5.4
Industry distribution by race, Characteristics of Business Owners (1992)

	White-Owned Firms	Asian-Owned Firms
Agricultural services	2.7%	2.1%
Construction	12.5%	3.9%
Manufacturing	3.4%	3.5%
Wholesale trade	3.6%	3.9%
Retail trade	14.7%	25.0%
Finance, insurance, and real estate	10.1%	8.7%
Transportation, communications, and public utilities	3.9%	4.2%
Personal services	25.9%	25.9%
Professional services	19.3%	18.8%
Uncoded industry	3.9%	4.0%
Sample size	15,872	6,321

Notes: (1) The sample includes businesses that are classified by the IRS as individual proprietorships or self-employed persons, partnerships, and subchapter S corporations, have sales of $500 or more, and have at least one owner who worked at least twelve weeks and ten hours per week in the business. (2) All estimates are calculated using sample weights provided by the Characteristics of Business Owners.

par with whites. Asians are slightly more likely to be found in the wholesale industry, which is also characterized by higher capital requirements for entry. Even within this industry, Asians use higher-than-average levels of startup capital (U.S. Census Bureau 1996).

Asians are much more likely to be found in the retail trade sector, with one quarter of Asian firms locating in this industry. This compares with 15 percent of white firms. There has been some concern in the literature that the concentration of Asians in the retail industry reflects less than optimal opportunities in salaried employment, especially for minorities (Kassoudji 1988; Borjas 1994; Bates 1997; Mar 2005). Yet Asians firms are about equally likely as white firms to be in the personal services industry with about 26 percent of each group locating in this industry. They are also about equally likely to be located in professional services, with 18.8 percent of Asian firms and 19.3 percent of white firms locating there. Thus, it appears that the concern that minority firms are limited to certain industries because of capital constraints does not appear to hold for Asians. The apparent dearth of Asian-owned firms in the construction industry is probably due in part to preferences or to industry-specific knowledge and experience. Another explanation may be that it is an industry in which there are considerable entry barriers created by existing networks and discrimination against outsiders.

Hours Worked

Are Asian-owned businesses more successful than white-owned businesses because Asian owners typically work long hours? Bates (1997) finds that the relative success of Asian immigrant firms disappears after adjusting for the number of hours worked by the owner. As previously discussed in chapter 3, we are concerned about including hours worked in the regression models or using them to create adjusted outcome measures, such as firm profits or sales per hour, because it assumes away the possibility that limited demand for products and services is responsible for why some business owners work less than full-time. We would be implicitly assuming that all business owners work their desired amount of hours, which is unlikely to be the case.

Even with these concerns, it is useful to examine whether Asian owners work more hours on average than other owners. We are especially interested in focusing on whether Asian owners are more likely to work long hours exceeding forty hours per week. Published estimates from the CBO indicate that Asian and other minority owners are slightly less likely than owners of all firms to report working forty-one to forty-nine hours per week and are slightly more likely to report working fifty to fifty-nine hours per week, compared with white firms (figure 5.4). The main difference is that Asian owners are more likely to work sixty hours or more: 22 percent of Asian owners work sixty or more hours per week compared with 14 percent of white owners. However, differences in the other categories are not large, and owners working very long hours represent a small fraction of all Asian business owners.

Examining sales by hours worked illustrates that Asian and other minority firms have better sales outcomes than whites-owned firms for each level of hours worked in the business. This implies that long hours are not the driving force behind the better outcomes of Asian-owned businesses. As shown in figure 5.5, Asian-owned businesses are more likely to have revenues of $100,000 or more in every hours worked category, not just at the higher end of the distribution. Previous researchers have noted that business owners have more flexibility in hours worked and are often willing to work more given a certain

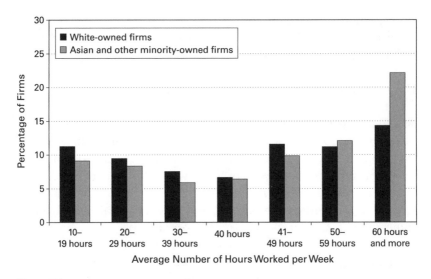

Figure 5.4
Hours worked by owner by race, published estimates from the Characteristics of Business Owners (1992)

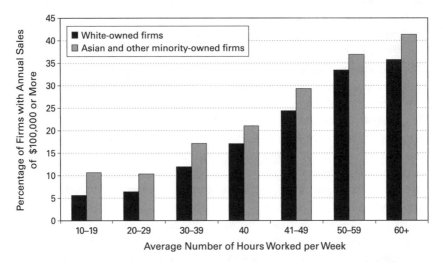

Figure 5.5
Firms with $100,000 or more in sales by race and hours worked (percent), published estimates from the Characteristics of Business Owners (1992)

return (Portes and Zhou 1996), suggesting that the long hours may be in response to significant demand for their goods or services and thus an indicator of success. Overall, Asian business owners may be more likely to work very long hours (sixty or more hours per week), but this represents only a fraction of Asian firms and even for this group, Asian firms perform better than white firms.

Asian Subgroups

Before turning to the explanations for why Asian-owned businesses outperform white-owned businesses on average, we address the issue of why we focus on Asian-owned businesses in general rather than on Asian immigrants or specific Asian subgroups. Many previous studies of Asian business ownership delineate immigrants from nonimmigrants. U.S.-born Asians and Asian immigrants may face different opportunities in the labor market and thus have different motives for entering business, ultimately leading to different business outcomes. While we analyze Asian immigrants separately from U.S.-born Asians, the results reported here are for all Asians. This is due to finding similar business outcomes for the two groups and limitations of releasing detailed tables through the Census Bureau's strict disclosure process for confidential and restricted-access data. Roughly 80 percent of Asian-owned businesses in the United States are owned by Asian immigrants. Therefore, the estimates of Asian business outcomes reported in chapter 2 and in this chapter are being driven primarily by businesses owned by Asian immigrants.

When comparing businesses owned by Asian immigrants and non-immigrants, we find similar business outcomes. Figure 5.6 reports the distribution of sales by immigrant status for Asian and other minority firms from published 1992 CBO data. Estimates from the 1992 CBO indicate that about 23 percent of Asian and other minority immigrant firms have employees, compared with 22 percent of those who were U.S. born. While the U.S.-born-owned firms are more heavily represented in the less than $5,000 category, the other differences in sales' distributions were not large across immigrant and nonimmigrant firms.

In our subsample of active firms from CBO microdata, business outcomes are remarkably similar between Asian immigrant and nonimmigrant firms. The percentages of firms that have employees or profits of at least $10,000 are virtually identical. Immigrant firms are slightly less

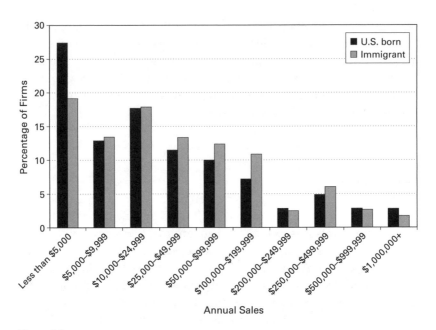

Figure 5.6
Sales and receipts by immigrant status for Asian and other minority-owned businesses, published estimates from the Characteristics of Business Owners (1992)

likely to close, but the difference is small. There are some differences, however, in the owner characteristics of immigrants and Asians who were born in the United States. For example, those who were born in the United States are younger and less likely to be married. They are also more likely to start businesses with little or no financial capital, more likely to have a family member who owned a business, and more likely to have worked for that business. Overall, however, Asian immigrant and U.S.-born owners are fairly similar, and the mean characteristics for all Asian firms are roughly similar to the mean characteristics for Asian immigrant firms.

Previous research using older CBO data yields similar outcomes among businesses owned by Asian immigrants and nonimmigrants. Using 1987 CBO data, Bates (1997) reports four business outcomes by immigrant status for Asians that are comparable to the ones we examine in this chapter. Immigrants are separated into two categories— those with a level of high fluency in English (Asian Indian and Filipino) and those with a low level of fluency (Korean and Chinese)— and are compared with nonimmigrant Asian Americans. The survival rates of firms in all three categories are virtually identical, ranging from 81.9 to 82.2 percent. While sales, employment, and profits are also similar, there are some slight variations. Koreans and Chinese average 1.7 employees, while nonimmigrant Asian Americans and high-fluency immigrants average 1.2 employees. Koreans and Chinese have the highest levels of sales but rank in the middle in terms of profits. In estimating regressions predicting firm survival, Bates also finds that both Asian immigrants and Asian nonimmigrant firms have higher rates of survival than white firms. The difference between Asian immigrants and nonimmigrants is relatively small and not statistically significant.

Census data on self-employed business owners from the 2000 Public Use Microdata Sample File (PUMS) provide additional support for grouping Asian immigrants and nonimmigrants together. Self-employed immigrants and nonimmigrants have nearly identical earnings at $53,400 and $56,600, respectively. Asian immigrants work slightly more hours in a given week but work nearly identical numbers of weeks during the year. While Asian immigrants are more likely to have dropped out of high school, the percentage that graduated from college is nearly identical to that of U.S.-born Asians. About 21 percent of immigrants have postgraduate education, compared with 23.5 percent of U.S.-born Asians. Interest income, which is often used as a proxy for wealth, is also similar for immigrants and nonimmigrants. Thus, while several previous studies delineate immigrants from nonimmigrants, these various data sources indicate that there are more similarities than differences in business outcomes and combining the two groups for our analyses may not be problematic.

A similar issue is grouping Asians from different countries of origin. Many previous studies of Asian self-employment have focused on a specific subgroup of Asians, such as Japanese Americans (Light 1972; Bonacich and Modell 1980), Chinese Americans (Bates 1997), and Korean Americans (Min 1988; Bates 1994; Yoon 1991, 1995). As discussed in chapter 2, differences in business outcomes exist across Asian subgroups, but the differences are relatively small when compared with differences between Asians and whites or blacks. Table 5.5 expands on these findings by reporting business outcomes from CBO microdata for the largest Asian subgroups. Comparing the various outcome measures, we do not find evidence that one subgroup outperforms the others across all measures. The results presented in chapter 2 from the 2002 SBO indicate similarly positive business outcomes across almost all of the larger Asian subgroups.

Table 5.5
Business outcomes among detailed Asian groups, Characteristics of Business Owners (1992)

	Percentage					
	All Asian Firms	Asian Indian Firms	Chinese Firms	Japanese Firms	Korean Firms	Other Asian Firms
Closure rate from 1992 to 1996	17.9%	12.4%	17.2%	16.1%	20.1%	20.8%
Net profit of $10,000 or more	29.9	38.8	29.4	26.8	31.8	26.3
Hire 1 or more employees	38.0	43.2	35.3	45.7	50.7	28.1

Notes: (1) The sample includes businesses that are classified by the IRS as individual proprietorships or self-employed persons, partnerships, and subchapter S corporations, have sales of $500 or more, and have at least one owner who worked at least twelve weeks and ten hours per week in the business. (2) All estimates are calculated using sample weights provided by the Characteristics of Business Owners.

We also experimented with business outcome regressions with detailed Asian subgroup dummies and find that the coefficients on these dummies are not statistically significant for any of the subgroups. This result is consistent with Bates (1997), who includes dummies for Asian Indian, Chinese, Korean, and Vietnamese in his survival regressions—none of which are statistically significant. Providing additional support of our grouping Asian subpopulations, Boyd (1991) finds that there are not statistically significant differences in self-employment earnings between Asian subgroups, such as Chinese, Japanese, Korean, Asian Indian, Filipino, Vietnamese, and other Asians. Given that the goal of this chapter is to compare the relative performance of Asian-owned businesses with that of whites, combining these subgroups seems reasonable.

In working with confidential data for this chapter, we were limited in the number of tabulations and regressions we could get released through the Census Bureau's lengthy disclosure process. This restriction limited our ability to conduct an extensive analysis delineating Asians by immigrant status or subgroup. Because our focus is on the outcomes of businesses and not the selection process into business ownership, we are interested in explaining the relative success of Asians as a group, whether they are immigrants or native born and irrespective of their country of origin. Further work examining these subpopulations will make a valuable contribution in better understanding this population, but it is beyond the scope of this chapter.

Identifying the Causes of Asian/White Differences in Business Outcomes

Asian business owners are more educated and use more startup capital, on average, than white business owners. To identify whether these differences, among others, can explain why Asian-owned businesses are more successful than white-owned businesses, we employ the same decomposition method used in chapter 4. This method, attributed to Blinder (1973) and Oaxaca (1973), decomposes racial differences in mean outcomes into those due to different observable characteristics (or *endowments*) between racial groups and those due to different effects of characteristics (or *coefficients*) of groups. We modify their technique to reflect the logit regressions that we use for our three binary outcomes of business performance (Fairlie 2005a). An extensive description of the technique is provided in chapter 4.

Table 5.6 reports estimates from this procedure for decomposing the Asian/white gaps in business outcomes. The separate contributions from racial differences in each set of independent variables are reported. Based on the concerns noted in the previous literature regarding potential endogeneity, we report decomposition results for the main owner and firm characteristics first and decomposition results that include startup capital and industry second. The means of all independent variables are reported in table 5.A.

Racial differences in the male and female composition of firms plays only a small role in explaining differences in outcomes with the exception of profits, in which case it explains 5.5 percent of the Asian/white gap. Marital status differences explain 3.9 percent of the gap in employment and 4.7 percent of the gap in profits but few of the other outcomes. In our sample, 82 percent of the Asian owners were married, compared with 77 percent of white owners.

Education plays a major role in explaining the Asian/white gap in outcomes. It explains 16 percent in both the profits and employer specifications, 24.2 percent in the closure specification, and 6.8 percent in the sales specification. These results indicate that a large part of the success of Asian-owned firms can be attributed to their higher education levels relative to whites. More than 22 percent of Asian owners have a postcollege education, compared with about 14 percent of whites, and nearly a quarter of Asian owners have a college degree, compared with 20 percent of whites. This holds true for both U.S.-born Asians and Asian immigrants.

Table 5.6
Decompositions of Asian/White gaps in small business outcomes, Characteristics of Business (1992)

	Specification			
	(1)	(2)	(3)	(4)
Dependent variable	Closure	Profits	Employer	Ln Sales
Asian mean	0.1896	0.3627	0.2628	10.6963
White mean	0.2282	0.3008	0.2065	10.0680
Asian/white gap	0.0386	−0.0619	−0.0562	−0.6283
Contributions from racial differences in:				
Sex	0.0006	−0.0034	−0.0004	−0.0141
	1.6%	5.5%	0.8%	2.2%
Marital status	0.0003	−0.0029	−0.0022	−0.0107
	0.9%	4.7%	3.9%	1.7%
Education	0.0093	−0.0099	−0.0091	−0.0429
	24.2%	16.0%	16.2%	6.8%
Region	0.0005	−0.0217	0.0019	−0.0647
	1.4%	35.0%	−3.3%	10.3%
Urban	−0.0032	−0.0096	0.0074	−0.0213
	−8.4%	15.5%	−13.1%	3.4%
Prior work experience	0.0028	−0.0144	−0.0084	−0.0377
	7.2%	23.2%	14.9%	6.0%
Prior work experience in a managerial capacity	0.0000	0.0003	0.0002	−0.0009
	0.0%	−0.4%	−0.4%	0.1%
Prior work experience in a similar business	−0.0013	0.0023	0.0010	0.0128
	−3.5%	−3.8%	−1.8%	−2.0%
Have a self-employed family member	−0.0014	0.0010	−0.0002	−0.0032
	−3.7%	−1.7%	0.4%	0.5%
Prior work experience in a family member's business	−0.0022	0.0018	0.0032	0.0204
	−5.8%	−2.9%	−5.8%	−3.2%
Inherited business	−0.0002	0.0009	0.0009	0.0048
	−0.6%	−1.5%	−1.5%	−0.8%
All included variables	0.0052	−0.0555	−0.0058	−0.1574
	13.4%	89.7%	10.3%	25.1%

Notes: (1) The samples and regression specifications are the same as those used in table 3.6. (2) Contribution estimates are mean values of the decomposition using 1,000 sub-samples of whites. See the text for more details.

Regional differences also play a role in explaining the higher profits (35 percent) and sales (10.3 percent) of Asian-owned businesses. Nearly 50 percent of Asian-owned firms are located in the Pacific region. Perhaps many of these firms have a wider market or trade relations with Asian countries. Region explains very little of the other two outcome variables, however. Urbanicity explains more than 15 percent of the Asian/white gap in profits. It also explains 8.4 percent of the gap in closure rates and 13.1 percent of the employer gap but just 3.4 percent of the gap in the log of sales. Nearly 95 percent of Asian-owned firms are located in urban areas, compared with about three quarters of white-owned firms. Locating in an urban area might also indicate a broader market area with greater growth potential.

Variations in previous work experience explain between 6 and 23 percent of the gaps in business outcomes. As shown in chapter 3, the estimated effects of prior work experience vary somewhat across outcome measures, although we find some evidence suggesting that individuals with twenty or more years of prior work experience and owners with very little previous work experience have worse outcomes, on average. Owners with long prior work experience may have moved into business ownership as a response to job loss (Farber 1999; Fairlie and Krashinsky 2005) or for lifestyles changes, while owners with very little experience may encounter difficulties identifying good business opportunities. Asian owners are more likely to have low levels of prior work experience and are less likely to have very high levels of prior work experience than white owners. It appears that lower incomes by the most experienced outweigh those of the least experienced, as variations in previous work experience explain between 6 and 23 percent of the gaps in business outcomes. It was most important in the profits outcome, which could indicate that very experienced business people are entering business ownership for lifestyle reasons rather than for profit motives.

Similar business experience and working in a family member's business actually increase the gaps. In other words, Asians have disadvantaged levels of these characteristics compared with whites. From tables 5.1 and 5.2, recall that Asians are less likely to have work experience in a family member's business prior to starting a firm and are less likely to have previously worked in a business with similar goods and services. If Asian owners had similar levels of theses characteristics as white owners then their businesses would be predicted to perform even better.

Managerial experience does not contribute to the racial differences in outcomes. In all cases, it is less than one half of 1 percent. Likewise, inheritances contribute very little to the gaps, which is consistent with our previous finding for black firms in chapter 4. The incidences of inheritances are too infrequent and the racial differences in inheritances are too small to result in inheritances contributing much to differences in business outcomes.

Our next decomposition includes the contributions from racial differences in both startup capital and industry. These results are reported in table 5.7. The contributions of the variables in the previous decomposition are similar to those in this decomposition. Racial differences in education continue to be important in explaining the Asian/white gaps in business outcomes. The inclusion of controls for startup capital and industry does not change the conclusion that Asian businesses are more successful partly because of higher education levels. The role of prior work experience also remains strong, explaining between 7.3 and 21.5 percent of the gaps in business outcomes.

Asian/white differences in business performance do not appear to be due to industry differences. Although racial differences in industry concentrations contribute to the gaps in closure, employment, and sales, it works in the other direction for profits. The industry distribution of Asian firms is less favorable for this outcome. Given the inconsistency of results across different outcomes, industry differences do not appear to contribute substantially to why Asian firms perform better on average than white firms.

Startup capital plays the most substantial role in explaining the gaps. Group differences in startup capital explain 57 percent of the gap in the log sales equation, 65 percent of the closure equation, 71 percent of the gap in the profit equation, and 100 percent of the gap in the employer equation. Fewer than 5 percent of white owned firms were started with more than $100,000 in capital, compared with 12 percent of Asian-owned firms. Also, nearly a quarter of Asian-owned firms were started with $25,000 to 100,000, compared with just 11 percent of firms owned by whites. Although more than 60 percent of white-owned firms were started with less than $5,000 in capital, only 36 percent of Asians did so. Clearly, firms with higher levels of startup capital are associated with more successful business outcomes. The contribution of higher levels of startup capital among Asian-owned businesses to their relative success is even larger than the contribution of lower levels of startup capital among black-owned businesses to their lower average outcomes.

Table 5.7
Decompositions of Asian/White gaps in small business outcomes, Characteristics of Business Owners (1992)

	Specification			
	(1)	(2)	(3)	(4)
Dependent variable	Closure	Profits	Employer	Ln Sales
Asian mean	0.1890	0.3637	0.2651	10.7037
White mean	0.2281	0.3003	0.2066	10.0615
Asian/white gap	0.0391	−0.0635	−0.0585	−0.6422
Contributions from racial differences in:				
Sex	0.0004	−0.0020	0.0002	−0.0127
	1.1%	3.1%	−0.3%	2.0%
Marital status	0.0005	−0.0027	−0.0012	−0.0084
	1.2%	4.3%	2.1%	1.3%
Education	0.0103	−0.0061	−0.0097	−0.0506
	26.3%	9.6%	16.6%	7.9%
Region	−0.0001	−0.0235	−0.0014	−0.0861
	−0.2%	37.0%	2.4%	13.4%
Urban	−0.0015	−0.0126	0.0028	−0.0385
	−3.8%	19.8%	−4.8%	6.0%
Prior work experience	0.0035	−0.0137	−0.0090	−0.0472
	8.9%	21.5%	15.5%	7.3%
Prior work experience in a managerial capacity	−0.0010	0.0001	0.0003	−0.0001
	−2.5%	−0.2%	−0.5%	0.0%
Prior work experience in a similar business	−0.0018	0.0028	0.0015	0.0132
	−4.5%	−4.4%	−2.5%	−2.1%
Have a self-employed family member	−0.0011	0.0000	−0.0005	−0.0058
	−2.9%	−0.1%	0.9%	0.9%
Prior work experience in a family member's business	−0.0014	0.0012	0.0020	0.0123
	−3.5%	−1.9%	−3.4%	−1.9%
Inherited business	0.0000	0.0008	0.0004	0.0028
	0.0%	−1.3%	−0.8%	−0.4%
Startup capital	0.0255	−0.0452	−0.0697	−0.3637
	65.3%	71.1%	119.2%	56.6%
Industry	0.0039	0.0061	−0.0096	−0.0357
	10.0%	−9.6%	16.4%	5.6%
All included variables	0.0373	−0.0946	−0.0941	−0.6206
	95.5%	149.0%	160.9%	96.6%

Notes: (1) The sample and regression specifications are the same as those used in table 3.14. (2) Contribution estimates are mean values of the decomposition using 1,000 subsamples of whites. See the text for more details.

Overall, racial differences in the explanatory variables explain a large percentage of the total Asian/white gaps in business outcomes, especially when startup capital is included. In the second set of specifications, the gaps in profits and employer status are fully explained, and less than 5 percent of the gaps in the closure and sales equations are left unexplained. Startup capital plays the strongest role, followed by education and prior work experience.

Conclusions

Estimates from the CBO indicate that Asian-owned businesses have better average outcomes than white-owned businesses. Asian firms are 16.9 percent less likely to close, 20.6 percent more likely to have profits of at least $10,000, and 27.2 percent more likely to hire employees than white firms. They also have mean annual sales that are roughly 60 percent higher than the mean sales of white-owned firms. These differences imply that Asian firms are also substantially more successful on average than are African American firms.

Asian business owners have relatively high levels of education: 46 percent of Asian business owners have a college degree, compared with 33 percent of white business owners. Asian business owners are also found to have very high levels of startup capital. Estimates from the CBO indicate that 12 percent of Asian-owned businesses started with more than $100,000 in capital, compared with only 5 percent of white-owned firms. In contrast to these results, we find that Asian business owners do not have advantaged family-business backgrounds when compared with whites. They are slightly less likely to have had a self-employed family member prior to starting their business and have prior work experience in a family member's business. Similar to white business owners, a very small percentage of Asian owners inherited their businesses.

We use a nonlinear decomposition technique to measure the contribution of racial differences in firm and owner characteristics to differences in business outcomes between Asian- and white-owned businesses. Asian-owned businesses are more successful than white-owned businesses largely for two reasons: the owners have high levels of human capital, and the businesses have substantial startup capital. Startup capital and education alone explain from 65 percent to the entire gap in business outcomes between Asians and whites. Racial differences in prior work experience are also found to be an important factor in explaining the Asian/white gaps in business outcomes. Our results indicate that group differences in prior work experience in family businesses do not contribute to Asian/white differences in closure probabilities, profits, employment, and sales. We also find no explanatory power from Asian/white differences in prior work experience in a similar business in determining racial differences in business outcomes.

Even with the relatively parsimonious models estimated using CBO data, we can explain virtually the entire gap between the outcomes of Asian-owned businesses and white-owned businesses. Admittedly, we do not explore whether other factors such as social capital and additional ethnic resources are important for the success of Asian-owned businesses. It is very difficult to find good exogenous measures of these factors. Furthermore, although social and ethnic resources may be important for the success of Asian-owned businesses, they are not easily affected by policy. Policies that increase human capital and access to financial capital, such as entrepreneurial training and loan-assistance programs, are easier to implement and expand.

Appendix

Table 5.A
Means of selected variables, Characteristics of Business Owners (1992)

	White-Owned Firms	Asian-Owned Firms
Firm no longer operating in 1996 (closure)	0.2282	0.1785
Net profit of at least $10,000	0.3004	0.3800
One or more paid employees	0.2067	0.2985
Log sales	10.07	10.71
Female-owned business	0.3268	0.3070
Married	0.7650	0.8200
Never married	0.1020	0.1010
High school graduate	0.2651	0.1590
Some college	0.3123	0.2482
College graduate	0.1962	0.2423
Graduate school	0.1353	0.2219
Northeast	0.0643	0.0221
Midatlantic	0.1469	0.1720
East North Central	0.1666	0.0699
West North Central	0.0847	0.0163

Table 5.A
(continued)

	White-Owned Firms	Asian-Owned Firms
South Atlantic	0.1597	0.1081
East South Central	0.0518	0.0121
West South Central	0.0999	0.0792
Mountain	0.0670	0.0327
Urban	0.7351	0.9467
Prior work experience: 1 year	0.0707	0.0946
Prior work experience: 2 to 5 years	0.1641	0.2255
Prior work experience: 6 to 9 years	0.1507	0.1607
Prior work experience: 10 to 19 years	0.2973	0.2474
Prior work experience: 20 years or more	0.2578	0.1313
Prior work experience in a managerial capacity	0.5552	0.5643
Prior work experience in a similar business	0.5030	0.4685
Have a self-employed family member	0.5231	0.4434
Prior work experience in a family member's business	0.2352	0.1796
Inherited business	0.0148	0.0132
Startup capital: $5,000 to $24,999	0.2374	0.2804
Startup capital: $25,000 to $99,999	0.1095	0.2412
Startup capital: $100,000 and over	0.0475	0.1198
Agricultural services	0.0269	0.0207
Mining and construction	0.1261	0.0388
Manufacturing	0.0330	0.0352
Wholesale	0.0360	0.0390
Finance, insurance, and real estate	0.0987	0.0865
Transportation, communications, and public utilities	0.0389	0.0420
Personal services	0.2616	0.2595
Professional services	0.1937	0.1885
Uncoded industry	0.0391	0.0402
Sample size	14,068	6,321

Notes: (1) The sample includes businesses that are classified by the IRS as individual proprietorships or self-employed persons, partnerships, and subchapter S corporations, have sales of $500 or more, and have at least one owner who worked at least twelve weeks and ten hours per week in the business. (2) All estimates are calculated using sample weights provided by the Characteristics of Business Owners.

6 Conclusions and Implications

African Americans are much less likely to own businesses than whites, and their businesses are less successful on average. Only 5.1 percent of black workers are self-employed business owners compared with 11.1 percent of white workers. Although there is some evidence of rising black business ownership rates in the past few years, racial disparities remain large, and a major convergence in business-ownership rates is unlikely in the near future. In fact, even in light of the substantial gains blacks have made in education, earnings, and civil rights during the twentieth century, black self-employment rates remained roughly constant relative to white rates.

Although a large number of businesses owned by African Americans are very successful, many more struggle with relatively low profits, sales, and employment. The result is that black-owned firms have lower average revenues and profits, are less likely to hire employees, and are more likely to close than white-owned firms. The disparities in these outcomes between black and white firms are quite large. For example, average annual sales of black firms are $74,018, which is less than one-fifth the level of average sales of white firms. Black-owned businesses are more successful now than they were in the past, but their average performance relative to white-owned businesses has not improved over the past two decades.

In contrast to these patterns, Asian Americans have high rates of business ownership, and Asian-owned businesses typically have better average outcomes than white-owned businesses. In the past few years, slightly more than 11 percent of Asian workers are self-employed business owners, which is comparable to the rate of business ownership among whites. Asian-owned firms are 16.9 percent less likely to close, 20.6 percent more likely to have profits of at least $10,000, and 27.2 percent more likely to hire employees than white-owned firms.

These large racial disparities in business ownership and outcomes are troubling because they are both a symptom and cause of broader economic inequality. We should be especially concerned about the implications for income and wealth inequality because business ownership provides the primary source of income for one out of ten Americans and business owners hold nearly 40 percent of total U.S. wealth (Bucks, Kennickell, and Moore 2006). Successful business ownership among disadvantaged minorities is also important for job creation, economic development, political power, and economic efficiency.

The lack of business ownership among African Americans and worse outcomes among black-owned businesses contribute substantially to overall earnings and wealth inequality. We estimate that total earnings inequality would drop by roughly 20 percent if black business ownership and performance improved to white levels. The impact of improving black business outcomes may reduce wealth inequality even more over the long run. Both black and white entrepreneurs have higher savings rates and accumulate more wealth than their counterparts working in the wage and salary sector (Bradford 2003).

The potential benefits of minority-owned businesses in terms of minority employment are also very important. The 3.9 million minority-owned firms in the United States hire 4.6 million employees. Many of these firms are located in predominately minority communities. In fact, more than 40 percent of black and Latino employer firms hire at least 90 percent minority employees (U.S. Census Bureau 1997), and 64 percent of the workforce of fast-growing black firms ("gazelles") is black (Boston 2003, 2006a).[1] It has been argued that promoting minority-business growth may be a more effective method of reducing minority unemployment than overall economic and employment growth (Boston 1999b). Making the conservative assumption that half of all employees at minority-owned firms are minorities, an increase in both the number of minority-owned firms and the average number of employees per firm by only 10 percent could result in nearly 1 million new jobs for minorities. An increase of 1 million jobs would be significant given there are roughly 3 million minorities currently unemployed in the United States (U.S. Bureau of Labor Statistics 2007).

Given the consequences of racial disparities in business ownership and outcomes, it is important to understand why these patterns exist. Why are African Americans less likely to start businesses, and why are their businesses less successful on average than white-owned businesses? Why do Asian-owned businesses, in contrast, have high rates of ownership and survivability and relatively high profits, employment, and sales compared with businesses owned by other groups? Although an extensive literature examines the causes of racial differences in business ownership, few studies explore the causes of racial differences in business outcomes, especially using business-level data. A better understanding of why businesses owned by some groups tend to outperform those owned by other groups is important.

Using confidential and restricted-access microdata from the Characteristics of Business Owners (CBO), we explore the factors associated with business success and the potential causes of racial disparities in closure rates, profits, employment, and sales. The detailed information on owner and business characteristics contained in the CBO microdata allows us to identify several key determinants of small business outcomes and underlying causes of racial disparities in business outcomes in the United States. We focus on the factors suggested by economic theory as being the most important for business success.

Three major barriers to successful minority businesses are revealed. First, the relative success among Asian-owned businesses and lack of success among black-owned businesses is partly due to high levels of startup capital among Asian firms and low levels of startup capital among black firms. Lower levels of startup capital among blacks appear to be partly due to low levels of personal wealth and possibly also lending discrimination. Second, relatively disadvantaged family-business backgrounds among black business owners contribute to worse outcomes. The lack of prior work experience in a family business among black business owners appears to limit their acquisition of general and specific business human capital useful for running successful businesses. Finally, other forms of human and business human capital, such as education and prior work experience in a related business, appear to limit the potential for business success among blacks. In contrast, highly educated owners are one of the main reasons behind the success of Asian-owned business in the United States. We discuss each of these explanations in more detail.

Financial Capital

The level of startup capital invested in the business is strongly associated with business success. Estimates from the CBO indicate that firms with higher levels of startup capital are less likely to close, have higher profits and sales, and are more likely to hire employees. The estimated positive relationship may be due to the inability of some entrepreneurs to obtain the optimal level of startup capital because of liquidity constraints. In this case, differences in startup capital may be due to differences in the personal wealth of the entrepreneur because this wealth can be invested directly in the business or used as collateral to obtain business loans. The positive relationship, however, may alternatively be due to potentially successful business ventures being more likely to attract startup capital than business ventures that are viewed as being potentially less successful. We provide some evidence from the literature suggesting that this alternative explanation is likely to be less important in explaining racial differences in business outcomes.

Personal wealth among African Americans is one eleventh that of whites. The median level of net worth, defined as the current value of all assets minus all liabilities on those assets, for black households is only $6,166 compared to $67,000 for white households. These figures imply that half of all black households have less than $6,166 in total wealth. Part of these disparities in wealth are due to blacks being less likely to own homes, having lower home values, and having lower equity to debt ratios in their homes. Recent research also indicates that black businesses may face lending discrimination (Blanchflower, Levine, and Zimmerman 2003; Cavalluzzo, Cavalluzzo, and Wolken 2002) and that blacks may have less access to family wealth through inheritances, loans, and equity investments. All of these factors may contribute to the substantially lower levels of startup capital among black business owners than among white business owners. Fewer than 2 percent of black firms start with $100,000 or more of capital, and 6.5 percent have between $25,000 and $100,000 in startup capital. Nearly two thirds of black businesses have less than $5,000 in startup capital. Although a large number of white firms also start with little capital, a much greater percentage start with large amounts of capital.

In contrast to the black experience, Asians have high levels of wealth and invested capital. The median level of net worth for Asian households is roughly similar to the white level of net worth. Asian businesses, however, start with substantially higher levels of capital. For example, 12 percent of Asian-owned firms have startup capital of $100,000 or more compared with fewer than 5 percent of white-owned firms.

Using a special statistical technique that accounts for the contributions of additional factors such as education, family-business backgrounds, and prior work experience, we find that racial differences in startup capital are the single most important factor explaining racial disparities in business outcomes. Decomposition estimates indicate that lower levels of startup capital among black firms explain from 14.5 to 43.2 percent of black/white gaps in business outcomes. Higher levels of startup capital among Asian firms explain an even larger share of the Asian/white gaps in business outcomes. The primary reason behind Asian firms having lower closure rates and higher profits, employment, and sales is that they invest more financial capital at startup than white or black firms.

Family-Business Experience

Our analysis of the CBO microdata reveals new findings on the importance of the owner's family-business background in determining business ownership and outcomes. More than half of all business owners had a self-employed family member prior to starting their business. Conditional on having a self-employed family member, less than half of small business owners worked in that family member's business. On the other hand, we find that only 1.6 percent of all small businesses in the United States are inherited. These results suggest that the strong intergenerational links in business ownership found in previous studies are partly but not entirely driven by opportunities to acquire both general and specific business human capital from working in family members' businesses. Business inheritances and partnerships with family members appear to play only a minor role.

A thorough examination of the determinants of business outcomes reveals a more nuanced role for the owner's family-business background in contributing to success in business ownership. Simply having a self-employed family member has no significant effect on business outcomes. In contrast, working in that family member's business leads to a more successful business. Business outcomes are 15 to 27 percent better if the owner worked in a family business prior to starting his or her own business.

The rich detail of the CBO microdata also allows us to control for prior similar business work experience and management experience. The inclusion of these controls suggests that the positive effects of working for a self-employed family on small business outcomes are not simply capturing the effects of management experience or specific business human capital. Instead, the independent effects of prior work experience in a family member's business on business outcomes appear to be partly due to the acquisition of less formal or more general business human capital. Estimates from the regression analysis also indicate that inherited businesses are more successful on average than noninherited businesses. However, their limited representation among the population of small businesses suggests that business inheritances are only a minor determinant of small business outcomes.

Black business owners have a relatively disadvantaged family-business background compared with white business owners. Black business owners are much less likely than white business owners to have had a self-employed family member prior to starting their businesses and are less likely to have worked in that family member's business. Only 12.6 percent of black business owners had prior work experience in a family member's business compared with 23.3 percent of white business owners. Racial differences and overall rates of business inheritances are much smaller: 1.4 percent of black owners and 1.7 percent of white owners inherit their firms.

Using a nonlinear decomposition technique that accounts for the contributions of additional factors such as education and startup capital, we find that the lower probability of having a self-employed family member prior to business startup among blacks than among whites does not generally contribute to racial differences in small business outcomes. Instead, the lack of prior work experience in family businesses among future black business owners, perhaps by restricting their acquisition of general and specific business human capital, limits the successfulness of their businesses relative to whites. Providing some additional evidence on the importance of limited opportunities for acquiring business human capital, racial differences in prior work experience in similar businesses also consistently explain part of the gaps in small business outcomes. Furthermore, the combination of these two factors suggests that racial differences in general opportunities to acquire business human capital contribute substantially to black/white differences in small business outcomes. On the other hand, racial differences in business inheritances are found to explain virtually none of the gaps in small business outcomes. The overall likelihood of business inheritances is just too small to play a major role in explaining racial differences in business outcomes.

The success of Asian firms does not appear to be due to advantageous family-business backgrounds. In fact, estimates from the CBO indicate that Asian business owners are less likely than white owners to have a family member who owned a business prior to starting their business, to have worked for a family business, and to inherit their business. The differences in having a self-employed family member and prior work experience in a family business, however, are smaller than they are between white and black business owners. Estimates from our decompositions indicate that Asian firms would be even more successful relative to white firms if they had more similar family-business backgrounds.

Human Capital

Similar to previous findings from the literature, we find evidence of a strong positive relationship between the education level of the owner and business outcomes. The general and specific knowledge and skills acquired through formal education may be useful for running a successful business, and the owner's level of education may also serve as a proxy for his or her overall ability or as a positive signal to potential customers, lenders, or other businesses. The estimated relationships between owner's education and small business outcomes are strong even after controlling for family-business background measures, startup capital levels, and industries.

Although blacks have made substantial gains in education, large racial disparities remain. For example, only 17.6 percent of black adults have a college education compared with 28.2 percent of whites. Marked disparities in education levels reveal themselves among business owners as well. Roughly one third of white business owners are college educated, whereas only one quarter of black business owners have the same level of education. In stark contrast to these patterns, Asians have extremely high levels of education. Nearly 50 percent of Asian adults and 50 percent of Asian business owners have a college degree.

Lower levels of education among black business owners and higher levels of education among Asian business owners translate into disparities in business outcomes. Our decomposition estimates indicate that differences in owner's education do not contribute substantially to disparities in business outcomes between black and white firms, but they do indicate that differences in education contribute to disparities in business outcomes between Asians and whites. Higher levels of education are a major reason that Asian-owned businesses are more successful than white-owned businesses and black-owned businesses in the United States.

Policy Implications

The desire for entrepreneurship is strong around the world. When individuals are asked whether they would prefer "being an employee or being self-employed," a large percentage reported "self-employment" as their preference (Blanchflower, Oswald, and Stutzer 2001). Slightly more than 70 percent of respondents in the United States express a desire to be self-employed. In many other countries (including Germany, Italy, and Canada), more than half of all individuals report a desire for self-employment.[2] Interest in self-employment also appears to be strong among minorities. More than 75 percent of young blacks report being interested in starting their own business compared with 63 percent of young white respondents (Walstad and Kourilsky 1998).

Although many disadvantaged individuals possess a strong desire for entrepreneurship, they may ultimately be unsuccessful in running businesses because of a lack of human capital, business human capital, or financial capital. In particular, if minority entrepreneurs face constraints that limit their optimal level of business ownership or optimal scale of businesses, such as liquidity constraints, informational barriers, lending discrimination, or customer discrimination, there will be some efficiency loss in the economy. Although it would be difficult to determine the level of this loss, barriers to entry and expansion faced by minority businesses are potentially costly to U.S. productivity, especially as minorities represent an increasing share of the total population and possess a strong desire for entrepreneurship.

Many efforts have been made to address these concerns about barriers to entrepreneurship and successful business ownership in the United States. Policies to promote entrepreneurship and business ownership among disadvantaged groups are widespread. For example, there exist more than 500 nonprofit programs providing loans, training, or technical assistance to disadvantaged entrepreneurs (Aspen Institute 2005). Several states in the United States also have programs providing transfers to unemployment insurance recipients (U.S. Department of Labor 1992; Vroman 1997; Kosanovich et al. 2001).[3] The federal government and several states have also promoted self-employment as a way to leave the welfare rolls (Guy, Doolittle, and Fink 1991). New demonstration programs by the U.S. Department of Labor and SBA provide microenterprise training and assistance as well as microloans (Bellotti 2006).

The focus of many programs for minority and disadvantaged firms is on providing more access to financial capital. Perhaps the most well-known program is the U.S. Small Business Administration's 7(a) Loan Program, which is named for section 7(a) of the Small Business Act and provides government backing on loans by commercial lenders. The loans are awarded to businesses applying for loans that would not otherwise receive bank funding. Although the program does not target minority entrepreneurs, they are disproportionately affected. Of the 97,000 loans approved for nearly $15 billion in 2006, roughly one third of the number and dollars went to minority firms (U.S. Small Business Administration 2007b). Many microlenders also provide small loans to disadvantaged business owners (Servon 1999; Aspen Institute 2005).

The largest government policies aimed at promoting minority businesses in the United States, however, are affirmative action contracting and procurement programs.[4] During the late 1970s and 1980s, there was substantial growth in the value of federal, state, and local government contracts reserved or set aside for minority-owned businesses. The purpose of these minority-business contracting programs was to develop minority enterprise, counter the effects of past discrimination, and reduce unemployment among minorities in urban communities. These programs originated from government policies that were designed to strengthen the viability of small businesses. Set-asides were initially targeted to economically disadvantaged minorities with the goal of increasing the number of minority-owned firms during the late 1960s and early 1970s, but they were later expanded to target minority businesses that had greater future growth potential (Bates 1985). In 2005, small disadvantaged businesses (SDBs) were awarded $21.7 billion in federal contracts (U.S. Small Business Administration 2007a).

Set-aside programs typically specify a percentage of the number or total dollar value of government contracts allotted to minority-owned businesses. In some cases, prime contractors are required to allot a specified percentage of the total amount of government contracts to minority-owned subcontractors and suppliers (Rice 1991; Myers 1997). Many of the programs provide goals for minority participation and price breaks instead of actually setting aside a certain number of contracts for minority-owned businesses. Data on local set-aside programs listed in Minority Business Enterprise Legal Defense and Education Fund (1988) indicate that these goals range from 1 to 50 percent, with most programs having goals of 5 to 15 percent. A large proportion of the program coverage appears to target the construction sector. Set-aside programs are also often complemented with procurement officials who aid minority-owned businesses in obtaining assistance (Bates and Williams 1993).

Contracting programs exist at the federal, state, city, county, and special district level. Recently, however, these programs have been both judicially and legislatively challenged and in many cases dismantled. The constitutionality of government-sponsored set-aside programs has been seriously questioned in two U.S. Supreme Court decisions—*Richmond v. J. A. Croson Co.* (1989) and *Adarand Constructors Inc. v. Peña* (1995). State referendums, such as Proposition 209 in California and Initiative 200 in Washington, further jeopardize the future of government affirmative action contracting programs. In response, many minority-business-development programs have disappeared, and others have shifted focus to disadvantaged-business-enterprise (DBE) programs.

Although minority-business set-asides represent an extremely large annual governmental expenditure and are controversial both politically and judicially, relatively little is known about their effectiveness. Previous research indicates that minority-business-contracting programs did not always increase utilization, can be costly, and may have led minority firms to overextend themselves (Myers and Chan 1996; Bates and Williams 1996; Marion 2007). The literature also indicates, however, that these programs may have increased the number of minority contracts and businesses in the United States, especially in the construction industry (Blanchflower and Wainwright 2005; Chay, Fairlie, and Chatterji 2005; Enchautegui et al. 1996; Boston 1998; Bates and Williams 1993). Given the heated debates over these programs, it is surprising that so little is known about their effects. More research is clearly needed.

Affirmative action contracting programs may have an impact on minority-business performance by reducing barriers to entry and expansion. In particular, the financial constraints identified above may be relaxed because smaller minority firms can grow through government work instead of borrowing from banks or other institutions. Government work may also provide a buffer against economic downturns in which small businesses may rely heavily on loans and personal wealth to survive. Given lower levels of wealth and less ability to borrow, this could be especially important for minority firms. On the other hand, government contracting represents a relatively small market share for minority firms and is focused on specific industries, such as construction (U.S. Census Bureau 2006a). Furthermore, the current trend toward reducing and eliminating affirmative action contracting programs suggests that these programs are likely to have less of an impact in the future.

New Policy Ideas

In light of these findings, future policies promoting minority businesses need to be creative. Government contracting programs and related loan programs for minority-owned or disadvantaged businesses are targeted toward alleviating financial constraints, but these programs do not provide opportunities for obtaining relevant work experience. Clearly, improving access to capital for minority entrepreneurs is important, especially in light of the striking wealth inequality that exists in the United States. However, increasing opportunities for the acquisition of human capital and business human capital should also be viewed as vital goals for minority-business development.

Before discussing specific policies ideas, an important distinction is needed between the goals of increasing the number of minority businesses and improving the performance of minority businesses. Although several constraints to minority-business ownership have been identified in the previous literature, it is difficult to know what the optimal level of business ownership would be given the risky nature of entrepreneurship. On the other hand, there is no disagreement over the importance of improving minority business-outcomes: better-performing businesses unambiguously make minorities better off. Therefore, we discuss policies that focus on relaxing the constraints to *successful* business ownership to address the problem of racial inequality. Furthermore, the policy ideas discussed below pertain to *all* disadvantaged business owners, not just those from minority groups, and also may have the broader effect of increasing the number of successful entrepreneurs in the U.S. economy.

Policies to promote educational attainment in general and among business owners more specifically would be a good start. The educational disparities between Asian and black business owners accentuate disparities in the general population. Asian business owners are found to be twice as likely to have a college education as black business owners. But in the general population, nearly half of all Asians have a college education compared with less than one out of every five blacks. Programs targeted at increasing educational opportunities for blacks may result in better business outcomes among black-owned businesses. These policies are also likely to contribute to reducing income and wealth inequality, which may further translate into reducing racial disparities in business outcomes. Wealth inequality may be directly addressed through expanding asset-building programs such as financial-education programs, individual development accounts (IDAs), and first-time home-ownership programs.

Our estimates indicate that blacks are less likely than whites to have previous work experience in a family member's business and are less likely to have previous work experience in a similar business. The relative scarcity of opportunities for acquiring general and specific business human capital apparently has a negative effect on the outcomes of black-owned firms. This finding is important because it suggests that a potentially effective emphasis for minority or disadvantaged business-development policies is to provide opportunities for relevant work experience for would-be entrepreneurs.

A few large national programs provide related mentoring services to entrepreneurs. For example, the Small Business Administration runs the Mentor-Protégé Program for disadvantaged firms under the 8(a) Program, which is named for section 8(a) of the Small Business Act. The program focuses on technical, management, and financial assistance, subcontract support, and assistance in performing prime contracts through joint-venture arrangements. Other federal agencies also have mentor-protégé programs. Another program is provided by the Service Corps of Retired Executives (SCORE). SCORE volunteers, who are working or retired business owners, executive, and corporate leaders, provide free advice and training to entrepreneurs and small business owners. These programs do not provide opportunities for would-be entrepreneurs to acquire general and specific business human capital by working for other business owners. Instead, the focus is on mentoring entrepreneurs as they start or run their own businesses.

The findings from our research suggest that governmental programs providing mentoring, internships, or apprenticeship-type training may help to reduce historical inequalities in business performance.[5] Training programs that are industry-specific, are targeted toward disadvantaged groups, and emphasize prior hands-on work experience are likely to be most useful for providing minority entrepreneurs with opportunities to acquire business human capital. In addition to the creation of these programs, the government could play a more active role in facilitating the placement of potential entrepreneurs in industry jobs where they would learn relevant skills for running future businesses. In each case, these policies may serve as a substitute for the lack of opportunities to work in family businesses for some disadvantaged groups.

All of these policies may be difficult and costly to implement, but a shift in the emphasis of entrepreneurial training programs away from writing business plans and finding capital and toward gaining related work experience would represent a step in the right direction. Potential entrepreneurs should be encouraged to find related work experience, especially in small businesses prior to launching new businesses. The work experience could be in a friend's or relative's business or in a similar industry as the one for the business idea. In an extreme case, entrepreneurial training programs could require relevant work experience as a prerequisite for participation in the program. The results from this study indicate that the benefits of this type of work experience could be large in terms of creating successful businesses. Although emphasizing the acquisition of relevant prior work experience may be especially valuable for disadvantaged entrepreneurs, it may help any would-be entrepreneurs in starting successful businesses. Prior industry work experience is one of the main factors considered in loan applications (U.S. Small Business Administration 2007a), and some potential entrepreneurs may realize that the initial chosen industry or business ownership, in general, is not for them.

An important issue is whether family-structure patterns among blacks may counteract some of the benefits of these policies. One reason that black business owners may be less likely to have a family member who owns a business and less likely to have worked in that family member's business is that relatively large numbers grow up in single-parent families. Having only one parent at home limits potential exposure to family businesses, particularly if the absent parent is the father because men have higher business ownership rates than women. For the current generation of black business owners, our best estimate is that more than 20 percent of them grew up in a single-parent family. Today, more than half of all black children live with only parent. These trends may limit the opportunities available to the current generation of black children to work in family businesses and acquire business human capital prior to starting their own businesses later in life.

Progress in business outcomes for future generations of black entrepreneurs thus may be dampened by recent trends in family structure.

To break the cycle of low rates of business ownership and relatively worse business outcomes from being passed from one generation of blacks to the next, programs that directly address deficiencies in family-business experience, possibly through an expansion of apprenticeship-type entrepreneurial training programs, may be needed. More research, however, is needed on the potential effectiveness of these types of programs, especially from rigorous evaluations of pilot programs, before a large-scale investment is made.

In conclusion, racial disparities in business success are a symptom of broader economic inequality. Policies that are targeted to alleviate barriers to raising capital and help people acquire business human capital through work experience may improve the outcomes of minority-owned businesses and disadvantaged businesses. More generally, policies that improve the education and wealth of African Americans and other disadvantaged groups will likely result in better performing businesses in the long run. Finally, any policies that increase education, business human capital, and access to financial capital are likely to increase the number of successful entrepreneurs in the U.S. economy.

Data Appendix

A major challenge for researchers in the area of minority business is finding data. Few datasets have both large samples of minority-owned businesses and detailed information on businesses characteristics and outcomes. It is particularly difficult to find detailed information on the characteristics of both owners and firms. This is important if we want to learn more about the relationship between owner characteristics (such as education and prior work experience) and business performance, for example. Many large nationally representative datasets are based on household surveys such as the Census and Current Population Survey (CPS), but these datasets include only limited information on the owner's business. Household surveys typically include only the owner's income from the business and the industry of the business. Business-level datasets, on the other hand, include more information on the business but typically include very limited information, if any, on the characteristics of the owners.

The Characteristics of Business Owners (CBO) is one of the only datasets that includes both a large sample of minority-owned businesses and detailed owner and firm characteristics. We use this dataset extensively to explore the owner and firm characteristics that are associated with business success, as well as the causes of racial differences in business outcomes.

In this data appendix, we describe the CBO and the dataset that it is drawn from—the Survey of Minority-Owned Business Enterprises (SMOBE). The recently released 2002 Survey of Business Owners (SBO), which replaced the SMOBE, is also discussed. Published estimates from the SMOBE and SBO are the most commonly cited and used estimates of the state of minority-owned businesses. The CPS is also described in detail because it provides the most up-to-date estimates of self-employed business ownership rates in the United States.

Unlike business-level data, the CPS includes information on wage and salary workers allowing one to easily calculate the percentage of the working population that owns a business, referred to as the self-employed business-ownership rate. Finally, we discuss a few additional data sources that can be used to study minority-owned businesses but are not used extensively in this study.

The Survey of Business Owners (SBO) and the Survey of Minority-Owned Business Enterprises (SMOBE)

The Survey of Business Owners (SBO) is conducted by the U.S. Census Bureau every five years to collect statistics that describe the composition of U.S. businesses by gender, race, and ethnicity. This survey was previously conducted as the Survey of Minority- and Women-Owned Business Enterprises (SMOBE/SWOBE). Data are compiled from several sources: IRS business tax returns, other Economic Census reports (such as the Annual Survey of Manufacturers and the Annual Retail Trade Survey), Social Security information on race and Hispanic or Latino origin, and a mailout and mailback survey. The universe for the most recent survey is all firms operating during 2002 with receipts of $1,000 or more that filed tax forms as individual proprietorships, partnerships, or any type of corporation.[1] Businesses that are classified as agricultural production, domestically scheduled airlines, railroads, U.S. Postal Service, mutual funds (except real estate investment trusts), religious grant operations, private households and religious organizations, public administration, and government are excluded.

The SMOBE and SBO data have undergone several major changes over time including the addition of C corporations and the removal of firms with annual receipts between $500 and $1,000 starting in 1997. Table A.1 includes a summary of the major changes in the SMOBE/SBO data from 1982 to 2002. Additional changes were made over time, which are described in more detail in table A.2. In chapter 2, we provide a new compilation of estimates from the SMOBE and SBO that makes these data as comparable as possible over the time period 1982 to 2002.

These surveys provide the most comprehensive data available on businesses by the race, ethnicity, and gender of the owners. Business ownership is defined as having 51 percent or more of the stock or equity in the business. Business ownership was categorized by gender (male, female, or equally male- and female-owned), ethnicity (His-

Table A.1
Major changes in survey methodology, Survey of Minority-Owned Business Enterprises
(1982 to 1997) and Survey of Business Owners (2002)

	1982	1987	1992	1997	2002
Dataset	SMOBE	SMOBE	SMOBE	SMOBE	SBO
Types of businesses included:					
Sole proprietorships	Yes	Yes	Yes	Yes	Yes
Partnerships	Yes	Yes	Yes	Yes	Yes
S corporations	Yes	Yes	Yes	Yes	Yes
All other corporations	No	No	No	Yes	Yes
Minimum business receipts	None	$500	$500	$1,000	$1,000

Source: U.S. Census Bureau (2005). For more details of changes, see table A.2.

panic, non-Hispanic), and race (white, black or African American, American Indian or Alaska native, Asian, native Hawaiian, or other Pacific Islander). For the first time, respondents could choose multiple race groups in the 2002 SBO survey.

Aggregate publications from this survey are available for each racial group, Hispanics, and women. Separate reports are not available for white firms, but estimates for non-Hispanic white firms and all white firms are reported in 1997 and 2002, respectively. Although not directly comparable over time, the number of non-Hispanic white or all white firms can be estimated by subtracting out all minority firms or Hispanic firms in other years.

The confidential microdata underlying these aggregate publications are available to approved researchers at the Center for Economic Studies.[2] Alternatively, special cross-tabulations of these data can be purchased from the U.S. Census Bureau. Prior to 2002, the SMOBE data contained information on businesses including legal form of organization (sole proprietorships, partnerships, S corporations, and, beginning in 1997, C corporations), industry, location, employment size, receipts size, and payroll. The 2002 SBO contains all of this information except legal form of organization.

The public use tables from the SBO/SMOBE are the most widely used source for tracking the number, performance, size, and industry composition of minority-owned businesses in the United States. Many researchers have used these data to try to better understand the role that minority- and female-owned businesses play in our economy (U.S. Small Business Administration 1999, 2001; Handy and Swinton 1983 and 1984; Robb 2000). Most research using the SMOBE data

Table A.2
Changes in survey methodology to the Survey of Business Owners (SBO) and Survey of Minority-Owned Business Enterprises (SMOBE) (1982 to 2002)

	1982	1987	1992	1997	2002
Legal form	IRS changed the rules for subchapter S corporations to allow for **up to 25** shareholders. However, the Census Bureau received data, **including** the number of shares owned, for up to only the first 10 owners. To determine the minority ownership of each S corporation with more than 10 owners, the number of shares listed for the first 10 shareholders was considered to be the number of shares for the entire corporation.	IRS changed rules for subchapter S corporations to allow for **up to 35** shareholders. The Census Bureau received data, **excluding** the number of shares owned, for up to only the first 10 owners. Census Bureau research indicated that 99.9% of all S corporations had all shareholders reporting the same race and ethnicity.	The use of select items from IRS and SSA administrative records to identify the owners of partnerships and subchapter S corporations was discontinued. Therefore, some partnerships and subchapter S corporations were subjected to being sampled to determine which were minority-owned. A small sample of C corporations was included in the SWOBE to provide estimates at the national level by industry division.	The universe was expanded to include all corporations in minority estimates for all tabulation levels.	Businesses were asked to report ownership by an American Indian tribal entity. These businesses are considered to be government-owned entities and are therefore excluded from the estimates of American Indian- and Alaska native-owned businesses. This distinction was not made in the previous surveys, so prior data are not directly comparable for this group.

Minority methods	The Census Bureau expanded its surname list to include more Hispanic surnames and some American Indian and Asian surnames. All owners, including those with "black" race codes, were subjected to the surname match to identify probable Hispanic or Asian ownership.	The Census Bureau's surname list was expanded to include nonminority surnames (i.e., non-Hispanic and non-Asian) to place minority/nonminority codes on each owner for use in an imputation of nonrespondents.		
Industry	Classifications for firm data were based on the 1972 Standard Industrial Classification (SIC) system.	Virtually all non-farm businesses were included. Classifications for firm data were based on the 1987 SIC system.	Virtually all non-farm businesses were included except those classified as agricultural production, airlines, railroads, U.S. Postal Service, mutual funds (except real estate investment trusts), religious grant operations, public administration, and government.	Virtually all non-farm businesses were included except those classified as agricultural production, domestically scheduled airlines, railroads, U.S. Postal Service, mutual funds (except real estate investment trusts), religious grant operations, public administration, and government.

Table A.2
(continued)

	1982	1987	1992	1997	2002
Receipts	Unknown receipts cutoff	Included all persons with business receipts over $500	Included all persons with business receipts over $500	Included all persons with business receipts over $1,000	Included all persons with business receipts over $1,000
Minority methodology	Black-owned businesses were directly identified using administrative records. Minority-owned C corporations were identified from other government agencies, public sources, and contacts with minority development agencies, and the data for these large corporations were obtained from the 1982 Economic Census. The data for these large corporations were included in the published tables.	Individual proprietorships owned by blacks were still identified using administrative records. A sample of partnerships and subchapter S corporations was taken to determine black ownership. In the past, only the nonblack race and ethnicity data were collected directly from respondents.	Based on the race, ethnicity, and gender of the majority of the number of owners, without regard to percentage of interest owned in the firm. All firms where 50 percent or more of the owners were minority were included in the tabs.	Based on 51 percent or more of the interests, claims, or rights in the business held by minorities to be included as a minority-owned business. Businesses in which ownership was shared among minority and non-minority groups with no single racial or ethnic group having majority interest were excluded from the minority business counts. Publicly held corporations, foreign-owned companies, and not-for-profit companies	Equal male/female ownership was based on equal shares of interest reported for businesses with male and female owners. Businesses could be tabulated in more than one minority group. The 2002 SBO was the first economic census in which each owner could self-identify with more than one racial group, so it was possible for a business to be classified and tabulated in more than one racial group. This can result because the sole owner

				reported more than one race, the majority owner reported more than one race, a majority combination of owners reported more than one race.
			tabulated and published as a separate category.	Two questionnaires: SBO-1: Sole proprietorships were asked to provide the percentage of ownership for the primary owner(s), his or her gender, ethnicity, and race. The equal male/female ownership option was eliminated from the sole proprietorship form.
		Four questionnaires: MB-1: Sole proprietorships were asked to provide information for the primary business owner. However, if a husband and wife owned the business equally, they were instructed to complete the form for both owners.	Two questionnaires: MB-1: Corporations and partnerships were asked to provide the percentage of ownership by gender, ethnicity, and race of the owners. Percentage of stock publicly held or owned by other organizations was also collected for partnerships and corporations.	
Questionnaires	Two questionnaires: MB-1: Sole proprietorship form instructed the respondent to mark the one box in race and the ethnicity question with which they most closely identify.	Two questionnaires: MB-1: Sole proprietorship form requested information for the primary business owner. However, if a husband and wife owned the business equally, they were instructed to complete the form for both owners. The respondent was asked to mark one box for race and ethnicity with which he/she most closely identifies.		

Table A.2
(continued)

	1982	1987	1992	1997	2002
	MB-2: Partnerships and corporations were asked to provide the name, social security number, and number of shares (if a corporation) and to mark the one box under race and ethnic background that the owner most closely identifies with.	MB-2: Partnerships and corporations were asked to provide the race and Spanish or Hispanic background or origin of the majority of partners or shareholders. Limited partnerships were asked to describe the general partner(s).	Partnerships and subchapter S corporations received separate forms (MB-2 and MB-3, respectively). They were asked to provide the number of partners or shareholders and to select the one box that best described the sex; Spanish, Hispanic, or Latino background; and race of the majority of their owners.	MB-2: Sole proprietorships were asked to mark the one box that best described the gender, ethnicity, and race of the primary owner(s). The gender question on the sole proprietorship questionnaire included an equal male/female ownership option.	SBO-2: Partnerships and corporations were asked to report the percentage of ownership, gender, ethnicity, and race for each of the three largest percentage owners. The Hispanic or Latino origin and racial response categories were updated in 2002 to meet the latest OMB guidelines.
Race or Ethnic groups	Five: Black-owned businesses, Hispanic-owned businesses, other minority-owned businesses, minority summary report.	Five: Black-owned businesses; Hispanic-owned businesses; Asian Americans, American Indians, and other minorities; minority summary report.	Five: Asian-, Pacific Islander-, American Indian-, and Alaska native-owned businesses, black-owned businesses, Hispanic-owned businesses, minority summary.	Seven: Asian- and Pacific islander-owned businesses, American Indian- and Alaska Native-owned businesses, black-owned businesses, Hispanic-owned businesses, minority summary, and company summary.	Seven: American Indian- and Alaska native-owned businesses; Asian-owned businesses; black-owned businesses, Hispanic-owned businesses, native Hawaiian- and other Pacific islander-owned businesses, and company summary.

Source: U.S. Census Bureau by special request (2005).

conduct cross-sectional analyses; however, Handy and Swinton (1983) link the 1972 and 1977 SMOBE microdata, and Robb (2000) links the 1992 SMOBE to a longitudinal file of employer businesses to create panel data.

The Characteristics of Business Owners (CBO)

The 1992 Characteristics of Business Owners (CBO) Survey is the third survey of its kind conducted by the U.S. Census Bureau. The first two surveys were conducted for 1982 and 1987. The 1997 CBO was cancelled, and the 2002 CBO contains substantially less information on the owner and business and has only recently accepted applications for restricted-access use by the U.S. Census Bureau. Minorities and women are oversampled in the 1992 CBO to allow researchers to more reliably study these businesses and business owners. The sample for the CBO is a subsample of the SMOBE and drawn from the businesses that responded to the SMOBE (the 1992 SMOBE had a 77 percent response rate).

The 1992 CBO survey was conducted by the U.S. Census Bureau to provide economic, demographic, and sociological data on business owners and their business activities (for more deteails on the CBO, see U.S. Census Bureau 1997, Bates 1990a, Headd 1999, and Robb 2000). The survey was sent to more than 75,000 firms and 115,000 owners who filed an IRS form 1040 Schedule C (individual proprietorship or self-employed person), 1065 (partnership), or 1120S (subchapter S corporation).[3] Only firms with $500 or more in sales were included. The businesses included in the CBO represent nearly 90 percent of all businesses in the United States (U.S. Census Bureau 1997). Response rates for the firm and owners surveys were approximately 60 percent. All estimates reported below use sample weights that adjust for survey nonresponse (Headd 1999).

The CBO is unique in that it contains detailed information on the characteristics of both business owners and their businesses. For example, owner characteristics include education, detailed work experience, hours worked in the business, and the way that the business was acquired. Business characteristics include closure, profits, sales, employment, and industry. Most business characteristics refer to 1992, with the main exception being closure, which is measured over the period 1992 to 1996. Additional advantages of the CBO over other nationally representative datasets for this analysis are the availability of measures of business ownership among family members and the large oversample of minority-owned businesses. In particular, the CBO contains rare or unique information on business inheritances, business ownership among family members, prior work experience in a family member's business, and prior work experience in a business whose goods or services were similar to those provided by the owner's business. The CBO allows us to conduct a detailed analysis of the determinants of several business outcomes, such as closure rates, sales, profits, and employment size.

Unfortunately, future CBO surveys are likely to contain substantially less information on owner and firm characteristics. For example, the survey used for the 2002 CBO does not contain information on key variables of interest such as the amount of startup capital, family business experience, prior work experience, and profits. We use the 1992 CBO microdata for the main analysis and report published estimates on business outcomes from the 2002 data. The estimates indicate that racial disparities in business performance have not changed over this period.

The CBO sample used in most analyses conducted in this study includes firms that meet a minimum weeks and hours restriction. Specifically, at least one owner must report working for the business at least twelve weeks in 1992 and at least ten hours per week. This restriction excludes 22.1 percent of firms in the original sample. The weeks and hours restrictions are imposed to rule out very small-scale business activities such as casual or side businesses owned by wage and salary workers. For the main results, we did not choose tighter hours- and weeks-worked criteria because of concerns about removing unsuccessful business owners. For example, a business owner who is working twenty-five hours per week may not be doing this by choice and may be working less than full-time only because of lack of demand for his or her products or services. There is a tradeoff between being overinclusive and throwing out unsuccessful businesses with no perfect delineating point. We follow some of the previous self-employment literature, which includes only self-employed business owners with at least fifteen hours worked per week and twenty weeks worked per year. We could not match these criteria exactly because the CBO only includes a categorical measure of hours and weeks worked limiting the flexibility of choosing cutoffs. We also try tighter hours and weeks restrictions and comment on the findings below.

In multiowner firms, which represent 20.6 percent of the sample, we identify one person as the primary owner of the business. The primary owner is identified as the owner working the most annual hours in 1992 (weeks*hours). In the case of ties, we identify the primary owner as the person who founded the business. Finally, all remaining ties are resolved by assigning a random owner. The primary business owner is used to identify all owner characteristics of the firm, such as marital status, education, prior work experience, and family business background. The race and sex of the firm, however, are identified by majority ownership, which is the method used by the underlying SMOBE/SWOBE (U.S. Census Bureau 1997; Robb 2000).[4]

Given the detailed information on both owner and business characteristics, the oversamples of minority-owned businesses, and availability since 1982, it is surprising that the CBO microdata have only been used by a handful of researchers to study minority-owned businesses (Bates 1997 and many other studies; Christopher 1993, 1998; Kijakazi 1997; Robb 2000, 2002). The lack of use appears to be primarily due to difficulties in accessing and reporting results from these confidential, restricted-access data. All research using the CBO must be conducted in a Census Research Data Center or at the Center for Economic Studies (CES) after approval by the CES and IRS, and all output must pass strict disclosure regulations.

The Current Population Survey (CPS)

Rates of minority business ownership are examined using the Current Population Survey (CPS). Microdata from the 1979 to 2006 Outgoing Rotation Group Files to the CPS are used to estimate self-employed business ownership rates by race and ethnicity. The survey, conducted by the U.S. Census Bureau and the Bureau of Labor Statistics, is representative of the entire U.S. population and interviews more than 50,000 households and 130,000 people per month. It contains detailed information on labor-force and demographic characteristics.

The CPS provides the most up-to-date estimates of the rate of business ownership in the United States. The new estimates of business-ownership rates from CPS microdata presented in this study improve on published estimates from the same source by the Bureau of Labor Statistics (BLS). Regularly published estimates from the BLS, such as those reported in *Employment and Earnings*, do not include incorpo-

rated business owners, which represent roughly one third and a growing share of all business owners.[5] Using CPS microdata, owners of
both unincorporated and incorporated businesses can be identified.

These data also provide a different, individual-based representation
of recent trends in minority business ownership than estimates of the
number of businesses from the SBO/SMOBE. Estimates from the CPS
do not suffer from two problems facing the SMOBE. The scope of businesses included in the SMOBE has changed over the past two decades,
and the data include a large number of side or "casual" businesses
owned by wage and salary workers or individuals who are not in the
labor force.[6] The CPS microdata include all individuals who identify
themselves as self-employed in their own not incorporated or incorporated business on their main job and thus capture only primary business owners.

The CPS is also advantageous for calculating business ownership
rates because it provides estimates of the size of the population
employed in the wage and salary sector. This allows for the use of the
same definitions of race, ethnicity, and labor force attachment for
estimating both the number of self-employed business owners (numer-
ator) and the total number of wage and salary workers and self-
employed business owners (denominator).

The Current Population Survey (CPS) Outgoing Rotation Group
(ORG) files are used to calculate the self-employment series reported
in chapter 2. The ORG files contain annual samples that are roughly
three times larger than those from a monthly CPS, such as the commonly used March Annual Demographic Files. The large sample sizes
are useful for estimating trends in business ownership rates for smaller
demographic groups and provide more precise estimates of the number and rates of self-employed business ownership for all groups.

Self-employed business owners are defined as those individuals who
identify themselves as self-employed in their own not incorporated or
incorporated business on the class of worker question. The class of
worker question refers to the job with the most hours during the refer-
ence week. We restrict the sample to include only individuals age sixteen and over who worked at least fifteen hours during this week. The
hours restriction is imposed to rule out very small-scale business activities. As in most previous studies of self-employment, agricultural
industries are excluded. Agricultural industries are defined using the
North American Industry Classification System (NAICS).[7] Estimates

for 1979 to 1991, however, also exclude veterinary services because they cannot be separately identified.

Estimates of self-employment rates may not be perfectly comparable before and after 1994 when the CPS was redesigned. In a thorough analysis of the 1994 CPS redesign using a "parallel survey," Polivika and Miller (1998) conclude that self-employment rates increased by 0.44 percentage points for men and 1.58 for women. On the other hand, Fairlie and Meyer (2000) find by comparing estimates from the CPS ORG to estimates from the CPS Annual Demographic Files for the same year (but subject to the redesign in different years) that the redesign may have led to a fall in the reported white male self-employment rate of one percentage point. Using the same comparison, however, the redesign leads to an increase in the black male self-employment rate by almost a full percentage point.

We create five distinct ethnic or racial groups by interacting responses to the race and Spanish/Hispanic origin questions available in the CPS. The groups are white (non-Latino), black, Latino, Asian and Pacific Islander, and Native American (American Indian, Aleut, and Eskimo). The black, Asian, and Native American groups include individuals reporting Spanish ethnicity. This classification does not, however, lead to a substantial undercount of Latinos as few Latinos report being black, Asian, or Native American (Fairlie 2004b). Race and Spanish codes changed in 1989, 1996 and 2003. The largest change was in 2003, when respondents were allowed to report multiple races. Estimates starting in 2003 reported in chapter 2 only include individuals reporting a single race. Individuals reporting a multiple race only represent 1.7 percent of our 2003 to 2006 sample.

Individual- versus Business-Level Data

Estimates of the level of minority business activity in the United States can be generated from both individual-level datasets such as the CPS and business-level datasets such as the SBO/SMOBE and compared with each other. Of course, estimates of the total number of business owners and the total number of businesses are not perfectly comparable. Multiple businesses owned by one individual count only once in individual-level data, and businesses with multiple owners count only once in business-level data. These discrepancies are relatively minor, however. Estimates from the 1992 CBO indicate that the total number of business owners is only 12 percent larger than the total number of businesses (U.S. Census Bureau 1997). Similarly, Boden and Nucci (1997) find that less than 3 percent of small business records in the CBO pertain to owners of multiple businesses.

There are several additional reasons for discrepancies in the total number of self-employed business owners and the total number of businesses that are due to measurement issues, some of which are specific to the CPS and SBO/SMOBE. The most important is that business ownership in the CPS refers to the person's main job activity. In the 2002 SBO and 1997 SMOBE, all businesses resulting from filing tax forms to the IRS with at least $1,000 in annual sales are included. Thus, side businesses owned by wage and salary workers are counted in the SBO/SMOBE data but not in the CPS data. The focus on main job activity in the CPS may represent only a small part of the discrepancy, however. Headd (2005) finds that in the 2004 CPS, roughly 500,000 of the individuals who did not report self-employment as their main job activity did report self-employment in their secondary occupation.

As discussed previously, we impose hours-worked restrictions to the CPS sample to rule out small-scale businesses. Excluding these businesses further limits the comparability of our CPS estimates to the SBO/SMOBE estimates. The SBO/SMOBE data do not impose any restrictions on the size of the business other than the annual sales restriction. Using the CBO microdata, however, we are able to impose restrictions on hours and weeks worked to remove small-scale businesses.

Another cause of the discrepancy is that the SBO/SMOBE data refer to businesses that existed at any point in the calendar year. The CPS instead refers to self-employed business ownership at the time of the survey. Thus, the CPS is likely to capture fewer business owners because there is a considerable amount of volatility in business ownership. The CPS and SBO/SMOBE may also differ in how likely they are to capture some occupations, such as sales and real estate agents. These individuals may report working for an employer instead of self-employment on the CPS questionnaire, even when they file as sole proprietors (Headd 2005). In a recent preliminary study, Bjelland et al. (2006) find that a large percentage of individuals in the CPS are not found in the Census Bureau's comprehensive dataset of businesses, the Business Register, and vice versa. Their preliminary matching exercise, however, only includes unincorporated business owners, sole proprietorships, and businesses with positive earnings.

Overall, individual- and business-level data capture different measures of business activity. There are advantages and disadvantages to both types of data for studying racial business patterns. We present estimates from both sources and CBO microdata in chapter 2. The CBO microdata capture detailed information on owner and business characteristics and allow us to address some of the disadvantages of using business-level data based on tax filings.

Additional Data Sources for Studying Minority-Owned Businesses

There are several additional nationally representative datasets that can be used to study minority-owned businesses. These datasets, however, are limited in size, scope, or timeliness compared to the CPS, SBO/SMOBE, and CBO. We briefly discuss a few of the most commonly used datasets for studying minority entrepreneurship.

One of the only business-level datasets that provides information on the owner is the Survey of Small Business Finances (SSBF), which is conducted by the Board of Governors of the Federal Reserve System every five years. The 2003 SSBF contains a nationally representative sample of 4,240 for-profit, nongovernmental, nonagricultural businesses with fewer than 500 employees.[8] The SSBF provides detailed information on many owner and firm characteristics, including credit histories, recent borrowing experiences, balance-sheet data, and sources of financial products and services used (for more information, see Mach and Wolken 2006 and ⟨www.federalreserve.gov/ssbf⟩). A major limitation to the SSBF, however, is that it contains relatively small minority business sample sizes.[9]

A new nationally representative, business-level dataset from the Kauffman Foundation is the Kauffman Firm Survey (KFS). The KFS contains information on nearly 5,000 firms that started in 2004 and tracks them over a three-year period. The sample sizes are sufficiently large for analyses of several minority groups (Asians, Hispanics, and blacks). The KFS includes detailed information on business outcomes in addition to owner characteristics and information on sources of financial capital.

There are also several commonly used household surveys providing individual-level data on self-employed business owners in addition to the CPS.[10] A less frequent but larger source of data on self-employed business owners is the Census of Population 5% Public Use Microdata Sample (PUMS). The 5% PUMS is calculated every ten years with observations for 5 percent of the U.S. population. Although census microdata is available as far back as 1850, the 1910 Census was the first census to include information on self-employment (see ⟨www.census .gov⟩ and ⟨www.ipums.org/usa⟩). The information available in the U.S. Census is very similar to the CPS.

Estimates of self-employed business owners can also be obtained from panel data allowing for the analysis of entry and exit over time.[11] The Survey of Income and Program Participation (SIPP), conducted by the U.S. Census Bureau, provides monthly data for a large sample of individuals (see ⟨www.sipp.census.gov/sipp⟩). The Panel Study of Income Dynamics (PSID) provides annual data for a large sample of individuals starting in 1968. The dataset, which contains an oversample of minority households, is conducted at the Survey Research Center, Institute for Social Research, University of Michigan (see ⟨http:// psidonline.isr.umich.edu⟩ for more details). The National Longitudinal Surveys (NLS) are a set of surveys containing detailed longitudinal information on demographic characteristics and labor-market activities for several age cohorts of the population (see ⟨www.bls.gov/nls⟩). The National Longitudinal Survey of Youth 1979 (NLSY79) is perhaps the most widely used NLS. It contains a nationally representative sample of individuals who were age fourteen to twenty-two when they were first interviewed in 1979 with oversamples of black and Latino youth (see Center for Human Resource Research 2005 for more information).[12] In most cases, these longitudinal datasets provide more detailed information on owner characteristics than the CPS, but they have much smaller sample sizes and are generally not as representative of the current U.S. population.

Summary

In this data appendix, we provide a description of the three main datasets used in this study—the SBO/SMOBE, CBO, and CPS. The SBO/ SMOBE and CPS are the most widely used, up-to-date sources of estimates for business outcomes and ownership by race and ethnicity in the United States, respectively. In this study, the SBO/SMOBE data are used to provide estimates of business outcomes by ethnicity and race, and the CPS microdata are used to estimate self-employed business ownership rates by ethnicity and race. The number of minority-owned businesses in the United States can also be estimated from the SBO/SMOBE and compared to estimates of the number of minority self-employed business owners in the CPS.

The CBO data are also described in detail. The CBO is a unique and relatively underutilized data source for examining racial differences in business outcomes and the causes of these differences. The CBO is unique in that it contains information on both the characteristics of the business and the business owner. It also contains detailed information on family background experiences of the owners. The CBO appears to be underutilized because of the difficulties in accessing and reporting results from these confidential and restricted-access data. All research using the CBO must be conducted in a Census Research Data Center or at the Center for Economic Studies (CES) after approval by the CES and IRS, and all output must pass strict disclosure regulations. CBO microdata and published estimates from the CBO (U.S. Census Bureau 1997) are used extensively in this study.

Notes

Chapter 1

1. There are 22,678 black-owned firms with $500,000 or more in annual sales and revenues in the United States (U.S. Census Bureau 2006b).

2. See Glazer and Moynihan (1970), Loewen (1971), Light (1972, 1979), Baron, Kahan, and Gross (1975), Bonacich and Modell (1980), Sowell (1981), and Moore (1983).

3. Racial disparities in business ownership also appear to contribute to racial tensions in urban areas and business owners (see Min 1996 and Yoon 1997, for example).

4. Survey data indicate strong interest in entrepreneurship among minorities. Seventy-five percent of young blacks, compared with 63 percent of young whites, report being interested in starting a business (Walstad and Kourilsky 1998). These patterns suggest that constraints may limit business ownership among blacks.

5. See Blanchflower (2004) and Parker (2004) for more discussion of the broader question of whether more self-employment is better.

Chapter 2

1. Published estimates from the CPS from government sources generally do not include owners of incorporated businesses. See the book's data appendix for more details.

2. The inclusion of agricultural industries results in larger racial differences in self-employment rates. The white, black, Latino, and Asian self-employment rates are 11.8, 5.1, 7.5, and 11.9 percent, respectively.

3. The Latino/white and black/white ratios of self-employment rates are similar for men and women separately. Asian women, however, have higher rates of self-employment than white women, and Asian men have lower rates than white men. For all groups, women have substantially lower rates of business ownership than men.

4. There is also evidence of relatively low black self-employment rates and high Asian self-employment rates in Canada and the United Kingdom and substantially lower Latino rates than white non-Latino rates in Canada (Clark and Drinkwater 1998, 2000; Fairlie 2006).

5. Estimates reported in Aronson (1991), Blau (1987), and Fairlie and Meyer (2000) indicate that the upward trend in the self-employment rate dates back to the early 1970s.

6. The decline from 1993 to 1994 may partly be due to the 1994 CPS redesign. See Polivika and Miller (1998) and Fairlie and Meyer (2000) for more discussion.

7. The inclusion of agriculture results in similar rates of self-employment between white and black men in 1910 (see Levenstein 1995).

8. See House-Soremekun (2002) for a discussion of African American business development in Cleveland from 1795 to the present.

9. A larger literature examines the overall determinants of business ownership. See Aronson (1991), Parker (2004), and van Praag (2005) for reviews of the literature.

10. The most common method of identifying the relative important of factors is the decomposition technique described in Blinder (1973) and Oaxaca (1973). The technique combines coefficient estimates from multivariate regressions and group differences in mean characteristics.

11. Black youth are also more likely than white youth to report that it is important "for our nation's schools to teach students about entrepreneurship and starting a business" (Walstad and Kourilsky 1998).

12. Evans and Jovanovic (1989), Evans and Leighton (1989), Meyer (1990), Holtz-Eakin, Joulfaian, and Rosen (1994a, 1994b), Lindh and Ohlsson (1996, 1998), Bates (1997), Blanchflower and Oswald (1998), Dunn and Holtz-Eakin (2000), Fairlie (1999), Johansson (2000), Taylor (2001), Zissimopoulos and Karoly (2003), Hurst and Lusardi (2004), Holtz-Eakin and Rosen (2004), Giannetti and Simonov (2004), Fairlie and Krashinsky (2005), and Nykvist (2005).

13. See Blau and Graham (1990), Oliver and Shapiro (1995), Menchik and Jianakoplos (1997), Altonji and Doraszelski (2001), and Gittleman and Wolff (2004) for a few recent studies on racial differences in asset levels. See Bradford (2003) on wealth holdings among black and white entrepreneurs.

14. Bates (1997) finds a very strong relationship between wealth and self-employment entry and large racial differences in wealth levels using the 1988 SIPP. Although estimates of the relative contribution of racial differences in wealth are not reported, these findings suggest that they explain a large part of the gap in self-employment entry rates.

15. Using data from the Panel Study of Entrepreneurial Dynamics (PSED), however, Kim, Aldich, and Keister (2006) do not find evidence that individuals who have self-employed parents are more likely to be nascent entrepreneurs. The results may differ because nascent entrepreneurs are defined as individuals who are "now trying to start a new business" and are not current business owners.

16. Earlier studies making this argument include Kinzer and Sagarin (1950), Glazer and Moynihan (1970), and Light (1972).

17. We thank Valerie Strang, Anthony Caruso, and James Jarzabkowski at the U.S. Census Bureau for providing estimates from the SBO and SMOBE.

18. To find the most recently available data, we used newer reports to find revised estimates for previous years whenever possible (for example, we used the 1987 report for

1982 estimates). We did not make any other adjustments to the data. See U.S. Small Business Administration (2007a) for adjustments to the number of Asian and Hispanic firms in 1982 and 1987.

19. To make the data as comparable as possible, we exclude publicly held, foreign-owned, not-for-profit and other firms from the published estimates for all firms. These types of firms are not included in the estimates for ethnic or racial groups, making comparisons between minority and total estimates problematic with unadjusted published data.

20. Estimates for white-owned firms reported in table 2.3 are not directly comparable over time because of changes in measurement.

21. These estimates required special tabulations prepared for us by the Census Bureau.

22. Published estimates from the 1992 CBO, which exclude C corporations, indicate that the total number of business owners is 11.8 percent higher than the total number of businesses (U.S. Census Bureau 1997). The numbers of black and Latino business owners are 2.8 and 5.1 percent higher than the number of black and Latino businesses, respectively.

23. Estimates from the 2004 March CPS indicate that 500,000 of the individuals not reporting self-employment as their main job activity report self-employment in their secondary occupation (Headd 2005).

24. In a comparison of estimates from the CBO to estimates from the CPS Annual Demographic Files, Boden and Nucci (1997) also find higher growth rates for white business owners from 1982 to 1987 using the CBO. This is even after removing S corporations from the CBO and incorporated business owners from the CPS and including all individuals receiving any self-employment income in the CPS to make the data more comparable.

25. Unpaid family workers are not included in these estimates.

26. We can apply these restrictions to the estimate of the total number of businesses from the 1992 SMOBE by reducing them by 22.1 percent. The resulting estimate of the total number of businesses is 13.4 million, which is more similar to the CPS estimate of the total number of self-employed business owners of 10.7 million. We should not expect these estimates to match perfectly because of the reasons noted above, but it is useful to note that they are closer than using the unadjusted SMOBE estimates.

27. The CBO includes only a categorical measure of profits.

28. Although sample weights are used that correct for nonresponse, there is some concern that closure rates are underestimated for the period from 1992 to 1996. Many businesses closed or moved over this period and did not respond to the survey which was sent out at the end of the period. Indeed, Robb (2000) showed, through matching administrative records, that nonrespondents had a much higher rate of closure than respondents. Racial differences in closure rates, however, were similar for the respondent and nonrespondent samples.

29. Estimates of the profit distribution for Asian- and other minority-owned firms clearly indicate that these businesses are overrepresented in higher profit categories (U.S. Census Bureau 1997). Asian- and Pacific Islander-owned businesses comprise 85 percent of all businesses in this group (U.S. Census Bureau 1996).

Chapter 3

1. See van der Sluis, van Praag, and Vijverberg (2004) and Moutray (2007) for recent reviews of the literature on the relationship between education and entrepreneurship. See Card (1999) for a review of the literature on the returns to education in the labor market.

2. Due to disclosure restrictions limiting the amount of output that can be removed from our analysis of CBO microdata, we rely on published estimates for some of the tables and figures reported in this chapter. As noted in chapter 2 and the book's data appendix, published estimates from the CBO include all businesses and not just those with an adequate hours-worked commitment to the business (which is the sample restriction used with the CBO microdata). We are also limited to examining only sales and employment using the published CBO data.

3. Recent evidence from developing countries also indicates a strong intergenerational link in business ownership (see Djankov et al. 2005, 2006, 2007, for example).

4. These correlations may be caused by heritability of self-employment. See Nicolaou et al. (2007) for recent evidence on the importance of genetic factors in determining who becomes self-employed.

5. The questions ask (1) "Prior to beginning/acquiring this business, had any of your close relatives ever owned a business OR been self-employed? (Close relatives refer to spouses, parents/guardians, brothers, sisters, or immediate family)" and (2) "If 'Yes,' did you work for any of these relatives?" (U.S. Census Bureau 1997, p. C-4).

6. A recent survey of small employer firms by the NFIB, indicates that 45.1 percent of businesses employ a family member. However, they use a broader definition of family members than in the CBO and only include firms with 1 to 249 employees (National Federation of Independent Business 2002).

7. The survey question asks whether the owner worked "for a business whose goods/ service(s) were similar to those provided by this business" (U.S. Census Bureau 1997, p. C-4).

8. Personal interview with a business loan officer at Bank of America.

9. We estimate a logit model for profits of $10,000 or more because only a categorical measure is available. We also estimate an ordered probit for profits and compare the results below. We use a logit model for the employment probability because most of the variation in employment among small businesses is between 0 and 1 employees. Roughly 80 percent of firms have no employees and only a small percentage have more than five employees.

10. The use of logs is common in the literature examining economic variables, such as income or sales, because it fits the data better and downplays the influence of observations with very large values. The coefficient estimates in the log specification can also be interpreted approximately as the percentage change in sales from a one-unit increase in the variable. A robustness check concluded that our estimates from the log sales specification are not sensitive to the exclusion of firms with extremely large annual sales.

11. See Portes and Zhou (1996) for a discussion of the problems associated with including hours worked as an explanatory variable or adjusting earnings by it. They note that

business owners have more flexibility in hours worked and are often willing to work more given a certain return.

12. Another problem arises in both of these cases because only categorical measures of hours and profits are available in the CBO.

13. We approximate by multiplying the coefficient estimate from the logit model by $\bar{p}(1 - \bar{p})$, where $\bar{p}$ is the mean of the dependent variable.

14. These findings are also consistent with evidence from household surveys indicating large differences in earnings between self-employed men and women (Aronson 1991; Devine 1994; Hundley 2000; U.S. Bureau of Labor Statistics 2004).

15. See also Gatewood et al. (2003) and Parker (2004) for recent reviews of the literature and Coleman (2001) for a discussion of constraints faced by female-owned firms.

16. Published estimates from the CBO indicate that a higher percentage of female owners report that the reason they started the business was "to have more freedom in meeting family responsibilities" than men, but a similarly high percentage of women as men reported that it was "to have a primary source of income" or "to be my own boss" (U.S. Census Bureau 1997).

17. As expected, the removal of business inheritances from the specifications does not affect the coefficients on other variables.

18. The cutoffs for the ordered probit are (1) negative, (2) 0 to $9,999, (3) $10,000 to $24,999, (4) $25,000 to $99,999, and (5) $100,000 or more.

19. Aldrich and Kim (2007) using a sample of nascent entrepreneurs and a comparison group also find that men are more likely to report working in their parent's business than are women.

20. Race, gender, region, and urban are from administrative records and have no missing values.

21. The technique has been used to impute income and wealth variables in the Survey of Consumer Finances (Kennickell 1998).

22. Information from all of the independent variables in the main specification and on financial capital, industry, and start year was used in the correlations.

23. The gains in efficiency are small after increasing the number of imputations above five (Schafer and Olsen 1998).

24. The CBO does not include any measure of the owner's net worth. Using the 1987 CBO, Astebro and Bernhardt (2004) instead use instrumented household income as a proxy for household wealth and find a positive relationship between this variable and startup capital controlling for other owner and business characteristics.

25. Astebro and Berhardt (2003) find a positive relationship between business survival and having a bank loan at startup after controlling for owner and business characteristics.

26. We find that the effects of startup capital and industry do not differ substantially for male- and female-owned businesses.

Chapter 4

1. The questions ask (1) "Prior to beginning/acquiring this business, had any of your close relatives ever owned a business OR been self-employed? (Close relatives refer to spouses, parents/guardians, brothers, sisters, or immediate family)" and (2) "If 'Yes,' did you work for any of these relatives?" (U.S. Census Bureau 1997, p. C-4).

2. These patterns may in part be due to lower employment levels among black-owned firms.

3. Fairlie and Krashinsky (2007) find evidence that housing appreciation is associated with higher levels of business creation.

4. Unfortunately, the CBO does not contain separate information for equity investments made by family members.

5. Dunn and Holtz-Eakin (2000) consider an additional explanation. Successful business owners may be more likely to transfer financial wealth to their children potentially making it easier for them to become self-employed. Their empirical results, however, suggest that it plays only a modest role. As mentioned earlier, we find that financial transfers from parents to children are not a common source of startup capital among small business owners.

6. Earlier empirical research using the partially SBA funded survey, Access to Capital by Subcategories of Firms, also found evidence consistent with lending discrimination. Ando (1988) finds that blacks were much more likely to have their loan application denied than whites, even after controlling for a variety of creditworthiness factors.

7. The recently released 2002 Survey of Business Owners yielded similar patterns. Black-owned businesses were more likely to use credit cards or business loans from the government, while white-owned businesses were twice as likely to use a bank loan. Whites were also more likely to use personal savings and other personal/family assets to start there businesses than were blacks. See U.S. Census Bureau (2006a) for more information.

8. See Shane and Cable (2002) for evidence on the impact of network ties on financing of new firms.

9. Note that the Blinder-Oaxaca decomposition is a special case of (4.2).

10. A useful property of the logit regression that includes a constant term is that the average of the predicted probabilities must equal the proportion of ones in the sample. In contrast, the predicted probability evaluated at the means of the independent variables is not necessarily equal to the proportion of ones, and in the sample used below it is larger because the logit function is concave for values greater than 0.5.

11. A black dummy variable is included in estimating the logit model with the pooled sample of blacks and whites but is not used to calculate the decomposition.

12. Unlike in the linear case, the independent contributions of X_1 and X_2 depend on the value of the other variable. This implies that the choice of a variable as X_1 or X_2 (or the order of switching the distributions) is potentially important in calculating its contribution to the racial gap. We return to this issue below.

Chapter 5

1. See Boyd (1991), Fratoe (1986), and Borjas (1986), for example.

2. Excellent reviews of the literature can be found in Aldrich and Waldinger (1990), Boyd (1991), and Bates (1997). Zhou (2004) and Light (2004) provide more recent reviews of the ethnic entrepreneurship literature.

3. Another line of research hypothesizes that Asians have a high rate of self-employment because they come from countries with high rates (or culture) of self-employment. Although estimates of self-employment rates are not available for all Asian countries with large immigrant populations in the United States, wide variation in self-employment rates exists across available countries in Asia (International Labour Organization 2005). Asian countries also do not have notably higher self-employment rates compared to other regions of the world. Previous research on the correlation between U.S. self-employment rates and home country rates is also mixed (Yuengert 1995; Fairlie and Meyer 1996).

4. We are thankful to Lingxin Hao for providing these estimates.

5. In our subsample of active firms using the CBO microdata, we are able to isolate Asians from Native Americans and find that 11.5 percent of Asians had a loan from family members, compared with 6.2 percent of white owners.

6. The recently released 2002 SBO suggests that these patterns continue. About 55 percent of white firms reported using personal or family savings to start their businesses, compared with 61.4 percent of Asians. Asians were also more likely than whites to use personal or business credit cards to finance their startups. About 9.6 percent of Asians reported using this source, compared with 8.8 percent of whites. Amounts of capital used were not available from this survey.

7. In addition, previous research finds that this unregulated source of funding comes with usurious interest rates that can negatively impact the chance for a business to succeed (Light, Kwuon, and Zhong 1990; Bates 1997).

Chapter 6

1. More 30 percent of other minority-owned employer firms hire at least 90 percent minority employees (U.S. Census Bureau 1997).

2. Job satisfaction is also much higher among the self-employed than wage and salary workers (Blanchflower, Oswald, and Stutzer 2001).

3. Many countries also have programs providing financial and other assistance to the unemployed to start businesses. See OECD (1992) for descriptions of programs in Belgium, Canada, Finland, France, Greece, Netherlands, Portugal, Spain, and the United Kingdom.

4. See Bates (1993b) and Boston (1999a) for a more thorough discussion of these programs.

5. Apprenticeships are common in the manufacturing sector in some developing countries and are associated with substantial returns in self-employment (Frazer 2003).

Data Appendix

1. Sole proprietorships complete a 1040C form, partnerships complete a 1065 form, S corporations complete a 1120S form, and C corporations complete a 1120 form.

2. See ⟨www.ces.census.gov⟩ for information on how to apply for access to these data.

3. C corporations were not included. C corporations as a tax filing status, however, are becoming less popular relative to S corporations due to changes in tax laws (Headd 1999).

4. The race of the primary owner is not available in the CBO.

5. See Hipple (2004) for recent estimates of the number of unincorporated and incorporated business owners.

6. Estimates from the 1992 CBO, which is drawn from the SMOBE, indicate that 44.2 percent of owners in the survey report that their businesses provided less than 25 percent of their total personal income (U.S. Census Bureau 1997). This estimate, however, does not include the hours-worked restriction used in our analyses of the CBO microdata.

7. A major change included in the NAICS was that landscaping and veterinary services were removed from agriculture.

8. The underlying sample frame for the SSBF was the Dun's Market Identifiers (DMI) file produced by the Dun & Bradstreet Corporation. The DMI data may undercount minority businesses (Haggerty et al. 1999). To address this concern the SSBF relies on its own screener question on minority ownership.

9. The 2003 sample includes 119 black-owned firms, 170 Asian-owned firms, and 149 Hispanic-owned firms (Mach and Wolken 2006). The 1998 survey includes larger minority sample sizes with 273 black-owned firms, 214 Asian-owned firms, and 260 Hispanic-owned firms (Bitler, Robb, and Wolken 2001).

10. Information on nascent entrepreneurs can be obtained from the Panel Study of Entrepreneurial Dynamics (PSED). See ⟨http://projects.isr.umich.edu/psed⟩ for more information.

11. Panel data can also be created using the CPS by matching records over time. See Fairlie (2007) for estimates of monthly entrepreneurship rates, which are defined as month-to-month entry into business ownership, by race for 1996 to 2006.

12. See also Fairlie (2005b) for review of the literature using the NLSY79 to study self-employment.

References

Aldrich, Howard, John Carter, Travor Jones, David McEnvoy, and Paul Vellemen. 1985. "Ethnic Residential Segregation and the Protected Market Hypothesis." *Social Forces* 63(4): 996–1009.

Aldrich, Howard E., and Phillip H. Kim. 2007. "A Life Course Perspective on Occupational Inheritance: Self-employed Parents and Their Children." In Martin Ruef and Michael Lounsbury, eds., *Research on the Sociology of Organizations* (pp. 33–82). Amsterdam: Elsevier JAI.

Aldrich, Howard E., and Roger Waldinger. 1990. "Ethnicity and Entrepreneurship." *Annual Review of Sociology* 16(1): 111–135.

Allen, W. David. 2000. "Social Networks and Self-Employment." *Journal of Socio-Economics* 29: 487–501.

Altonji, Joseph G., and Rebecca M. Blank. 1999. "Race and Gender in the Labor Market." In Orley Ashenfelter and David Card, eds., *Handbook of Labor Economics* (vol. 3C, pp. 3143–3259). Amsterdam: Elsevier.

Altonji, Joseph G., and Ulrich Doraszelski. 2001. "The Role of Permanent Income and Demographics in Black/White Differences in Wealth." National Bureau for Economic Research Working Paper No. 8473.

Amato, Paul R. 2000. "The Consequences of Divorce for Adults and Children." *Journal of Marriage and Family* 62(4): 1269–1287.

Ando, Faith. 1988. "Capital Issues and Minority-Owned Business." *Review of Black Political Economy* 16(4): 77–109.

Aronson, Robert L. 1991. *Self-Employment: A Labor Market Perspective.* Ithaca: ILR Press.

Aspen Institute. 2005. "2005 Online Directory of Microenterprise Programs." FIELD Microenterprise Fund for Innovation, Effectiveness, Learning and Dissemination, ⟨http://fieldus.org/Publications/Directory.asp⟩.

Astebro, Thomas, and Irwin Bernhardt. 2003. "Start-Up Financing, Owner Characteristics and Survival." *Journal of Economics and Business* 55(4): 303–320.

Astebro, T., and I. Bernhardt. 2004. "The Winners Curse of Human Capital." *Small Business Economics* 24(1): 63–78.

Avery, Robert B., Raphael W. Bostic, and Katherine A. Samolyk. 1998. "The Role of Personal Wealth in Small Business Finance." *Journal of Banking and Finance* 22: 1019–1061.

Avery, Robert B., and Michael S. Rendall. 1997. "The Contribution of Inheritances to Black-White Wealth Disparities in the United States." Bronfenbrenner Life Course Center Working Paper 97-08.

Avery, R. B., and M. S. Rendall. 2002. "Lifetime Inheritances of Three Generations of Whites and Blacks." *American Journal of Sociology* 107(5): 1300–1346.

Baron, Salo W., Arcadius Kahan, and Nachum Gross. 1975. *Economic History of the Jews.* New York: Schocken Books.

Bates, Timothy. 1985. "Impact of Preferential Procurement Policies on Minority-Owned Businesses." *Review of Black Political Economy* (Summer): 51–65.

Bates, Timothy. 1989. "The Changing Nature of Minority Business: A Comparative Analysis of Asian, Nonminority, and Black-Owned Businesses." *Review of Black Political Economy* 18 (Fall): 25–42.

Bates, Timothy. 1990a. "The Characteristics of Business Owners Data Base." *Journal of Human Resources* 25(4): 752–756.

Bates, Timothy. 1990b. "Entrepreneur Human Capital Inputs and Small Business Longevity." *Review of Economics and Statistics* 72(4): 551–559.

Bates, Timothy. 1993a. *Assessment of State and Local Government Minority Business Development Programs: Report to the U.S. Department of Commerce Minority Business Development Agency.* Washington, DC: U.S. Department of Commerce.

Bates, Timothy. 1993b. *Banking on Black Enterprise.* Washington, DC: Joint Center for Political and Economic Studies.

Bates, Timothy. 1994. "An Analysis of Korean-Immigrant-Owned Small-Business Start-Ups with Comparisons to African-American and Nonminority-Owned Firms." *Urban Affairs Quarterly* 30(2): 227–248.

Bates, Timothy. 1997. *Race, Self-Employment and Upward Mobility: An Illusive American Dream.* Washington, DC: Woodrow Wilson Center Press and Baltimore: Johns Hopkins University Press.

Bates, Timothy. 2005. "Financing Disadvantaged Firms." In Patrick Bolton and Howard Rosenthal, eds., *Credit Markets for the Poor* (pp. 149–178). New York: Russell Sage Foundation.

Bates, Timothy, and David Howell. 1997. "The Declining Status of African American Men in the New York City Construction Industry." In Patrick Mason and Rhonda Williams, eds., *Race, Markets, and Social Outcomes.* Boston: Kluwer.

Bates, Timothy, and Alicia M. Robb. 2007. "Analysis of Young Neighborhood Firms Serving Urban Minority Clients." Working paper. Note: Forthcoming in *Journal of Economics and Business* (January 2008).

Bates, Timothy, and Darrell L. Williams. 1993. "Racial Politics: Does It Pay?" *Social Science Quarterly* 74(3): 507–522.

Bates, Timothy, and Darrell Williams. 1996. "Do Preferential Procurement Programs Benefit Minority Business?" *American Economic Review* 86(2): 294–297.

Becker, G. 1971/1957. *The Economics of Discrimination.* Chicago: University of Chicago Press.

Bellotti, Jeanne. 2006. "First Findings from the Evaluation of Project GATE." Paper presented at the 2006 Association for Public Policy Analysis and Management Conference, Madison, WI, November 2.

Benus, J. M., Johnson, T. R., Wood, M., Grover, N., and Shen, T. 1995. *Self-Employment Programs: A New Reemployment Strategy. Final Report on the UI Self-Employment Demonstration.* Unemployment Insurance Occasional Paper 95-4. Washington, DC: U.S. Department of Labor, Employment and Training Administration, Unemployment Insurance Service.

Bitler, Marianne, Alicia Robb, and John Wolken, 2001. "Financial Services Used by Small Businesses: Evidence from the 1998 Survey of Small Business Finances." *Federal Reserve Bulletin* 87 (April): 183–205.

Bjelland, Melissa, John Haltiwanger, Kristin Sandusky, and James Spletzer. 2006. "Reconciling Household and Administrative Measures of Self-Employment and Entrepreneurship." U.S. Census Bureau Working Paper.

Black, Jane, David de Meza, and David Jeffreys. 1996. "House Prices, the Supply of Collateral and the Enterprise Economy." *Economic Journal* 106(434): 60–75.

Blanchard, Lloyd, John Yinger, and Bo Zhao. 2004. "Do Credit Market Barriers Exist for Minority and Women Entrepreneurs?" Syracuse University Working Paper.

Blanchflower, David G. 2004. "Self-Employment: More May Not Be Better." Dartmouth University Working Paper.

Blanchflower, David G., P. Levine, and D. Zimmerman. 2003. "Discrimination in the Small Business Credit Market." *Review of Economics and Statistics* 85(4) (November): 930–943.

Blanchflower, David G., and Andrew J. Oswald. 1998. "What Makes an Entrepreneur?" *Journal of Labor Economics* 16(1): 26–60.

Blanchflower, David G., Andrew Oswald, and Alois Stutzer. 2001. "Latent Entrepreneurship across Nations." *European Economic Review* 45: 680–691.

Blanchflower, D. G., and Wainwright, J. 2005. "An Analysis of the Impact of Affirmative Action Programs on Self-Employment in the Construction Industry." National Bureau of Economic Research Working Paper No. 11793.

Blau, David M. 1987. "A Time-Series Analysis of Self-Employment in the United States." *Journal of Political Economy* 95: 445–467.

Blau, Francine, and David Graham. 1990. "Black-White Differences in Wealth and Asset Composition." *Quarterly Journal of Economics* 105(2): 321–339.

Blinder, Alan S. 1973. "Wage Discrimination: Reduced Form and Structural Variables." *Journal of Human Resources* 8: 436–455.

Boden, Rick. 1996. "Gender and Self-Employment Selection: An Empirical Assessment." *Journal of Socio-Economics* 25(6): 671–682.

Boden, Richard J. 1999. "Flexible Working Hours, Family Responsibilities, and Female Self-Employment: Gender Differences in Self-Employment Selection." *American Journal of Economic Sociology* 58(1): 71–76.

Boden, Rick, and Brian Headd. 2002. "Race and Gender Differences in Business Ownership and Business Turnover." *Business Economics* (October): 61–71.

Boden, Richard J., and Alfred R. Nucci. 1997. "Counting the Self-Employed Using House-hold and Business Sample Data." *Small Business Economics* 9(5): 427–436.

Boden, Richard J., and Alfred Nucci. 2000. "On the Survival Prospects of Men's and Women's New Business Ventures." *Journal of Business Venturing* 15(4): 347–362.

Bonacich, Edna, and Ivan Light. 1988. *Immigrant Entrepreneurs: Koreans in Los Angeles 1965–1982*. Berkeley: University of California Press.

Bonacich, Edna, and John Modell. 1980. *The Economic Basis of Ethnic Solidarity in the Japa-nese American Community*. Berkeley: University of California Press.

Borjas, George. 1986. "The Self-Employment Experience of Immigrants." *Journal of Human Resources* 21 (Fall): 487–506.

Borjas, George. 1990. *Friends or Strangers: The Impact of Immigrants on the U.S. Economy*. New York: Basic Books.

Borjas, George. 1994. "The Economics of Migration," *Journal of Economic Literature* 32(4): 1667–1717.

Borjas, George J. 1999. "The Wage Structure and Self-Selection into Self-Employment." Harvard University Working Paper.

Borjas, George, and Stephen Bronars. 1989. "Consumer Discrimination and Self-Employment." *Journal of Political Economy* 97: 581–605.

Bostic, R., and K. P. Lampani. 1999. "Racial Differences in Patterns of Small Business Fi-nance: The Importance of Local Geography." Working paper.

Boston, Thomas D. 1998. "Trends in Minority-Owned Businesses." Paper presented at the National Research Council Research Conference on Racial Trends in the United States, Washington, DC, October 15.

Boston, Thomas D. 1999a. *Affirmative Action and Black Entrepreneurship*. New York: Routledge.

Boston, Thomas D. 1999b. "Generating Jobs through African American Business Devel-opment." In J. Whitehead and C. Harris, eds., *Readings in Black Political Economy* (pp. 305–310). Dubuque: Kendall-Hunt.

Boston, Thomas D. 2003. "The ING Gazelle Index, Third Quarter, 2003." Available at ⟨www.inggazelleindex.com⟩.

Boston, Thomas D. 2005. "Black Patronage of Black-owned Businesses and Black Em-ployment." In J. Whitehead, J. Stewart and C. Conrad, eds., *African Americans in the United States* (pp. 373–377). New York: Rowman & Littlefield.

Boston, Thomas D. 2006b. "The Role of Black-Owned Businesses in Black Community Development." Paul Ong, ed., *Jobs and Economic Development in Minority Communities: Realities, Challenges, and Innovation* (pp. 161–175). Philadelphia: Temple University Press.

Boston, Thomas D., and Linje R. Boston. 2007. "Secrets of Gazelles: The Differences between High-Growth and Low-Growth Businesses Owned by African American Entre-preneurs." *Annals of the American Academy of Political and Social Science* 613 (September): 108–130.

Boyd, Robert L. 1990. "Black and Asian Self-Employment in Large Metropolitan Areas: A Comparative Analysis." *Social Problems* 37(2): 258–274.

Boyd, Robert L. 1991. "Inequality in the Earnings of Self-Employed African and Asian Americans." *Sociological Perspectives* 34(4): 447–472.

Bradford, William D. 2003. "The Wealth Dynamics of Entrepreneurship for Black and White Families in the U.S." *Review of Income and Wealth* 49(1): 89–116.

Brownstone, David, and Robert Valletta. 2001. "The Bootstrap and Multiple Imputations: Harnessing Increased Computing Power for Improved Statistical Tests." *Journal of Economic Perspectives* 15(4): 129–141.

Bruce, Donald. 1999. "Do Husbands Matter? Married Women Entering Self-Employment." *Small Business Economics* 13: 317–329.

Bruderl, Josef, and Peter Preisendorfer. 1998. "Network Support and the Success of Newly Founded Businesses." *Small Business Economics* 10: 213–225.

Brush, Candida, Nancy Carter, Elizabeth Gatewood, Patricia Greene, and Myra Hart. 2004. *Gatekeepers of Venture Growth: A Diana Project Report on the Role and Participation of Women in the Venture Capital Industry.* Kansas City, MO: Ewing Marion Kauffman Foundation.

Bucks, Brian K., Arthur B. Kennickell, and Kevin B. Moore. 2006. "Recent Changes in U.S. Family Finances: Evidence from the 2001 and 2004 Survey of Consumer Finances." *Federal Reserve Bulletin* 92: A1–A38.

Cain, Glen G. 1987. "The Economic Analysis of Labor Market Discrimination: A Survey." Orley Ashenfelter and R. Laynard, eds., *Handbook of Labor Economics* (vol. 1, pp. 693–781). Amsterdam: Elsevier.

Card, David. 1999. "The Causal Effect of Education on Earnings." Orley Ashenfelter and David Card, eds., *Handbook of Labor Economics* (vol. 3A, pp. 1801–1863). Amsterdam: Elsevier.

Carr, Deborah. 1996. "Two Paths to Self-Employment? Women's and Men's Self-Employment in the United States, 1980." *Work and Occupations* 23: 26–53.

Cavalluzzo, Ken, Linda Cavalluzzo, and John Wolken. 2002. "Competition, Small Business Financing, and Discrimination: Evidence from a New Survey." *Journal of Business* 75(4): 641–679.

Cavalluzzo, Ken, and John Wolken. 2005. "Small Business Loan Turndowns, Personal Wealth and Discrimination." *Journal of Business* 78(6): 2153–2177.

Cayton, Horace R., and St. Clair Drake. 1946. *Black Metropolis.* London: Jonathan Cape.

Center for Human Resource Research. 2005. *NLSY79 Users' Guide.* Columbus: Ohio State University.

Chaganti, Radha, and Patricia Greene. 2002. "Who Are Ethnic Entrepreneurs? A Study of Entrepreneurs' Ethnic Involvement and Business Characteristics." *Journal of Small Business Management* 40(2): 126–143.

Charles, Kerwin Kofi, and Erik Hurst. 2002. "The Transition to Home-Ownership and the Black-White Wealth Gap." *Review of Economics and Statistics* 84(2): 281–297.

Chay, Kenneth, Robert Fairlie, and Ronnie Chatterji. 2005. "The Impact of Contracting Set-Asides on Minority Business Ownership." University of California Working Paper.

Christopher, Jan. 1993. "Empirical Analyses of the Factors Influencing Business Performance." Ph.D. dissertation, Howard University.

Christopher, Jan. 1998. "Minority Business Formation and Survival: Evidence on Business Performance and Viability." *Review of Black Political Economy* 26(3): (Summer): 37–72.

Clark, Kenneth, and Stephen Drinkwater. 1998. "Ethnicity and Self-Employment in Britain." *Oxford Bulletin of Economics and Statistics* 60: 383–407.

Clark, Kenneth, and Stephen Drinkwater. 2000. "Pushed Out or Pulled In? Self-Employment among Ethnic Minorities in England and Wales." *Labour Economics* 7: 603–628.

Clark, Kenneth, and Stephen Drinkwater. 2002. "Enclaves, Neighbourhood Effects and Employment Outcomes: Ethnic Minorities in England and Wales." *Journal of Population Economics* 15: 5–29.

Coate, Stephen, and Sharon Tennyson. 1992. "Labor Market Discrimination, Imperfect Information and Self-Employment." *Oxford Economic Papers* 44: 272–288.

Cobb-Clark, Deborah A., and Vincent Hildebrand. 2006. "The Wealth of Mexican Americans." *Journal of Human Resources* 41(4): 841–868.

Coleman, Susan. 2001. "Constraints Faced by Women Small Business Owners: Evidence from the Data." Paper presented at the United States Association for Small Business and Entrepreneurship Annual Meetings, Orlando, February 8.

Coleman, Susan. 2002. "The Borrowing Experience of Black and Hispanic-Owned Small Firms: Evidence from the 1998 Survey of Small Business Finances." *Academy of Entrepreneurship Journal* 8(1): 1–20.

Coleman, Susan. 2003. "Borrowing Patterns for Small Firms: A Comparison by Race and Ethnicity." *Journal of Entrepreneurial Finance and Business Ventures* 7(3): 87–108.

Conley, Dalton. 1999. *Being Black, Living in the Red: Race, Wealth and Social Policy in America*. Los Angeles: University of California Press.

Davidsson, Per, and Benson Honig. 2003. "The Role of Social and Human Capital among Nascent Entrepreneurs." *Journal of Business Venturing* 18(3): 301–331.

Dawkins, Casey J. 2007. "Race, Space, and the Dynamics of Self-Employment." Virginia Tech Working Paper.

Devine, Theresa J. 1994. "Characteristics of Self-Employed Women in the United States." *Monthly Labor Review* 117(3): 20–34.

Djankov, Simeon, Edward Miguel, Yingyi Qian, Gerald Roland, and Ekaterina Zhuravskaya. 2005. "Who Are Russia's Entrepreneurs?" *Journal of the European Economic Association, Papers and Proceedings* 3(2–3): 587–597.

Djankov, Simeon, Yingyi Qian, Gerald Roland, and Ekaterina Zhuravskaya. 2006. "Who Are China's Entrepreneurs?" *American Economic Review* 96(2): 348–352.

Djankov, Simeon, Yingyi Qian, Gerald Roland, and Ekaterina Zhuravskaya. 2007. "What Makes a Successful Entrepreneur? Evidence from Brazil." World Bank Working Paper: Washington, DC.

Du Bois, W. E. B. 1899. *The Philadelphia Negro*. Philadelphia: University of Pennsylvania.

Dunn, Thomas A., and Douglas J. Holtz-Eakin. 2000. "Financial Capital, Human Capital, and the Transition to Self-Employment: Evidence from Intergenerational Links." *Journal of Labor Economics* 18(2): 282–305.

Earle, John S., and Zuzana Sakova. 2000. "Business Start-Ups or Disguised Unemployment? Evidence on the Character of Self-Employment from Transition Economies." *Labour Economics* 7(5): 575–601.

Enchautegui, Maria E., Michael Fix, Pamela Loprest, Sarah von der Lippe, and Douglas Wissoker. 1996. *Do Minority-Owned Businesses Get a Fair Share of Government Contracts.* Washington, DC: Urban Institute.

Evans, David, and Boyan Jovanovic. 1989. "An Estimated Model of Entrepreneurial Choice under Liquidity Constraints." *Journal of Political Economy* 97(4): 808–827.

Evans, David, and Linda Leighton. 1989. "Some Empirical Aspects of Entrepreneurship." *American Economic Review* 79: 519–535.

Fairlie, Robert W. 1999. "The Absence of the African-American Owned Business: An Analysis of the Dynamics of Self-Employment." *Journal of Labor Economics* 17(1): 80–108.

Fairlie, Robert W. 2002. "Drug Dealing and Legitimate Self-Employment." *Journal of Labor Economics* 20(3): 538–567.

Fairlie, Robert W. 2004a. "Does Business Ownership Provide a Source of Upward Mobility for Blacks and Hispanics?" Doug Holtz-Eakin and Harvey S. Rosen, eds., *Public Policy and the Economics of Entrepreneurship* (pp. 153–180). Cambridge, MA: MIT Press.

Fairlie, Robert W. 2004b. "Recent Trends in Ethnic and Racial Business Ownership." *Small Business Economics* 23: 203–218.

Fairlie, Robert W. 2004c. *Self-Employed Business Ownership Rates in the United States: 1979–2003.* Washington, DC: U.S. Small Business Administration, Office of Advocacy.

Fairlie, Robert W. 2005a. "An Extension of the Blinder-Oaxaca Decomposition Technique to Logit and Probit Models." *Journal of Economic and Social Measurement* 30(4): 305–316.

Fairlie, Robert W. 2005b. "Self-Employment, Entrepreneurship and the National Longitudinal Survey of Youth." *Monthly Labor Review* (Special issue commemorating the twenty-fifth anniversary of the NLSY79) 128(2): 40–47.

Fairlie, Robert W. 2006. "Entrepreneurship among Disadvantaged Groups: An Analysis of the Dynamics of Self-Employment by Gender, Race and Education." In Simon Parker, ed., *The Life Cycle of Entrepreneurial Ventures,* International Handbook Series on Entrepreneurship (vol. 3, pp. 437–475). New York: Springer.

Fairlie, Robert W. 2007. *The Kauffman Index of Entrepreneurial Activity: 1996–2006.* Kansas City, MO: Ewing Marion Kauffman Foundation.

Fairlie, Robert W., and Harry A. Krashinsky, 2005. "Liquidity Constraints, Household Wealth, and Entrepreneurship Revisited." Working paper.

Fairlie, Robert W., and Bruce D. Meyer. 1996. "Ethnic and Racial Self-Employment Differences and Possible Explanations." *Journal of Human Resources* 31 (Fall): 757–793.

Fairlie, Robert W., and Bruce D. Meyer. 2000. "Trends in Self-Employment among Black and White Men: 1910–1990." *Journal of Human Resources* 35(4): 643–669.

Fairlie, Robert W., and Alicia M. Robb. 2007. "Why Are Black-Owned Businesses Less Successful than White-Owned Businesses: The Role of Families, Inheritances, and Business Human Capital." *Journal of Labor Economics* 25(2): 289–323.

Fairlie, Robert W., and Christopher Woodruff. 2005. "Mexican Entrepreneurship: A Comparison of Self-Employment in Mexico and the United States." George Borjas, ed., *Mexican Immigration* (pp. 123–158). Cambridge, MA: National Bureau of Economic Research.

Fairlie, Robert W., and Christopher Woodruff. 2007. "Mexican-American Entrepreneurship." University of California Working Paper.

Farber, Henry S. 1999. "Alternative and Part-Time Employment Arrangements as a Response to Job Loss" (pt. 2). *Journal of Labor Economics* 17(4): S142–S169.

Feagin, Joe R., and Nikitah Imani. 1994. "Racial Barriers to African American Entrepreneurship: An Exploratory Study." *Social Problems* 41(4): 562–585.

Fratoe, Frank. 1986. "A Sociological Analysis of Minority Business." *Review of Black Political Economy* 15(2): 5–29.

Fratoe, F. 1988. "Social Capital of Black Business Owners." *Review of Black Political Economy* (Spring): 33–50.

Frazer, Garth. 2003. "Learning the Master's Trade: Apprenticeship and Firm-Specific Human Capital." University of Toronto Working Paper.

Frazier, E. Franklin. 1957. *The Negro in the United States* (2nd ed.). New York: McMillan.

Gatewood, Elizabeth J., Nancy M. Carter, Candida G. Brush, Patricia G. Greene, and Myra M. Hart. 2003. *Women Entrepreneurs, Their Ventures, and the Venture Capital Industry: An Annotated Bibliography*. Stockholm: Entrepreneurship and Small Business Research Institute.

Giannetti, M., and A. Simonov. 2004. "On the Determinants of Entrepreneurial Activity: Social Norms, Economic Environment and Individual Characteristics." *Swedish Economic Policy Review* 11(2): 271–313.

Gil, Ricard, and Wesley R. Hartmann. 2007. "Airing Your Dirty Laundry: Vertical Integration, Reputational Capital and Social Networks." University of California, Santa Cruz, Working Paper.

Gittleman, Maury, and Edward N. Wolff. 2000. "Racial Wealth Disparities: Is the Gap Closing?" Working paper.

Gittleman, Maury, and Edward N. Wolff. 2004. "Racial Differences in Patterns of Wealth Accumulation." *Journal of Human Resources* 34(1): 193–227.

Glazer, Nathan, and Daniel P. Moynihan. 1970. *Beyond the Melting Pot: the Negroes, Puerto Ricans, Jews, Italians, and Irish of New York City* (2nd ed). Cambridge, MA: MIT Press.

Guy, Cynthia, Fred Doolittle, and Barbara Fink. 1991. *Self-Employment for Welfare Recipients: Implementation of the SEID Program*. New York: Manpower Demonstration Research Corporation.

Haggerty, Catherine, Karen Grigorian, Rachel Harter, and John Wolken. 1999. "The 1998 Survey of Small Business Finances: Sampling and Level of Effort Associated with Gaining Cooperation from Minority-Owned Businesses." NORC and Federal Reserve Working Paper.

Handy, John, and David Swinton. 1983. *The Determinants of the Growth of Black-Owned Businesses: A Preliminary Analysis.* Washington, DC: U.S. Department of Commerce.

Handy, John, and David Swinton. 1984. "The Determinants of the Rate of Growth of Black-Owned Businesses." *Review of Black Political Economy* 12: 85–110.

Hao, Lingxin. 2007. *Color Lines, Country Lines: Race, Immigration, and Wealth Stratification in America.* New York: Russell Sage Foundation.

Headd, Brian. 1999. "The Characteristics of Business Owners Database, 1992." U.S. Census Bureau, Center for Economic Studies, Working Paper CES-WP-99-8.

Headd, Brian. 2003. "Redefining Business Success: Distinguishing between Closure and Failure." *Small Business Economics* 21(1): 51–61.

Headd, Brian. 2005. "Measuring Microenterprise: Data on Self-Employment and Nonemployers." Working paper.

Hipple, Steven. 2004. "Self-Employment in the United States: An Update." *Monthly Labor Review* 127(7): 13–23.

Holtz-Eakin, Douglas, David Joulfaian, and Harvey Rosen. 1994a. "Entrepreneurial Decisions and Liquidity Constraints." *RAND Journal of Economics* 23: 334–347.

Holtz-Eakin, Douglas, David Joulfaian, and Harvey Rosen. 1994b. "Sticking It Out: Entrepreneurial Survival and Liquidity Constraints." *Journal of Political Economy* 102(1): 53–75.

Holtz-Eakin, Douglas, and Harvey Rosen. 2004. "Cash Constraints and Business Start-Ups: Deutschmarks versus Dollars." Syracuse University Working Paper.

Holtz-Eakin, Douglas, Harvey S. Rosen, and Robert Weathers. 2000. "Horatio Alger Meets the Mobility Tables." *Small Business Economics* 14: 243–274.

House-Soremekun, Bessie. 2002. *Confronting the Odds: African-American Entrepreneurship in Cleveland, Ohio.* Kent, OH: Kent State University Press.

Hout, Michael, and Harvey S. Rosen. 2000. "Self-Employment, Family Background, and Race." *Journal of Human Resources* 35(4): 670–692.

Hundley, Greg. 2000. "Male/Female Earnings Differences in Self-Employment: The Effects of Marriage, Children, and the Household Division of Labor." *Industrial and Labor Relations Review* 54(1): 95–104.

Hurst, Erik, and Annamaria Lusardi. 2004. "Liquidity Constraints, Household Wealth, and Entrepreneurship." *Journal of Political Economy* 112(2): 319–347.

International Labour Organization. 2005. *Labour Statistics Database.* Available at ⟨http://laborsta.ilo.org⟩.

Johansson, Edvard. 2000. "Self-Employment and Liquidity Constraints: Evidence from Finland." *Scandinavian Journal of Economics* 102(1): 123–134.

Joint Center for Political and Economic Studies. 1994. *Assessment of Minority Business Development Programs.* Report to the U.S. Department of Commerce Minority Business Development Agency, Washington, DC.

Jones, F. L. 1983. "On Decomposing the Wage Gap: A Critical Comment on Blinder's Method." *Journal of Human Resources* 18(1): 126–130.

Jovanovic, Boyan. 1982. "Selection and the Evolution of Industry." *Econometrica* 50(3): 649–670.

Kalnins, Arturs, and Wilbur Chung. 2006. "Social Capital, Geography, and Survival: Gujarati Immigrant Entrepreneurs in the U.S. Lodging Industry." *Management Science* 52(2): 233–247.

Kassoudji, Sherrie. 1988. "English Language Abilities and the Labor Market Opportunities of Hispanic and East Asian Men." *Journal of Labor Economics* 6(2): 205–228.

Kawaguchi, Daiji. 2004. "Positive, Non-Earnings Aspects of Self-Employment: Evidence from Job Satisfaction Scores." University of Tsukuba Institute of Policy and Planning Sciences Working Paper.

Kawaguchi, Daiji. 2005. "Negative Self Selection into Self-Employment among African Americans." *Topics in Economic Analysis and Policy* 5(1): art. 9, 1–25.

Kennickell, Arthur B. 1998. "Multiple Imputation in the Survey of Consumer Finances." Paper prepared for the August 1998 Joint Statistical Meetings, Dallas.

Kihlstrom, Richard, and Jean-Jacques Laffont. 1979. "A General Equilibrium Entrepreneurial Theory of Firm Formation Based on Risk Aversion." *Journal of Political Economy* 87(4): 719–748.

Kijakazi, K. 1997. *African-American Economics Development and Small Business Ownership.* New York: Garland Press.

Kim, Kwang Chung, and Won Moo Hurh. 1985. "Ethnic Resources Utilization of Korean Immigrant Entrepreneurs in the Chicago Minority Area." *International Migration Review* 19(1): 82–111.

Kim, Kwang, Won Hurh, and Marilyn Fernandez. 1989. "Intragroup Differences in Business Participation: Three Asian Immigrant Groups." *International Migration Review* 23(1): 73–95.

Kim, Phillip H., Howard E. Aldrich, and Lisa A. Keister. 2006. "Access (Not) Denied: The Impact of Financial, Human, and Cultural Capital on Entrepreneurial Entry in the United States." *Small Business Economics* 27(1): 5–22.

Kinzer, Robert H., and Edward Sagarin. 1950. *The Negro in American Business: the Conflict between Separatism and Integration.* New York: Greenberg.

Knight, Frank. 1921. *Risk Uncertainty, and Profit.* New York: Houghton Mifflin.

Kosanovich, William T., Heather Fleck, Berwood Yost, Wendy Armon, and Sandra Siliezar. 2001. *Comprehensive Assessment of Self-Employment Assistance Programs.* U.S. Department of Labor Report.

Lentz, Bernard, and David Laband. 1990. "Entrepreneurial Success and Occupational Inheritance among Proprietors." *Canadian Journal of Economics* 23(3): 563–579.

Levenstein, Margaret. 1995. "African American Entrepreneurship: The View from the 1910 Census." *Business and Economic History* 24(1): 106–122.

Light, Ivan. 1972. *Ethnic Enterprise in America.* Berkeley: University of California Press.

Light, Ivan. 1979. "Disadvantaged Minorities in Self Employment." *International Journal of Comparative Sociology* 20(1–2): 31–45.

Light, Ivan. 2004. "The Ethnic Economy." In Neil Smelser and Richard Swedberg, eds., *Handbook of Economic Sociology* (2nd ed.). New York: Russell Sage Foundation.

Light, Ivan, Im Jung Kwuon, and Deng Zhong. 1990. "Korean Rotating Credit Associations in Los Angeles." *Amerasia Journal* 16(2): 35–54.

Lindh, Thomas, and Henry Ohlsson. 1996. "Self-Employment and Windfall Gains: Evidence from the Swedish Lottery." *Economic Journal* 106(439): 1515–1526.

Lindh, Thomas, and Henry Ohlsson. 1998. "Self-Employment and Wealth Inequality." *Review of Income and Wealth* 44(1): 25–41.

Loewen, James W. 1971. *The Mississippi Chinese: Between Black and White.* Cambridge: Harvard University Press.

Lofstrom, Magnus, and Chunbei Wang. 2006. "Hispanic Self-Employment: A Dynamic Analysis of Business Ownership." Paper presented at the University of North Carolina Minority Entrepreneurship Bootcamp.

Lohmann, Henning. 2001. "Self-Employed or Employee, Full-Time or Part-Time? Gender Differences in the Determinants and Conditions for Self-Employment in Europe and the US." Mannheim Centre for European Social Research Working Paper 38.

Lombard, Karen V. 2001. "Female Self-Employment and Demand for Flexible, Nonstandard Work Schedules." *Economic Inquiry* 39(2): 214–237.

Lowrey, Ying. 2005. *Dynamics of Minority-Owned Employer Establishments, 1997–2001: An Analysis of Employer Data from the Survey of Minority-Owned Business Establishments.* Washington, DC: U.S. Small Business Administration, Office of Advocacy.

Lucas, Robert. 1978. "On the Size Distribution of Firms." *Bell Journal of Economics* 9(2): 508–523.

MacDonald, Heather. 1995. "Why Koreans Succeed." *City Journal* (Spring): 12–29.

Mach, Traci L., and John D. Wolken. 2006. "Financial Services Used by Small Businesses: Evidence from the 2003 Survey of Small Business Finances." *Federal Reserve Bulletin* 87: 167–195.

Mar, Don. 2005. "Individual Characteristics vs. City Structural Characteristics: Explaining Self-Employment Differences among Chinese, Japanese, and Filipinos in the United States." *Journal of Socio-Economics* 34: 341–359.

Marion, Justin. 2007. "How Costly Is Affirmative Action? Government Contracting and California's Proposition 209." University of Chicago Working Paper.

McLanahan, Sara, and Gary Sandefur. 1994. *Growing Up with a Single Parent: What Hurts, What Helps.* Cambridge, MA: Harvard University Press.

Menchik, Paul L., and Nancy A. Jianakoplos. 1997. "Black-White Wealth Inequality: Is Inheritance the Reason?" *Economic Inquiry* 35(2): 428–442.

Meyer, Bruce. 1990. "Why Are There So Few Black Entrepreneurs?" National Bureau of Economic Research Working Paper No. 3537.

Min, Pyong. 1984. "From White-Collar Occupations to Small Business: Korean Immigrants' Occupational Adjustment." *Sociological Quarterly* 25(3): 333–352.

Min, Pyong. 1986–1987. "Filipino and Korean Immigrants in Small Business: A Comparative Analysis." *Amerasia Journal* 13(1): 53–71.

Min, Pyong Gap. 1988. *Ethnic Business Enterprises: Korean Small Business in Atlanta*. New York: Center for Migration Studies.

Min, Pyong Gap. 1989. *Some Positive Functions of Ethnic Business for an Immigrant Community: Koreans in Los Angeles*. Final Report Submitted to the National Science Foundation, Washington, DC.

Min, Pyong Gap. 1993. "Korean Immigrants in Los Angeles." In Ivan Light and Parminder Bhachu, eds., *Immigration and Entrepreneurship: Culture, Capital, and Ethnic Networks*. New Brunswick, NJ: Transaction Publishers.

Min, Pyong Gap. 1996. *Caught in the Middle: Korean Merchants in America's Multiethnic Cities*. Berkeley: University of California Press.

Minority Business Enterprise Legal Defense and Education Fund. 1988. *Report on the Minority Business Enterprise Programs of State and Local Governments*. Washington, DC: Minority Business Enterprise Legal Defense and Education Fund.

Mitchell, K., and D. K. Pearce. 2004. *Availability of Financing to Small Firms using the Survey of Small Business Finances*. U.S. Small Business Administration, Office of Advocacy.

Moore, Robert L. 1983. "Employer Discrimination: Evidence from Self-employed Workers." *Review of Economics and Statistics* 65: 496–501.

Moutray, Chad. 2007. "Educational Attainment and Other Characteristics of the Self-Employed: An Examination Using the Panel Study of Income Dynamics Data." U.S. Small Business Administration Working Paper.

Myers, Samuel L., Jr. 1997. "Minority Business Set-Asides." In *Encyclopedia of African-American Business History*. Westport, CT: Greenwood Press.

Myers, Samuel L., Jr., and Tsze Chan. 1996. "Who Benefits from Minority Business Set-Asides? The Case of New Jersey." *Journal of Policy Analysis and Management* 15(2): 202–226.

Myrdal, Gunnar. 1944. *An American Dilemma*. New York: Harper.

National Center for Health Statistics. 2003. "Births: Final Data for 2003." *National Vital Statistics Reports* 51(2).

National Federation of Independent Business. 2002. *National Small Business Poll: Families in Business*. Washington, DC: NFIB.

Nicolaou, Nicos, Scott Shane, Lynn Cherkas, Janice Hunkin, and Tim D. Spector. 2007. "Is the Tendency to Engage in Self-Employment Genetic?" Imperial College London Working Paper.

Nykvist, Jenny. 2005. "Entrepreneurship and Liquidity Constraints: Evidence from Sweden." Uppsala University, Department of Economics, Working Paper 2005: 21.

Oaxaca, Ronald. 1973. "Male-Female Wage Differentials in Urban Labor Markets." *International Economic Review* 14: 693–709.

Oaxaca, Ronald, and Michael Ransom. 1994. "On Discrimination and the Decomposition of Wage Differentials." *Journal of Econometrics* 61: 5–21.

Oliver, Melvin L., and Thomas M. Shapiro. 1995. *Black Wealth/White Wealth: A New Perspective on Racial Inequality*. New York: Routledge.

Organization for Economic Cooperation and Development (OECD). 1992. *Employment Outlook 1992.* Paris: OECD. Available at ⟨http://www.oecd.org/dataoecd/4/8/2409984.pdf⟩.

Parker, Simon C. 2004. *The Economics of Self-Employment and Entrepreneurship.* Cambridge: Cambridge University Press.

Parker, Simon C. 2005. "Entrepreneurship among Married Couples in the United States: A Simultaneous Probit Approach." Institute for the Study of Labor (IZA) Discussion Paper 1712.

Polivka, Anne E., and Stephen M. Miller. 1998. "The CPS after the Redesign: Refocusing the Economic Lens." In John Haltiwanger, Marilyn E. Manser, and Robert Toel, eds., *Labor Statistics Measurement Issues* (pp. 249–286). Chicago: University of Chicago Press.

Porter, Michael. 1995. "The Competitive Advantage of the Inner City." *Harvard Business Review* 73(3): 55–71.

Portes, Alejandro, and R. L. Bach. 1985. *Latin Journey: Cuban and Mexican Immigrants in the United States.* Berkeley: University of California Press.

Portes, Alejandro, and Min Zhou. 1996. "Self-Employment and the Earnings of Immigrants." *American Sociological Review* (61): 219–230.

Rauch, James E. 2001. "Black Ties Only? Ethnic Business Networks, Intermediaries, and African-American Retail Entrepreneurship." In James E. Rauch and Alessandra Casella, eds., *Networks and Markets.* New York: Russell Sage Foundation.

Razin, Eran, and Andre Langlois. 1996. "Metropolitan Characteristics and Entrepreneurship among Immigrants and Ethnic Groups in Canada." *International Migration Review* 30(3): 703–727.

Rees, Hedley, and Anup Shah. 1986. "An Empirical Analysis of Self-Employment in the U.K." *Journal of Applied Econometrics* 1(1): 95–108.

Reynolds, Paul. 2005. *Entrepreneurship in the US: The Future Is Now.* New York: Springer.

Reynolds, P., and S. White. 1997. *The Entrepreneurial Process: Economic Growth, Men, Women, and Minorities.* Westport, CT: Quorum Books.

Rice, Mitchell F. 1991. "Government Set-Asides, Minority Business Enterprises, and the Supreme Court." *Public Administration Review* 51(2): 114–122.

Robb, Alicia. 2000. "The Role of Race, Gender, and Discrimination in Business Survival." Doctoral dissertation, University of Michigan Press.

Robb, Alicia. 2002. "Entrepreneurship: A Path for Economic Advancement for Women and Minorities?" *Journal of Developmental Entrepreneurship* 7(4): 383–397.

Robb, Alicia. 2005. "Fear in Financing: The Borrowing Experiences of Minority Firms." Working paper.

Robb, Alicia M., and Robert W. Fairlie 2006. "Tracing Access to Financial Capital among African-Americans from the Entrepreneurial Venture to the Established Business." University of California, Santa Cruz, Working Paper.

Rubin, Donald B. 1987. *Multiple Imputation for Nonresponse in Surveys.* New York: John Wiley.

Saxenian, AnnaLee. 2002. *Local and Global Networks of Immigrant Professionals in Silicon Valley*. San Francisco: Public Policy Institute of California.

Schafer, Joseph L. 1999. "Multiple Imputation: A Primer." *Statistical Methods in Medical Research* 8: 3–15.

Schafer, Joseph L., and Maren K. Olsen. 1998. "Multiple Imputation for Multivariate Missing-Data Problems: A Data Analyst's Perspective." *Multivariate Behavioral Research* 33(4): 545–571.

Scholz, John Karl, and Kara Levine. 2004. "U.S. Black-White Wealth Inequality." In K. Neckerman, ed., *Social Inequality* (pp. 895–929). New York: Russell Sage Foundation.

Schumpeter, J. A. 1934. *The Theory of Economic Development*. Cambridge, MA: Harvard University Press.

Seltzer, Judith. 1994. "The Consequences of Marital Dissolution for Children." *Annual Review of Sociology* 20: 235–266.

Servon, Lisa J. 1999. *Bootstrap Capital: Microenterprises and the American Poor*. Washington, DC: Brookings Institution Press.

Shane, Scott, and Daniel Cable. 2002. "Network Ties, Reputation, and the Financing of New Ventures." *Management Science* 48(3): 364–381.

Sowell, Thomas. 1981. *Markets and Minorities*. New York: Basic Books.

Srinivasan, R., C. Woo, and A. C. Cooper. 1994. "Performance Determinants for Male and Female Entrepreneurs." Working Paper 1053, Purdue University.

Taylor, Mark. 2001. "Self-Employment and Windfall Gains in Britain: Evidence from Panel Data." *Economica* 63: 539–565.

Tucker, M. Belinda, and Claudia Mitchell-Kernan. 1995. *The Decline in Marriage among African-Americans: Causes, Consequences, and Policy Implications*. New York: Russell Sage Foundation.

U.S. Bureau of Labor Statistics. 2004. "Median Weekly Earnings of Full-Time Wage and Salary Workers by Selected Characteristics." *Labor Force Statisticsw from the Current Population Survey*. Available at ⟨http://www.bls.gov/cps/cpsaat37.pdf⟩.

U.S. Bureau of Labor Statistics. 2007. "Table A-2. Employment Status of the Civilian Population by Race, Sex, and Age" and "Table A-3. Employment Status of the Hispanic or Latino Population by Sex and Age." Available at ⟨http://stats.bls.gov/news.release/empsit.toc.htm⟩.

U.S. Census Bureau. 1992. *1987 Economic Census: Characteristics of Business Owners*. Washington, DC: U.S. Government Printing Office.

U.S. Census Bureau. 1996. *1992 Economic Census: Survey of Minority-Owned Business Enterprises, Asians and Pacific Islanders, American Indians, and Alaska Natives*. Washington, DC: U.S. Government Printing Office.

U.S. Census Bureau. 1997. *1992 Economic Census: Characteristics of Business Owners*. Washington, DC: U.S. Government Printing Office.

U.S. Census Bureau. 2001. *1997 Economic Census: Company Summary*. Washington, DC: U.S. Government Printing Office.

U.S. Census Bureau. 2005a. "Educational Attainment in the United States: March 2004." *Current Population Reports, Population Characteristics, P20-476*. Washington, DC: U.S. Government Printing Office.

U.S. Census Bureau. 2005b. *Families and Living Arrangements*. Available at ⟨http://www.census.gov/population/www/socdemo/hh-fam.html#history⟩.

U.S. Census Bureau. 2006a. *Characteristics of Businesses: 2002: 2002 Economic Census, Survey of Business Owners Company Statistics Series*. Washington, DC: U.S. Government Printing Office.

U.S. Census Bureau. 2006b. *2002 Economic Census, Survey of Business Owners Company Statistics Series*. Washington, DC: U.S. Government Printing Office.

U.S. Census Bureau. 2007. "Wealth and Asset Ownership." Available at ⟨http://www.census.gov/hhes/www/wealth/1998_2000_tables.html⟩.

U.S. Department of Labor. 1992. *Self-Employment Programs for Unemployed Workers*. Unemployment Insurance Occasional Paper 92-2. Washington, DC: U.S. Government Printing Office.

U.S. Small Business Administration. 1999. *Minorities in Business*. Washington, DC: U.S. Small Business Administration, Office of Advocacy.

U.S. Small Business Administration. 2001. *Minorities in Business*. Washington, DC: U.S. Small Business Administration, Office of Advocacy.

U.S. Small Business Administration. 2007a. *Minorities in Business: A Demographic Review of Minority Business Ownership*. Washington, DC: U.S. Small Business Administration, Office of Advocacy.

U.S. Small Business Administration. 2007b. *Office of Financial Assistance Statistics on Small Business Administration Loan Approval*. Washington, DC: U.S. Small Business Administration, Office of Advocacy.

van der Sluis, J., van Praag, M., and Vijverberg, W. 2004. *Education and Entrepreneurship in Industrialized Countries: A Meta-Analysis*. Tinbergen InstituteWorking Paper No. TI 03–046/3. Amsterdam: Tinbergen Institute.

van Praag, Mirjam. 2005. "Successful Entrepreneurship: Confronting Economic Theory with Empirical Practice." Cheltenham, UK: Elgar.

Vroman, Wayne. 1997. "Self-Employment Assistance: Revised Report." Washington, DC: Urban Institute.

Waldinger, Roger. 1986. "Immigrant Enterprise: A Critique and Reformulation." *Theory and Society* 15(1–2): 249–285.

Waldinger, Rober, Howard Aldrich, and Robin Ward. 1990. *Ethnic Entrepreneurs*. Newbury Park, CA: Sage.

Walstad, William B., and Marilyn L. Kourilsky. 1998. "Entrepreneurial Attitudes and Knowledge of Black Youth." *Entrepreneurship Theory and Practice* 23(2): 5–18.

Wilson, James Q. 2002. *The Marriage Problem: How Our Culture Has Weakened Families*. New York: HarperCollins.

Wilson, William J. 1987. *The Truly Disadvantaged: The Inner City, the Underclass, and Public Policy*. Chicago: University of Chicago Press.

Wolff, Edward N. 2001. "Recent Trends in Wealth Ownership, from 1983 to 1998." In Thomas M. Shapiro and Edward N. Wolff, eds., *Assets for the Poor: The Benefits of Spreading Asset Ownership* (pp. 34–73). New York: Russell Sage Foundation.

Yoon, In-Jin. 1991. "The Changing Significance of Ethnic and Class Resources in Immigrant Business." *International Migration Review* 25(2): 303–331.

Yoon, In-Jin. 1993. "The Social Origins of Korean Immigration to the United States from 1965 to the Present." Paper No. 121, Papers of the Program on Population, East-West Center, Honolulu, Hawaii.

Yoon, In-Jin. 1995. "The Growth of Korean Immigrant Entrepreneurship in Chicago." *Ethnic and Racial Studies* 18(2): 315–335.

Yoon, In-Jin. 1997. *On My Own: Korean Businesses and Race Relations in America.* Chicago: University of Chicago Press.

Yuengert, Andrew M. 1995. "Testing Hypotheses of Immigrant Self-Employment." *Journal of Human Resources* 30(1): 194–204.

Zhou, M. 1992. *Chinatown: The Socioeconomic Potential of an Urban Enclave.* Philadelphia: Temple University Press.

Zhou, M. 1995. "Low-Wage Employment and Social Mobility: The Experience of Immigrant Chinese Women in New York City." *National Journal of Sociology* 9(1): 1–30.

Zhou, M. 2004. "Revisiting Ethnic Entrepreneurship: Convergencies, Controversies, and Conceptual Advancements." *International Migration Review* 38(3): 1040–1074.

Zissimopoulos, Julie, and Lynn Karoly. 2003. "Transitions to Self-Employment at Older Ages." RAND Working Paper.

Index